GOD OF GRACE
AND
GOD OF GLORY

GOD OF GRACE
AND
GOD OF GLORY

An Account of the Theology of Jonathan Edwards

STEPHEN R. HOLMES

William B. Eerdmans Publishing Company
Grand Rapids, Michigan

Published in Great Britain by T&T Clark Ltd,
59 George Street, Edinburgh EH2 2LQ, Scotland

www.tandtclark.co.uk

This edition published 2001 in the USA
under license from T&T Clark Ltd by
Wm. B. Eerdmans Publishing Co.
255 Jefferson Ave. S.E.
Grand Rapids
Michigan 49503

www.eerdmans.com

First published 2001

ISBN 0–8028–3914–2

Typeset by Fakenham Photosetting Limited, Fakenham, Norfolk
Printed and bound in Great Britain by Bookcraft Ltd, Avon

For Heather
not because it is worthy of her,
but because she should have the first

Contents

Preface

One of the reasons why I, as an English Baptist minister, became interested in Edwards was his effect on my own denomination. In the 1780s, the Evangelical Revival was in danger of bypassing English Baptist life altogether. The General (*i.e.* Arminian) Baptists had largely fallen into Unitarianism and Deism, and were no longer a Christian denomination in any meaningful sense. Many or most of the Particular (*i.e.* Calvinist) Baptists were held captive by a hypercalvinist 'orthodoxy', usually considered to stem from the writings of John Gill and John Brine. (Interestingly, there is evidence that Edwards had read Brine and, probably, Gill. *Miscellanies* 1357 contains material reproduced from Brine's writings concerning defects in philosophical morality, and Edwards' *Catalogue* contains two references to Gill.) This hypercalvinism was distinguished by the argument that, since the reprobate could not respond to the gospel invitation, it was inappropriate to preach in an invitational manner. One could speak of Christ's salvation, but not exhort sinners to repent and believe. Unsurprisingly, under the influence of such theology, the denomination was in a parlous state. The escape from this came through the publication in 1785 of Andrew Fuller's *The Gospel Worthy of all Acceptation*, expressing an evangelical Calvinist theology that had taken root amongst a group of ministers in Northamptonshire and Cambridgeshire. Fuller based his arguments upon a close reading of Jonathan Edwards, particularly the *Freedom of the Will*.

Fullerism, as this transplanted Edwardsean Calvinism became known, led to a revitalisation of the denomination and the founding (by Fuller, William Carey and others) of the modern Protestant missionary movement in 1792, still my denomination's greatest gift to the Church Universal. Guided by Edwards' writings, the Baptists developed a missionary-minded, modern, confident and relevant orthodox Calvinist theology, which came to fullest flower in the ministry of Charles Haddon Spurgeon, the 'Prince of Preachers'. Amongst many other works, Spurgeon founded a college for the training of pastors, and it was as a student at Spurgeon's College that I was first introduced to the writings of Jonathan Edwards.

There is more to the story than that, however: under the guidance of my tutors at that college, I began to discover what Edwards taught Fuller two centuries before – that a confident, relevant, evangelistic, Reformed theology was both possible and attractive. It was reading Barth rather than Edwards that first opened my eyes to this, but the point is the same. Such Reformed and reforming theology has informed my thought and my preaching ever since, and I hold the tradition that bears the name in high honour.

However, it seems to me that something has gone badly wrong. In England at least, the title 'Reformed' too often refers to a theology and church praxis that apparently lacks confidence, relevance, and intellectual rigor: the (increasingly) desperate attempt to hold to a mythical golden age of theology and polity defined by forcing figures as diverse as Owen and Baxter into a theological bed of Procrustes. The Reformed tradition of theology is a noble one, and at its noblest when, as with Edwards or Barth, it is confident enough to welcome what is new, test it by the one canon of the gospel, and accept and hold on to whatever may be found useful or interesting. Edwards rewrote Reformed theology because he found the truth in the best secular philosophy – Locke – and science – Newton – of his day, and because he saw new things happening in the churches and was prepared to sift them and welcome the good. If a Reformed church must always be being reformed, as the noble slogan insists, then a Reformed theology must also always be open to what correction the Lord, in His mercy, may bring. This book is a modest attempt to honour a great Reformed theologian in the way that I believe Edwards would have wanted to be honoured: not by pretending that he had all things right, but by seeking, in humble dependence on God's Spirit, to be ever more faithful to the gospel of Jesus Christ.

Because only thus will God be glorified.

S. R. H.
Epiphany 2000

Acknowledgements

Lists of acknowledgements, particularly in a first book, can be in danger of reading like an Oscar acceptance speech, containing seemingly endless lists of people, and of no interest of all to anyone except those mentioned. I excuse myself, however, by citing a crucial difference: unlike the viewer of the award ceremony, the book reader can merely turn over the page. It is the case that my debt to a number of people should be publicly recorded, and it is a pleasure as well as a duty to do that here.

This book has its origin in a doctoral thesis that completed under the supervision of Professor Colin Gunton. I greatly value Colin's friendship; the manner of his supervision and the quality of his advice have contributed substantially to whatever value may be found in this book. I must also publicly acknowledge my debts to the Revd Dr John Colwell. John was formerly my tutor at Spurgeon's College, and first introduced me to Jonathan Edwards' writings. I taught at Spurgeon's under his guidance whilst working on my thesis, and he was kind enough to read the whole of that work whilst it was in progress, and to make many useful comments. Again, the book would be a much lesser work were it not for this help. John and Colin between them have taught me (and continue to teach me) by precept and example, what it is to be a scholar and a theologian; there are few people to whom I am more greatly indebted than these two.

My Ph.D. examiners, Professor Robert Jenson and Professor Alan Sell, were generous with their advice. Dr Mike Higton read parts of the thesis at an early stage, and Dr Murray Rae read it all just before I submitted it. When I decided that I would seek to write a book accessible to the famous 'intelligent non-specialist', as well as to Edwards' scholars, Dr Chris Goringe was kind enough to act as one such and look over a couple of chapters to advise me on where I was failing in this. Each will be able to see, should they care to, where I have taken their advice and where, having considered it carefully, I have gone with my own instincts; to each I am grateful.

The quality of the theological education I received from Spurgeon's College whilst preparing for ministry will not be adequately conveyed to the reader of this work, and the College's willingness to take me on as their Research Fellow provided the time and the funding that made the completion of the thesis which underlies this book possible. It was a happy coincidence, although not a happy occasion, when my time at Spurgeon's came to an end in the same week as my *viva voce*. Whilst working on the thesis and latterly on the book, I have been a part of another academic community, at King's College London. The Research Institute in Systematic Theology there, which brings together postgraduate students, staff, and others, has provided constant stimulation through its weekly seminars and occasional conferences, and has resulted in some close friendships.

I am of the fixed opinion that almost the sole use of electronic bibliographical aids is to demonstrate the indispensability of good librarians. Mrs Judy Powles, librarian of Spurgeon's College, has been invaluable. Staff at libraries in King's College, the University of London, Cambridge University, the British Library, and the Beinecke Rare Book and Manuscript Library of Yale University have been of great help at different times. My time at the Beinecke was also enriched by conversations with, and practical help from, Ken Minkema and Peter Thuesen, the editorial staff of the Yale University Press project to publish Edwards' works, who were generous with their time and expertise, and who gave me copies of some of the unpublished *Miscellanies*, as noted in the Author's Note below.

Finally, Heather, my wife these last seven years, and for many more to come, I hope and pray. Her patience, support and interest have been of more value than I can adequately say. To her this book is dedicated.

Author's Note

In recent years, the lack of a personal, gender-neutral, third person singular pronoun in English has become notorious. The days when Charlotte Brontë could unselfconsciously refer to herself as 'he' in a letter are gone, whether this is to be celebrated or bemoaned. No wholly satisfactory solution to the various questions raised has yet been proposed, and a writer can only make his or her (!) own attempts to use the language as well as possible. Here I have let gender-specific language in passages I am quoting pass without comment; cases where the sense is not obvious are extremely rare, and I see no reason to edit texts to conform to current linguistic practice on this point any more than on the issue of the old forms of the second person singular pronoun. In my own writing I have sought not to be gender-specific, on one occasion (only, I think) trusting the authority of the most recent Oxford dictionary sufficiently to use 'they' as a singular pronoun. This much, I trust, is uncontroversial. The more inflammatory issue concerns pronouns applied to God; here, I have reverted to the traditional practice of capitalising masculine forms. This has the twin advantages of preserving traditional usage whilst alerting readers to the fact that I do not intend to suggest that God is male and not female.

A second issue concerns citations from as-yet unpublished manuscripts; Edwards' use (or, rather, non-use) of punctuation in his own notebooks makes his style rather difficult to read, and he regularly uses a set of abbreviations which, whilst never obscuring the sense, are at least aesthetically difficult. When I have quoted from such material, however, I have chosen to perform only minimal editing on the text, regarding accuracy as a higher call than aesthetics in a work of this nature. I have expanded a few regular abbreviations without comment ('X' for Christ, 'G' for God, 'ch' for church, and so on), and have supplied punctuation where I think that the text verges on the incomprehensible without it. I have also not indicated places in the text where words had been crossed out. I do not think there is any point here where this level of editing is in any danger of determining, or changing, the meaning of the text. In the case of the *Miscellanies* entries, I have used Thomas Schafer's typewritten transcriptions, stored in the Beinecke Rare Book and Manuscript Library, Yale University, without further adjustment, with the exception of five longer entries for which the editorial team of the *Works of Jonathan Edwards*, Yale University were kind enough to give me printed copies of their more-or-less prepared edition. These entries were numbers 1091, 1174, 1219, 1245 and 1352, and I have used the copies given to me without variance. In the case of one or two other manuscripts which I have transcribed myself, I have indicated uncertain readings in footnotes.

Finally, I should indicate the abbreviations that are used here: For Edwards' works, I use *YEn* for volumes of the Yale edition and *BTn* for volumes of the older Banner of Truth edition. For other material, only 'Barth *CD*' for the English translation of Karl Barth's *Church Dogmatics* and 'Heppe' for the English translation of Heinrich Heppe's *Reformed Dogmatics* are used. Full details of all these editions may be found in the Bibliography.

An earlier version of chapter 6 appeared as 'The Justice of Hell and the Display of God's Glory in the Thought of Jonathan Edwards' in the Fall 2000 issue of *Pro Ecclesia*.

1
Jonathan Edwards, Theologian

If, as rumour has it, 'may you live in interesting times' is an ancient oriental curse, then Jonathan Edwards of all men was cursed. Locally, nationally and internationally, his times were very interesting indeed. Locally, he found himself as a pastor at the epicentre of the Great Awakening and as a missionary to the Indians during the French and Indian War. Nationally, whilst his early death prevented him from seeing the American colonies in revolt, Edwards has always been recognised as an iconic figure in the formation of American identity, which was the precursor to the Revolution.[1] Internationally, Edwards lived on the cusp of the Enlightenment, perhaps still the greatest change in Western intellectual self-understanding since the Renaissance of the fifteenth century. However, many people have the questionable distinction of having lived in interesting times; Edwards' significance lies both in his action as a shaper of major events, and also particularly in his reflection, as he sought to understand the historical events and intellectual changes of his day, using the categories of Christian theology of a specifically Reformed flavour.

Jonathan Edwards was born in 1703, the fifth child, and only son amongst ten daughters, of Timothy Edwards, minister of East Windsor parish and third-generation New Englander, and Esther, née Stoddard. His mother had borne an honourable name; the Stoddards had been respected in the community even before Esther's father, Solomon, had begun his famous and productive ministry in Northampton in 1669, and already, as the century turned, his achievements added lustre, although he had nearly three decades more service to give. After five years' study at the Collegiate School, which was soon to become Yale, in its early and difficult

---

[1] On this see later.

years,[2] Edwards took up a preaching ministry, before his twentieth birthday, amongst a Presbyterian congregation in New York. Within a year, that congregation had decided, under Edwards' guidance, that reunion with its parent church was a necessary step, and Edwards left, apparently intending to accept a call to minister in the new town of Bolton. The events of the next few months appear confused, but by the middle of the next year, 1724, Edwards was serving as Tutor at Yale. Again, the post was short-lived, although again apparently useful and valued. He spent the last three months of 1725 very seriously ill, the first half of 1726 convalescing at his parents' house, and then in August an invitation came to assist his grandfather, now 83, in the work of ministry in Northampton. Soon Edwards was the heir apparent to the great man, and when Stoddard died, early in 1729, he succeeded to the eminent pulpit he was to occupy for the next twenty-one years.

In 1727 Edwards had married Sarah Pierrepont, in whose honour he had written his 'Apostrophe', a prose poem of great tenderness, four years before.[3] Their first child was born in August 1728, and ten more followed. Although seven years younger than he, Sarah would die a few months after her husband, before reaching her 50th year. The tale of Jonathan and Sarah Edwards has more than once been written as a love story:[4] around every great theologian, it seems, tales of humanity cluster, to remind us that this person, also, was no more than a human being just as we are; for Jonathan Edwards, who is more forbidding than many, it is the story of the love he shared

[2] During the time Edwards was a student the college was split, with three towns seeking to become its permanent home. Even after the Connecticut General Assembly decreed that New Haven should be the site, many of the students, including Edwards, returned to an alternative site at Wethersfield because they doubted the orthodoxy of Samuel Johnson, then tutor at New Haven.

[3] YE16, pp. 789–90.

[4] Elisabeth D. Dodds, *Marriage to a Difficult Man: The 'Uncommon Union' of Jonathan and Sarah Edwards* (Philadelphia: Westminster Press, 1971); James W. McClendon, *Systematic Theology: vol. 1: Ethics* (Nashville, TN: Abingdon Press, 1986) pp. 110–31.

with Sarah that may finally move us from respecting the theology to admiring the man.

Local revivals of religion were not uncommon in Puritan New England. Edwards tells us that he had lived through at least one such in his father's church,[5] and that Stoddard claimed five 'harvests' during his time at Northampton.[6] These revivals, however, were generally very brief, and confined to one parish. Whilst of immense significance to those touched by them, they were not events that changed the nature of society in the way that Edwards observed in 1734–5. For six months Northampton was seized by a deep and serious concern for religion. Over three hundred people appeared to have been converted; 'the town seemed to be full of the presence of God: it never was so full of love, nor so full of joy .... There were remarkable tokens of God's presence in almost every house ... God's day was a delight ... everyone earnestly intent on the public worship, every hearer eager to drink in the words of the minister as they came from his mouth ....'[7] Emanating from Northampton, this new spirit touched almost every community in the Connecticut River valley. With the old Puritan dream of the colonies being a 'city on a hill', displaying godliness, still alive, these were heady times indeed.

They came to an end, too soon, and for five years Edwards laboured to rekindle the flame. That work was to be another's, however. George Whitefield landed at Rhode Island on 14 September 1740 for a tour of the colonies. He began as he meant to go on, preaching six times in the first three days of his visit. Little over a month later, he arrived at Edwards' church. His *Journal* tells the story of 'the joyful news that Northampton people have recovered their first love' as 'Good Mr. Edwards wept ...'.[8] For the two years following, religious fervour was common in New England and was regularly accompanied by physical

---

[5] In the 'Personal Narrative'. See *YE16*, p. 790.
[6] In the 'Faithful Narrative'. See *YE4*, p. 146.
[7] Edwards' words, from the 'Faithful Narrative'. *YE4*, p. 151.
[8] Whitefield's *Journal* for Sunday, 19 October 1740.

manifestations, fainting, weeping, shouting, and more bizarre behaviour. Edwards took his part in preaching for conversions, most famously at Enfield in 1741, where he spoke to 'Sinners in the Hands of an Angry God'.[9] His most lasting labour, however, was a series of books describing and defending the revivals against both those who would have no emotion in true religion and those who would have nothing but emotion. The last, longest and greatest of these works, the *Treatise Concerning the Religious Affections* was the first great book that Edwards wrote, and still takes a high place amongst theological (rather than psychological) analyses of religious experience.

By the time *Religious Affections* was published, however, in 1746, not only was the revival apparently over once again, but Edwards was also engaged in controversy over church order in Northampton. The New England communities had struggled with the place of unconverted children who became unconverted adults and had children of their own. The towns were organised around the churches, and so the original polity of the Pilgrim Fathers would condemn non-Christian men and women to life in an underclass, excluded from formal civic life, as well as the informal but more important social life of the church. The answer to this was the 'half-way covenant', under which those who were prepared to acknowledge the truth of the Christian gospel and live under the discipline of the church were permitted membership of the church, Christian marriage and baptism for their children, but were not allowed to the Lord's Table, the eucharistic service, unless they could show reason to hope they were converted. Under a Calvinist scheme, that is, those who believed the scheme but regarded themselves as reprobate or elect but not yet saved could find a place in society.

Edwards' predecessor and grandfather, Stoddard, had taken this one step further. Recognising that many who regarded themselves as Christian used the half-way covenant as a comfortable way to maintain religious

---

[9] I shall have more to say about this most famous of Edwards' sermons in chapter 6. See p. 217.

standing whilst avoiding the challenges which Christianity puts in the way of its adherents, he had admitted all who could profess belief in the Christian scheme to the table, and encouraged them to participate. Presumably as a result of the attention that he had given to the nature and proof of true religious experience in the various defences of the revivals, Edwards became convinced that this practice, which he had adopted from his grandfather, was inappropriate, and resolved to stop it.[10] Around the same time came what has become known as the 'bad book affair', when some youths of the town got hold of a midwifery manual, presumably the nearest thing to pornography that inland New England had to offer. Edwards' response showed a lack of pastoral tact, and offended a number of leading families. In addition, there was a continuing complaint over the size of Edwards' salary on the part of the townsfolk, and its repeatedly late payment on Edwards' part. Whilst it was the communion issue that finally brought matters to a head, all these different disagreements are symptoms of a failing relationship between Edwards and his people. In June 1750 a council of local ministers and church 'messengers' and a meeting of the Northampton church both recommended that Edwards should leave his pastorate. On 1 July, Edwards preached his 'farewell sermon'.

For some months afterwards, however, having no place to go to, the family continued to live in Northampton, and Edwards was even often asked, albeit grudgingly, to fill the pulpit during the interregnum. In December 1750 he received an invitation to combine missionary duties to the Housatonic Indian settlement at Stockbridge with the pastorate of a very small church composed of those Indians who had converted, together with those New Englanders who lived in the town. By the following August, he had accepted the call and was installed.

The six and a half years Edwards spent at Stockbridge were unquestionably hard, and yet there he produced a

---

[10] I shall deal with the theological issues raised by 'Stoddardianism' in chapter 5. See pp. 184–91.

series of writings of genuine greatness. To begin with, the family was poor: they struggled to sell their house in Northampton, were living on a reduced income, and the older daughters were beginning to marry, and so needed dowries. The Edwards Collection in the Beinecke Library contains some notebooks that demonstrate this in a most pathetic way. The unmarried daughters made painted paper fans to sell; paper being difficult to acquire and expensive on the frontier, Edwards would take the offcuts of the fan paper and, combining it with the odd blank half-page from a letter he had received and the empty margin of a Boston newspaper, would carefully stitch the fragments into something that would pass for a book. In such, in a tiny hand, presumably to conserve even these stocks of paper, Edwards recorded notes that were eventually to be incorporated into the *Freedom of the Will* or *True Virtue*.

Poverty was not the only problem, however. The leading citizen of the little town was one Ephraim Williams, a relative of those who had led the opposition to Edwards in Northampton. Williams apparently regarded the frontier as a place of great commercial opportunity, and had set about improving his position in life. As always with commercial gains, someone else had to lose, and in this case it was the Native American population. Edwards saw the importance of friendship with the Indians, not merely for missionary purposes, but also to aid the British cause against the French, who were seeking to link their territories in Canada and Louisiana with the help of the Six Nations. Such a conflict of interest, with old familial distrust to fuel it, resulted in a protracted power struggle for control of the Stockbridge mission, a struggle that Edwards eventually won early in 1754.

During these few years of hardship Edwards produced the works on which his reputation has rested ever since. His first production from Stockbridge was his last word on the communion controversy, *Misrepresentations Corrected*, but he followed this with the famous *Enquiry into the modern prevailing Notions of the Freedom of the Will*. Next came *The Great Christian Doctrine of Original Sin Defended*, and, although their publication was posthumous, the *Two Dissertations: Concerning the End for which God Created the World* and *True Virtue* also date from these years. These were all preparatory for '*A History of the Work of Redemption*, a body of divinity in an entire new method, being thrown into the form of a history, considering the affair of Christian theology, as the whole of it, in each part, stands in reference to the great work of redemption by Jesus Christ; which I suppose is to be the grand design of all God's designs . . . .'[11] Before this could be written, Calvinism needed to be defended philosophically and exegetically, and the propriety of placing the work of Christ at the centre of creation, and so at the centre of ethics, needed to be demonstrated, hence the earlier works.

Those words indicate Edwards' intention to produce a work which, like the greatest writings of the theological canon, would seek to transcend its time; a work like the *Summa Theologica* of St Thomas, John Calvin's *Institutes* or Karl Barth's *Church Dogmatics*, which, although alert to the particularities of their context, attempt a coherent and lasting statement of the whole of Christian doctrine. Other thinkers, arguably as great, have by choice or necessity devoted themselves solely to contextual writings, applying gospel categories to the needs and questions of the day. In this connection we might think of SS. Athanasius and Augustine, who fought the Church's battles and so had little or no time to reflect at leisure,[12] or Martin Luther, whose greatest works are the product of controversy. By tragic accident, Jonathan Edwards belongs in this second group. When he was only 54, before he could write his *magnum opus*, the imperfections of the new technique of vaccination put an end to his life. He had been called to succeed his son-in-law, Aaron Burr, as President of Nassau Hall in Princeton. The smallpox was then rife, and so he, like

---

[11] *YE16*, pp. 727–8.
[12] Augustine's one great non-polemic work, *De Trinitate*, appeared in an unfinished state after more than twenty years of work. See his *Retractions* ii.15.

others, was given the vaccine. That was on 23 February
1758. One day short of a month later, he died. His last
recorded words perhaps sum up his life. He spoke of his
great love for Sarah, encouraged his children to find
faith in God, asked that he not be given an elaborate
funeral, but that the money saved should go to charity,
and then looked to Jesus. After this, when it seemed that
he was unconscious and those around spoke of the loss
that the college and God's Church would have to bear,
he spoke one last sentence: 'Trust in God, and you need
not fear.'

There is not room here to attempt a more adequate
biography of Edwards than this brief outline of his life.
Edwards is, unhappily, in need of a biographer. There has,
to be sure, been no shortage of books,[13] but none of the
volumes currently available can be regarded as satisfactory.
The standard modern biography is still Ola Winslow's
Jonathan Edwards,[14] originally published in 1940, and so
unable to take account of the intellectual progress made in
the last half-century, not just in understanding Edwards'
thought, but in our grasp of colonial American life, or such
important advances as the patient work that has resulted in
accurate dates for Edwards' manuscripts. Nine years later,
Perry Miller published the book that rekindled interest in
Edwards as a seminal thinker, rather than simply as a
historically important figure.[15] This was not, however,
strictly a biography, although the basic details of Edwards'
life are included; rather, it was an attempt to understand
Edwards' thought. Thus its great strengths, and thus its
limitations, at least considered as biography.

There have been a number of book-length biographies of

---

[13] Two early biographies by Samuel Hopkins and Sereno Dwight remain
indispensable. An abridged form of Dwight's biography can be found in
BT1 pp. xi–cxcvii; Hopkins is reprinted in David Levin (ed.), *Jonathan
Edwards: A Profile* (American Profiles Series) (New York: Hill & Wang,
1969).
[14] Ola E. Winslow, *Jonathan Edwards 1703–1758: A Biography* (New York:
Octagon Books, 1973).
[15] Perry Miller, *Jonathan Edwards* (n.p.: William Sloane Associates, 1949).

Edwards since Winslow and Miller, but in every case they are unsatisfactory for one reason or another. Perhaps the best is Iain Murray's *Jonathan Edwards: A New Biography* (1987), both the most ambitious and most useful of the more recent biographies. It is well written, careful and comprehensive factually, and sympathetic to Edwards. Not unusually for Murray, however (one thinks of his volume on Spurgeon) the reader cannot help feeling that the author's apologetic concern for a particular brand of Reformed piety is in constant danger of obscuring the subject.[16] This is, finally, a great shame, as this should have been the biography for which students of Edwards are waiting. A standard biography to replace Winslow is desperately needed, and Edwards students can only hope that even now an able scholar with an eye to the tercentenary in 2003 is at work.

To tell the story of Edwards' life in such a brief compass as I have attempted can only give a glimmering of an idea of the currents that flowed around him. He has been called the 'last Puritan',[17] and certainly the old Puritan ideals and traditions were important in shaping him. A great hope filled the Puritans who left English shores and settled in a 'new' England during the second quarter of the seventeenth century. There they would found a pure Christian society on gospel principles. Without the cautious reformers who had defeated the cry of 'Reformation without tarrying for any' in the old country, there would be the opportunity to show what glories godly communities could rise to, to build a 'city on the hill' that would indeed be seen by the nations and serve as a witness to bring true Christian religion back to England and to

[16] To cite merely one example: throughout his book, Murray does not have a positive word to say about Perry Miller's study. Whilst I share the current consensus view that Miller fails badly to understand Edwards' theology, and so finally fails badly to understand Edwards, there remains much of interest and value in his book – not least in the attempt to place Edwards philosophically. Murray is apparently blinded to these strengths because of the seriousness he ascribes to the fault, and so has little or no time for philosophical issues, leading finally to a failure to see what is distinctive about Edwards' version of Calvinism.

[17] David C. Brand, *Profile of the Last Puritan* (Atlanta, GA: Scholars' Press, 1991).

Europe. God was leading them into the promised land, where they would build a temple and a kingdom which, like Solomon's of old, would be a wonder of the world.

Such Biblical metaphors abound in early Puritan history, and demonstrate the self-understanding of the original settlers. The first Governor of the Massachusetts Bay colony, John Winthrop, was even compared to Nehemiah by Cotton Mather in his great chronicle of the colonies. These were people who believed they had a divinely-given mission: the Church of England had only half-Reformed, aligning its doctrine to the pure Word of God, but retaining the old Roman hierarchy and ceremony; many Anglicans[18] who could not accept this half-way settlement found safety from politics (and from Archbishop Laud) in the new land, where they could order the churches as they felt the Scriptures commanded them to, and so demonstrate to the world that they were sure was watching what a truly Reformed nation could and should be. This was, to use one last metaphor, a Babylonian captivity, a time of growth and prosperity in a far land before the opportunity to return and re-establish a purified religion, which God would inevitably bring.

But the land was harder than Babylon had been of old, and the purity of the society was embarrassingly less obvious in the second and third generations. A polity that had been built round the church, on the assumption that every citizen was Christian, found itself confronted by questions of what to do with adult unbelievers who wanted to be a part of the town, and wanted their children baptised.[19] The 'half-way covenant' and 'Stoddardianism' (see pp. 4–5 above) were just two manifestations of the need

[18] It is important to realise that before the ejection of 1662 the majority of Puritans were not separatists, and certainly that those who founded the Massachusetts colony were not. They believed in the propriety of the Anglican settlement, that the Monarch should be supreme governor of the church, and should compel obedience to church order; they merely disagreed over the particular church order to which the Monarch should compel obedience.

[19] This demonstrates the point about Anglicanism in the previous note. Unbelieving children would not be a problem (other than pastorally) for a separatist church.

to adapt the vision – the foundational myth of the society – to an uncomfortably foreign reality. The 'awakenings' or revivals that occurred from time to time in one town or another throughout the land were in part attempts to be once more the society that the people had been told they should be, and when Edwards and others saw the uncommonly extensive revival in Northampton in 1734–5, and then the province-wide awakening of the early 1740s, there must have been hopes that a return to the old society was on its way. History, however, tells us that these marked the end of the old way of life. After 1750, for a whole complex of reasons, the New Englanders could no longer be thought of as Puritan English exiles; they were Yankees and Americans.

The word 'Puritan' was originally a term of abuse, and certainly is so now. H. L. Mencken's definition of Puritanism as 'the haunting fear that someone, somewhere, may be happy' catches the modern usage, which perceives the Puritan as a killjoy, probably a religious hypocrite, who covers up his (usually) own emptiness by laying burdens on others. This may be a useful word, but it is not fair to those of whom it was first used. The Puritans were not hedonists, certainly; they did not share the pervasive modern assumption that 'self-fulfilment' is the final goal of every man or woman. They were also religiously serious, believing that if God exists, then that should change everything in our lives. They were, however, neither joyless nor killjoys. They were a big-hearted breed, the greatness of their vision of God and the suffering they had undergone from the Establishment in old England and from the land itself in New England somehow enlarged their capacities. Jonathan Edwards' ability to be transported by the beauty of nature, or Sarah's mystical experiences that he documented,[20] or the strong love they shared are all typical. When they had something to celebrate, they knew how, and the strong cider of New England would flow long into the night. Shakespeare's religious contemporaries

[20] The example of piety that Edwards gave in 'Some Thoughts Concerning the Present Revival of Religion' is Sarah's story. See *YE4*, pp. 331–41.

(and their descendants) believed no more than he did that because one was virtuous there should be no more cakes and ale.

The problem, perhaps, is that the modern meaning of the word is read back to the history. We all know that Puritanism was a hard, cold creed, infected by hypocrisy, and so when we hear of Puritans enjoying themselves, it can only be as hypocrites. The truth is somewhat different: in a rather particular way, these Calvinists were more optimistic and life-affirming than most. They believed in a God who was totally committed to His people, who had created this world as the perfect place for them, and who still promised eternal joy and pleasures at His right hand. True, sin and fallenness complicated the picture, but they were merely passing black linings on a basically silver cloud. Faced with trouble and hardship, Puritan theologians – and all Puritans were to some extent theologians – knew it was something that was never intended for them, and indeed was passing. What is more, in the doctrine of perseverance they had a promise that they would overcome the trials and troubles of life. Certain of victory, they enjoyed the good things of life as gifts from God's hand, and endured the bad things knowing that in God's hands they were safe, and this too would pass. They had no illusions, and knew life was hard; but they also had a strong hope that things would be better, and were able to enjoy those joys that they were granted. They did not share the cheap hedonism of today, but that does not allow us to ridicule or caricature our parents. Theirs was a piety with much to commend it.

More important for studying Edwards' theology is the intellectual character of Puritanism. The idea that New England was a backwater in the eighteenth century has long been laid to rest; books and journals flowed across the Atlantic regularly and in quantity. Nor was their religion an impediment to learning: the Puritans believed that all truth was God's truth, and so gave themselves with seriousness to every branch of study, thinking to advance themselves in godliness thereby. The earliest writings of Jonathan Edwards demonstrate this: they consist of careful observations of flying insects,[21] which ended with an improvement considering how their lives and deaths demonstrated God's wisdom in creating the world as He had done. Puritan learning retained, however, the marks of medieval and Renaissance scholasticism. Two in particular are of relevance here: firstly, there was a confidence in the use of 'reason', or human linguistic discourse, as a method adequately suited to understanding every area of knowledge; and secondly, all truth was assumed to be unitary, and so the height of scholarly achievement was the production of a 'technologia'.

A technologia was a survey of the different branches of knowledge showing their inter-relations and dependencies on each other. Its antecedents are Alexander Richardson's appropriation of the logic of Peter Ramus and the 'Technometria' of William Ames (who had also been influenced by Ramus). The *Dialecticae Libri Duo*, Ramus' little book that summed up his views on the nature of human reasoning, was published in Paris in 1556, three years before the final edition of Calvin's *Institutes of the Christian Religion*. These two books between them could be said to define English and American Puritanism; Calvin offering the subject matter and Ramus the method that would enable its development. Richardson (who was a tutor at Queens' College, Cambridge, the university where early Puritan theology was in great measure forged[22]) and Ames, the first great Puritan theologian, adapted Ramus' system to fit a key theological axiom, that in the mind of God all knowledge was one. It was this baptised Ramism that in great measure lay behind the technologia of New England scholarship.

When God created the world, He thought of the processes, components and, since He is eternal, the history of the creation. So, in the mind of God, all possible

---

[21] 'On Insects' in *YE6*.
[22] Ramist logic was rigorously opposed by Richard Hooker at Oxford at the same time. The existence of distinct theological traditions in Oxford and Cambridge in the second half of the sixteenth century ensured that in the later debates both Puritans and Anglicans had robust theological systems and traditions from which to argue.

knowledge is unified and coherent. Thus, it should be possible to trace the interconnections of the different branches of knowledge and to draw up an exhaustive plan of their arrangements. Indeed, only with such a plan in view would the various branches of knowledge be properly understood: the relationship of astronomy to history, for example, was misunderstood by those who practised astrology. The final aim of all this was to relate all of human knowledge to God's wisdom, which ordered all these disparate elements perfectly in the first place.

Both this and the confidence in the adequacy of human reason to the task of understanding the world, which has its origin and defence in a particular way of understanding the creation of humanity 'in the image of God' in Genesis, can be seen to be theologically construed methods of reasoning. This incidentally suggests good reason for the apparent conservatism of Puritan learning; Samuel Johnson complained that (just a few years before Edwards went up to Yale) the college had 'heard indeed of a new philosophy that of late was all in vogue and of such names as Descartes, Boyle, Locke and Newton, but they were cautioned against thinking anything of them because the new philosophy it was said would soon bring in a new divinity and corrupt the pure religion of the country'.[23] The fear was understandable: the current method had been brought in line with the gospel; a new way of organising knowledge and constructing arguments would be inimical to the gospel unless it, too, could be baptised. I will suggest later, particularly in chapter 3, that Edwards took up this task.

In common with this Puritan heritage, the 'Reformed Orthodox' tradition of theology,[24] which flourished on the European mainland, was influential in New England. It is

[23] Quoted in *YE6*, p. 13.
[24] The theological movement which, between c.1570 and c.1700, sought to codify and systematise the thought of the Reformers is variously known as 'Protestant Scholasticism' and 'Protestant Orthodoxy', with 'Reformed' or 'Lutheran' replacing 'Protestant' when more precision is required. The titles are not, I think, especially well-suited, but are customary, and so will be used here. For some historical details of the movements, see Carl R. Trueman and R. S. Clark (eds), *Protestant Scholasticism: Essays in Reassessment* (Carlisle: Paternoster Press, 1999).

not easy to define the differences between this movement and Puritanism, which itself is a notoriously difficult word. In part, I think, they are sociological: the continental Reformed churches were state churches, and so owned the universities and had the leisure to pursue their reflection; Puritans in their homeland were dissenters and nonconformists, often suffering persecution, and rarely more than tolerated. So the continental Reformed literature produced great theological systems written in Latin, and offering ever more careful statements and definitions of disputed theological points, whilst the characteristic Puritan literature is a published sermon or series of sermons, written in the vernacular, and dealing with very practical issues of the living out of the Christian life. This distinction is overstated (amongst the Puritans, Baxter and Owen wrote major dogmatic works, for example), but might give the flavour of a genuine difference that any reader of the texts will feel.

If my suggestion of a sociological reason behind this divergence is correct, then we might expect the New Englanders to gradually feel more at home with the continental tradition. Whilst still under various types of colonial rule until the Revolution, the church polity was practically a Congregationalist state church, and there was little or no need to offer continuous self-justifications such as had been required of the Puritans in England. Equally, whilst the various colleges were not the great universities of Europe, there was leisure to explore the finer points of theological reasoning in a way that few could in the home country after Oxford and Cambridge were closed to nonconformists. There is plenty of evidence that the great Reformed systems were read and appreciated in Harvard and Yale; Jonathan Edwards, in a letter to a friend, recommends two of them, François Turretin's *Institutes of Elenctic Theology* and Petrus van Mastricht's *Theoretico-Practica Theologia*.[25] When considering Edwards' theology, then, the positions and questions of this continental tradition are at least as relevant as those of the Anglophone Puritan tradition. This background has

[25] See *YE16*, p. 217.

been largely ignored by secondary literature, however, as a glance under 'Turretin' or 'Mastricht' in the indices of the standard texts will demonstrate. I hope my use of this tradition in this study will demonstrate how illuminating for Edwards' theology it can be.

If this theological background has been too much ignored, the same emphatically cannot be said of aspects of Edwards' philosophical background, at least since Perry Miller attempted his reconstruction of Edwards as a prototype Lockean empiricist. Certainly, he read Locke and Newton early in his life, and was deeply affected by them in all sorts of ways. Like others of the day (Samuel Johnson, Cotton Mather), he realised that the implied critique of the old way that these writers offered was devastating. Locke's rejection of any categories innate in the human mind that are suited to knowing the world and Newton's demonstration that the mathematics of mechanical objects can describe at least some properties of all objects without distinction together undermined the logic, the way in which ideas could properly be connected, that had served New England very well for the first century of its existence. However, as even the outline of a biography I have included will clearly demonstrate, Edwards was a Puritan pastor, preaching for revival, defending Calvinism, and understanding the events of the world around him in thoroughly theological terms. For the last century and a half, this has been the chief riddle concerning Edwards: how could someone of undoubted genius, clearly alert to the implications of the new science and new philosophy that were to launch the Enlightenment, remain wedded to such an outmoded system of thought and, indeed, way of life?

There is widespread agreement that the single most significant text in sparking the renewal of interest in Edwards that has taken place during this century is Perry Miller's *Jonathan Edwards*.[26] At the point when Miller's study appeared, Edwards had for some decades been

---

[26] Miller, *Jonathan Edwards*.

remembered as little more than a fiery Puritan preacher, and even within the churches only by groups on the fringes, in intellectual and theological terms at least: traditional Calvinists knew him as a powerful exponent of their position; revivalists knew him as *the* preacher of the Great Awakening; the supporters of the Evangelical missions knew him as Brainerd's biographer.[27] Miller highlighted Edwards' philosophical genius, and the use he had made of Locke and Newton. He also (as one of the most significant historians of colonial America) introduced Edwards as a key figure in interpreting the American culture, whilst down-playing the significance of Edwards' theology – for Miller, Calvinist dogmatics was merely the medium Edwards used to express his art, which could as well (or better) have been expressed in poetry or literature or perhaps even music. Edwards was great precisely because it was not necessary to view him as a theologian.

The first impression that will confront anyone attempting a survey of the scholarship since Miller's work will be the bewildering array of approaches that is available. That book was designed to focus on the importance of Edwards as a figure in American history, and his writing style is sufficiently powerful to gain him a place in the American literary canon as well. I have mentioned a philosophical puzzle, and I write as a theologian. In these four fields, at least, Edwards occupies a sufficiently major place for regular studies to appear still, and there are yet other areas where he deserves notice (the history of science, for example). The student may legitimately ask, then, which of these fields is primary: was he a philosopher who was a Calvinist because that was the only option in his culture, or a theologian whose philosophy served his account of the faith? Or is his true genius as a writer, a user of language, and philosophy and theology alike are merely what he happened to write? In the remainder of this chapter, I will

---

[27] It is perhaps instructive to ask just how much of the revival of interest in Edwards' thought has been due to the intellectual mainstream recognising that its dismissal of traditional theological orthodoxies and evangelistically-minded Christian practice was too hasty and unjustified – not to say arrogant.

argue that, although the revival of scholarly interest in
Edwards that has taken place during the latter half of the
twentieth century began with Miller's assertion that
Edwards could be interesting only if his theology was
bracketed, it has led to the recognition that Edwards' life
and writings make sense only when it is realised that the
controlling vision was theological.

Nineteenth-century America solved the philosophical
problem by postulating a radical break in Edwards' intellectual history. The philosophical works were all early; at
some point Edwards laid down these interests in order to
concentrate on theology. In his biography, Hopkins gave
us the memorable image of a thirteen-year-old boy poring
over Locke's *Essay* with 'more Satisfaction and Pleasure in
studying it, than the most Greedy miser in gathering up
handsful of Silver and Gold from some new discover'd
Treasure.'[28] Edwards' other early biographer, Sereno
Dwight, first published the *Notes on the Mind*, the most
purely philosophical of Edwards' notebooks, on which his
reputation as a philosopher was largely built. It was the
contents of the *Mind*, held to be purely early work, that led
to most nineteenth-century studies describing Edwards as
an idealist, and to a series of attempts to discover from
whence came this idealism, which was remarkably similar
to Bishop Berkeley's system, with all of reality existing in
the mind of God,[29] was derived. For some reason, and
tragically, according to this reconstruction, Edwards gave
up his philosophical work and devoted himself purely to
sermonising from pulpit and page. His Calvinism, and
hence all his theology, was an embarrassment; his sermons
so many abhorrent barbarisms, unfit for civilized ears. As
Murray says, '... [t]hey were certain that if Edwards were
to be appreciated at all it must *not* be in terms of his

[28] See *YE6*, p. 17 for the relevant paragraph. It is now universally
accepted that this picture is wrong. Edwards either read Locke as a
student but only grasped his full significance later, or came to him whilst
as a tutor at Yale. See *YE6*, pp. 24–6 for a summary of the evidence.
[29] See chapter 3, pp. 94–9 for more on Edwards' philosophy, and a brief
comparison with Berkeley.

theology.... Only as a "philosopher", it seemed, could he retain some respectability.'[30]

Miller's study, as I have already noted, depicted Edwards as a Lockean, and so an empiricist, rather than an idealist. 'In Edwards,' he claims, ' "idealism" is an incidental argument, and except for the fact that his mind moved for a few paragraphs along the same path as Berkeley's, a path that was unmistakably laid out by Locke, Edwards and Berkeley have little in common.'[31] I will offer my own assessment of the similarities and differences between Edwards and Berkeley later; the present point is the impetus Miller gave to the study of Edwards' philosophy. It was no longer sufficient to regard Edwards' philosophy as the juvenile idealism of a genius who unfortunately devoted his mature thought to less profitable subjects; for Miller everything Edwards wrote was determined in its form by these early philosophical commitments, and the need was not to trace the source of these teenage speculations, but to trace their issue, to find that there was philosophical gold in the Calvinistic dross of the mature treatises – or perhaps, that the common stone of Puritan dogmatics had been sculpted into philosophically beautiful forms by Edwards' consummate artistry.

This is not however Miller's only contribution to the understanding of Edwards' philosophy. As well as making much of Locke, he recognises the significance for Edwards of an early reading of Newton.[32] Anderson, who has edited Edwards' early scientific manuscripts, regards him as 'nearly unique' amongst naturalists in the American colonies in focusing his interest on problems of physics, rather than those of botany or zoology.[33] However, Edwards' interest was not in becoming a Newtonian physicist – in a reassuring glimpse of humanity in the genius, he became one of the first of many students who could make neither head nor tail of the differential

---

[30] Murray, *Jonathan Edwards*, p. xx; italics original.
[31] Miller, *Jonathan Edwards*, p. 62.
[32] Miller, *Jonathan Edwards*, pp. 72–4.
[33] *YE6*, p. 39.

calculus! Edwards' use of Newton, as Miller was the first to recognise, was once again philosophical. Miller offered the example of the collapse of causality: from the Aristotelian profusion of pre-Newtonian physics, Edwards was left with one meaningful cause, the instrumental, and (suggests Miller) one of his most carefully-argued sermons can be read as an attempt to rewrite the doctrine of justification by faith alone within constraints imposed by this reduction.[34] It must be said that Miller's reconstruction of Edwards' philosophical genius is now widely regarded as wrong-headed at almost every turn, but that is not the point. His book is important not because it is right, but because it opened up vistas in Edwards' thought that few had imagined were there.

After Miller, many studies have sought to explore these wide open spaces. Whilst some continue the nineteenth-century project of seeking to trace the sources of Edwards' philosophy,[35] the majority address the challenge of finding an interpretation that will demonstrate the coherence that runs through the corpus. A recurrent theme has been aesthetics.[36] As a result of this work the centrality of the third of the classical transcendentals for Edwards has been established. The use Edwards makes of it is distinctive, however: as I will indicate in chapter 3, beauty is finally an ontological category (i.e. it is a way of talking about being or existence simply considered), and so theological (as Edwards regularly identifies God as 'being-in-general'). As a result of this, again and again, when asking about reasons for God's actions, Edwards will claim that such and such a

---

[34] Miller, *Jonathan Edwards*, pp. 74–9.
[35] The best of these are probably Norman Fiering, *Jonathan Edwards's Moral Thought and its British Context* (Chapel Hill, NC: University of North Carolina Press, 1981) and W. S. Morris, *The Young Jonathan Edwards: A Reconstruction* (Brooklyn: Carlson, 1991). This latter work is an unrevised posthumous publication of a thesis completed in 1955, and shows its age in one or two particulars, but it is astonishingly comprehensive, and so remains useful.
[36] The major works in this area are Roland A. Delattre, *Beauty and Sensibility in the Thought of Jonathan Edwards* (London: Yale University Press, 1968) and Terrence Erdt, *Jonathan Edwards: Art and the Sense of the Heart* (Amherst, MA: University of Massachusetts Press, 1980).

course is appropriate for God because, in the light of who God is, it is beautiful.

Aesthetics has importance in every area of Edwards' thought, but particularly perhaps in ethical discussions. This relationship was established and first explored by Clyde Holbrook,[37] whose study was also the first of the recent works to trace the distinctions Edwards makes between redeemed and unredeemed virtuous action, a distinction which should now be recognised as key to his ethics. The new field of 'moral philosophy', which was built on the new psychology of Locke, contained significant secularising tendencies. Edwards, clearly aware of this nascent discipline, attempted to reverse this in his own ethical works. Writers such as Shaftesbury and Hutcheson had explored a morality based on Lockean psychology, which (potentially) had no need for divine reward and retribution in its account of motives; Edwards argued vigorously in response that ethics must be theocentric – 'True Virtue' could exist only in a God-directed, Spirit-empowered, Christ-like life. His ethics are clearly God-centred, built around the recognition that it is impossible to speak of moral action without reference to God.

Perhaps most interestingly in the philosophical realm, a number of scholars have used Edwards' writings to advance or explore characteristically postmodern themes. Stephen Daniel's discussion of semiotics assumes and asserts that Edwards is not a modernist thinker,[38] and even compares his thought to that of such leading postmodernists as Michel Foucault and Julia Kristeva. Another writer similarly uses Edwards as one of a number of conversation partners in his discussion of the nature of reasoning in an implicit attack on the modernist

---

[37] Clyde A. Holbrook, *The Ethics of Jonathan Edwards: Morality and Aesthetics* (Ann Arbor, MI: University of Michigan Press, 1973).
[38] Stephen H. Daniel, *The Philosophy of Jonathan Edwards: A Study in Divine Semiotics* (The Indiana Series in the Philosophy of Religion) (Bloomington, IN: Indiana University Press, 1994). For the particular point see, for example, p. 4: 'Edwards's texts assume practices which are simply unimaginable in terms of modernity.'

paradigm.[39] Clearly Edwards was not 'postmodern'; the etymology of that title alone should convince us of that. The use of these studies, however, is that they highlight the possibility of a different account of the history of ideas from the Enlightenment myth of progress. Edwards' Calvinism need not be thought of as 'primitive', just as incompatible with the dominant thought-forms of nineteenth-century America, and thus difficult for people in that culture to cope with. When Jenson suggests that Edwards shows a different way of being American, and so offers a theological challenge to a nation that came to birth after his death, it is this sort of theme he is implicitly drawing on.[40] What is perhaps missing in these postmodernist interpretations of Edwards is the realisation, central to Jenson, that this is a *theological* critique, that its basis and power come from an assertion of the priority of God.

In order to suggest a way of drawing together this range of approaches to Edwards' philosophy, I have indicated my conviction, as I have discussed each approach, that any common ground will be theological rather than philosophical. In a recent article, Michael McClymond has argued this point persuasively. He suggests that the theocentric nature of Edwards' thought will establish the connections and he offers indications of how this might work with regard to ontology, epistemology, idealism and aesthetics.[41] Miller had sought to paint Edwards as a

---

[39] W. J. Wainwright, *Reason and the Heart: A Prolegomenon to a Critique of Passional Reason* (London: Cornell University Press, 1995). Also to be mentioned here is Leon Chai, *Jonathan Edwards and the Limits of Enlightenment Philosophy* (Oxford: Oxford University Press, 1998), which pursues a similar programme.
[40] R. W. Jenson, *America's Theologian: A Recommendation of Jonathan Edwards* (Oxford: Oxford University Press, 1988) *passim*, but particularly pp. 11–12, 194–6, and the entire section entitled 'Community', pp. 139–85.
[41] Michael J. McClymond, 'God the Measure: Towards an Understanding of Jonathan Edwards' Theocentric Metaphysics', *Scottish Journal of Theology* 47 (1994) pp. 43–59. This article has been incorporated into Professor McClymond's monograph on Edwards, *Encounters with God: An Approach to the Theology of Jonathan Edwards* (Oxford: Oxford University Press, 1998), where it forms chapter 2, without substantial alteration. Chapter 4 of the book extends the argument concerning theocentricity to include Edwards' ethics.

philosopher who happened to write his philosophy in the form of Calvinist dogmatics; McClymond shows that only by recognising Edwards as what might be termed a 'radical Calvinist' with an uncompromising assertion of the centrality and sovereignty of God, can his philosophy be understood. With this latter judgement I heartily concur.

So, Edwards' continuing philosophical interests can be made sense of only by understanding them within the context of his theology. Can the same be said of his position within the fields of American history and literature? Perry Miller's name regularly appears in works on Edwards mainly because of one book; his significance, however – and by any standards Miller was a significant scholar – lies more in his historical work on colonial America.[42] His work resulted in a new appreciation of early American history, and an interest in finding the genius of America in those early years. A major motif of this search, a motif which can already be found in Miller's own writings,[43] has been the polarity between Jonathan Edwards and Benjamin Franklin.[44]

This polarity has taken various forms. Sometimes it is clearly present, but its precise nature is indistinct, as when a recent history of American literature describes Edwards and Franklin as 'two men who between them seem to realize and sum up the changes of American thought and the variety within it'.[45] Sometimes Edwards is the bugbear, the personification of aristocracy, superstition and intellectual slavery from which the new, young nation was to

---

[42] See (amongst other works) *Orthodoxy in Massachusetts 1630–1650* (Boston: Beacon Press, 1959²), the two volumes of *The New England Mind: The Seventeenth Century* and *From Colony to Province* (both Cambridge, MA: Harvard University Press, 1954 and 1953, respectively); *The Puritans* (with Thomas H. Johnson, revised edition: New York: Harper and Row, 1963); *Errand Into the Wilderness* (Cambridge, MA: Harvard University Press, 1956).

[43] *Jonathan Edwards*, p. xiii.

[44] For a brief overview of the history of this comparison see the 'Introduction' in Barbara B. Oberg and Harry S. Stout (eds), *Benjamin Franklin, Jonathan Edwards, and the Representation of American Culture* (Oxford: Oxford University Press, 1993) pp. 3–8.

[45] Richard Ruland and Malcolm Bradbury, *From Puritanism to Postmodernity: A History of American Literature* (London: Penguin, 1992) p. 38.

free itself; and Franklin, as the personification of democracy, of the American dream of earning one's position in society, offers salvation from this bugbear.[46] In other versions, there is less of a value judgement implied, as when a complementarity is seen between the heirs of Edwards, the idealist philosopher in American academic life, and the heirs of Franklin, the utilitarian in business life.[47]

Alongside this attempt to use Edwards as an interpretative tool for American culture, there is a parallel (to the extent that the separation is not always recognised) attempt to use Edwards as an interpreter of American culture. For Miller, Edwards reminds the nation that sometimes, beyond the satisfaction and the solace that can be found in a new refrigerator, or a paid-off car (one can imagine Miller arguing, as the consumer boom of the 1950s began), there is something darker, and wilder and more elemental, that must occasionally be faced (the consumer boom, after all, took place in the shadow of the Bomb). For Jenson, Edwards is America's prophet as much as America's theologian. He sees with inspired clarity the failures and contradictions that will come from the nation's particular idolatries, and in theological treatise as much as jeremiad, calls the nation, not back, but to a different way of moving forward.

Clearly, what is at stake here is as much an interpretation of American culture as an interpretation of Edwards. But in fact the disagreements run deeper than that: as Jenson sees with some clarity, Edwards' vision, inspired by Locke and Newton, is of a different way of being

---

[46] So, for example, Vernon L. Parrington, *Main Currents in American Thought: An Interpretation of American Literature from the Beginnings to 1920: Vol. I: 1620–1800: The Colonial Mind* (New York: Harcourt, Brace & Co., 1930). See especially pp. 148–78.
[47] Thus Howard Mumford Jones, *O Strange New World: American Culture: The Formative Years* (London: Chatto & Windus, 1965) pp. 197–200, where he claims to have found the idea in Brooks. Van Wyck Brooks published a number of works around the turn of the century in the area of what would now be called American Studies, and several are listed in Jones's bibliography. He gives no precise reference to where this idea may be found in Brooks, and I have not been able to trace it.

Enlightened than that which the Enlightenment in fact followed, personified so well in Benjamin Franklin.[48] The Declaration of Independence and the nation that was born from it represent, in a sense, the great Enlightenment social experiment.[49] Edwards was out of step with that experiment, a representative of a different possible Enlightenment and a different possible America, and interpretations of his place in the history of American culture will depend in large part upon evaluations of that experiment.

Prior to Miller's study, there seems to have been substantial agreement that Edwards was to be considered as anachronistic even in his own day: Puritan, even medieval, a representative of an old order that was even then passing and has now long passed.[50] Miller, in seeking to paint Edwards as a Lockean philosopher, argues for a thoroughly Enlightened Edwards, so modern, in fact, that in some ways we are only just catching up with him.[51] In either case, there is a shared premise: that of human progress. On the one hand, Edwards, however brilliant, is left behind by the march of progress. On the other, his brilliance is shown by the way that he steals a march on progress. Either way, the assumption is that there is a general forward movement in human history, that every century, if not every day, in every way, we are getting better and better.

Perhaps beginning with Auschwitz, or perhaps much earlier, this attitude has been seriously damaged this century. Richard Bauckham has recently argued that we are witnessing 'the end of secular eschatology'[52] – the final

---

[48] Again, the point can be found *passim*, but see particularly the closing comments on pp. 194–6.

[49] Or one of the two great Enlightenment social experiments, but the other, beginning with the French Revolution, has a far messier history, being entangled in European wars from the beginning and often since.

[50] Parrington, *Main Currents*, will again serve as an example of this attitude.

[51] '... he speaks from an insight into science and psychology so much ahead of his time that our own can hardly be said to have caught up with him.' Miller, *Jonathan Edwards*, p. xiii.

[52] The title of the Drew Lecture, 1998; unpublished as-yet, but the text is held by the library of Spurgeon's College.

failure of the forward-looking optimism that has characterised post-Enlightenment Western societies. This is not to
say that the 'myth of progress' is dead – studies making all
the same assumptions are still regularly published[53] – but
it is to say that this attitude should no longer be assumed,
that it, too, is open to question, that, perhaps, the next great
intellectual step forward will be to realise that great intellectual steps go in directions other than simply forward.

If the Enlightenment was not the historically necessary
next step from Newton and Locke, if the Declaration of
Independence and the Constitution that followed were not
fated – or 'self-evident' – but merely one possible
movement, then Edwards' relationship to American
culture is capable of a multiplicity of interpretations. The
options are no longer restricted to a series of points on a
(temporal) linear scale – anachronistic, prophetic, or some
ambiguous mixture of the two. A two-dimensional map is
now available, and Edwards (or Franklin) might be
pointing down different roads from the one the Founding
Fathers walked, might even have been far-sighted enough
to see some of the difficulties on that road, and other paths
that were clearer. This is certainly, as I have indicated, the
opinion of Professor Jenson.

My interest is not particularly in Edwards as an interpreter of America – that, surely, is a theme for Americans –
and I claim no specialist knowledge of Franklin. But the
history of scholarship since Miller's writings in this area
represents an opening up of possibilities for discussing
Edwards in terms of the Enlightenment and modernity.
What a theologian may take with some gratitude from the

---

[53]   An attractive illustration may be found in A. Owen Aldridge's paper
in Oberg and Stout (eds), *American Culture*, 'Enlightenment and
Awakening in Edwards and Franklin' (pp. 27–41). The whole paper
demonstrates this attitude, but it is encapsulated in a pair of literary
comparisons – Edwards with Shakespeare, bard of an old world and an
older age, and Franklin with Pope, a contemporary author who may be
described as the chief hymnographer of the anglophone Enlightenment.
Again, Elizabeth Dunn's paper in the same volume, ' "A Wall Between
Them Up to Heaven" ' (pp. 58–74) contains a long endnote categorising
commentators according to whether they describe Edwards as 'modern',
'premodern' or some mixture of the two.

field of American Studies is that Edwards need not be judged by modern categories, but may, in some senses, stand himself as a judge of modernity. And what a theologian may perhaps offer to this other field is the suggestion that it is explicitly theological analysis, a thoroughgoing criticism based on the gospel, rather than any independent insight, that enables Edwards to speak so penetratingly and so searingly to his nation.

So, to the theology. Miller's attempted rehabilitation of Edwards proceeded in spite of Edwards' theology. At one point he quotes Holmes as saying that 'Edwards' system seems, in the light of to-day, to the last degree barbaric, mechanical, materialistic, pessimistic,' and Miller heartily concurs: 'No civilized man in our day, any more than in Dr. Holmes', can say otherwise if he dwells only on the doctrinal positions.'[54] This is presumably a calculated rebuke to the Princeton theologians who had until a decade or two before Miller wrote held Edwards' name in high honour precisely as a theologian.

This is, in many respects, a continuation of the early nineteenth century evaluation of Edwards. On the one hand, defenders of a version of Christian orthodoxy saw him as the head and founder of their school; on the other hand novelists and philosophers recognised a man of genius but found his ideas abhorrent and (once again) remnants of an older world that had, thankfully, passed. The theme is becoming recurrent: Edwards was out of step with an Enlightenment liberalism that has been the most intolerant of all intellectual systems, regarding any other way of thought not as a rival to be argued against, but as an anachronism to be dismissed or patronised. The continuance of this attitude is evident today in (even the most serious) media commentary. Islamic attitudes, for example, are often treated as unintelligible objects of wonderment or amusement, rather than engaged with the respect they deserve.[55]

[54] *Jonathan Edwards*, p. 328.
[55] To add a personal example, I recall a situation from my student days in which I was told, with no hint of irony, 'You can't say that – we're tolerant here.'

But the response too is becoming recurrent, and this we owe to Miller. Edwards was not an anachronism, a backwoods preacher a century behind the times. He grasped the implications of Locke and Newton decades before almost anyone else on the American continent. Miller, however, sees Edwards as modern – 'he speaks with an insight into science and psychology so much ahead of his time that our own can hardly be said to have caught up with him' – despite his theology – 'he speaks from a primitive religious conception which often seems hopelessly out of touch with even his own day'.[56] Miller is still a child of the Enlightenment and tries to make Edwards one too. Perhaps, half a century after Miller wrote, our own day has finally caught up with Edwards: there are other answers, other ways forward, where the doubts of Hume lack force and so Kant's erection of a noumenal barrier is no longer necessary; where the imposing systems of thought based on 'self-evident' truths can be deconstructed and exposed as power games, as deceitful operations of self-love, in Edwards' terms. But where Edwards differs from the thinkers moving in the same directions two centuries later is in his recognition that all this can, indeed must, be done theologically.

Probably the most significant single text in the decades after Miller in this area was Conrad Cherry's *The Theology of Jonathan Edwards: A Reappraisal*.[57] Cherry patiently and carefully unravels Edwards' thought from the perspective of his understanding of faith, but this particular focus is less significant than the general claim: 'for good or for ill, Edwards was a Calvinist theologian'.[58] An intellectually respectable Calvinist theologian was something novel; and a series of studies of greater or lesser length followed, examining Edwards' theology. Amongst this diversity of published work, two themes may be picked out with relative ease. Firstly, the most well-covered area has been conversion, particularly the nature of the 'new sense of the

---

[56] Miller, *Jonathan Edwards*, p. xiii.
[57] Conrad Cherry, *The Theology of Jonathan Edwards: A Reappraisal* (Garden City, NY: Doubleday, 1966).
[58] Cherry, *Reappraisal*, p. 3.

heart' about which Edwards talked so frequently.[59] This theme has been seen to link together Lockean psychological positions and Puritan questions about the nature and morphology of conversion, and so offers fertile ground for an exploration of the theological use to which Edwards put his philosophical positions.

Secondly, a steady stream of works interpreting Edwards from within a traditional Calvinist position have appeared. The best of these (amongst which Cherry may be counted) illuminate the study of Edwards by placing him within another intellectual context: Puritan and Orthodox Reformed theology.[60] Others suffer from a too-obvious apologetic intent: authors who lack knowledge of, or interest in, Edwards' philosophical commitments expound his thought in classic Reformed categories in order to reclaim him for a particular theological school. I suspect, but make no attempt to demonstrate here, that a version of the Scottish 'Common Sense Realism' is retained as a part of commitment to these particular theological schools, and so Edwards is read as if he operated using such a philosophy. One may say many things of Edwards' philosophical commitments, but that they were determined by 'common sense' is not one of them! The result of such a procedure is usually to offer a system that differs little from that of (say) Warfield and lacks penetration into the distinctive elements of Edwards' thought.[61]

---

[59] Book-length studies focusing here include Harold P. Simonson, *Jonathan Edwards: Theologian of the Heart* (Grand Rapids, MI: Eerdmans, 1974) and Erdt, *Art.* Cherry, *Reappraisal* and Wainwright, *Reason* both devote considerable attention to the topic. A significant number of other articles and papers have also been published.

[60] In addition to Cherry, Paul Helm's insightful introduction to Edwards' *Treatise on Grace and Other Writings* (Cambridge: James Clarke, 1971) may be included in this category.

[61] The best of these works is John H. Gerstner's three-volume *The Rational Biblical Theology of Jonathan Edwards* (Powhatan, VA: Berea Publications, 1991-3). Gerstner organises Edwards' thoughts in a meticulous and extremely helpful manner, but rarely offers commentary that is at all incisive, and at times is guilty of simple anachronism. No matter how dear the position may have been to Dr Gerstner's heart, Edwards was not a Biblical inerrantist, and indeed, provides precisely the theological positions required to avoid the total capitulation to Enlightened values that the doctrine of inerrancy represents. Murray's biographical volume, as earlier noted, is open to a similar set of criticisms.

I have already suggested that Edwards has not yet been sufficiently well placed within the Reformed tradition of theology, particularly in its continental forms. He is, however, creatively within this tradition: his is a distinctively Enlightened Puritanism, a Calvinism that has found (particularly in the doctrine of the Trinity) ways to reshape its own distinctives so that they can stand without apology in an intellectual climate shaped by the heirs of Locke and Newton. This is necessarily a different orthodoxy (but orthodox nonetheless) from that which Edwards would have learnt from van Mastricht and Turretin; it is also a different system from that developed by the Edwardsean tradition that followed him, precisely because this clearsighted appreciation of the significance of Locke and Newton was lacking in that tradition.[62]

Jonathan Edwards was a Reformed preacher and theologian. His undoubted greatness as a writer, a philosopher, even his early promise as a scientist, should not be allowed to obscure this truth. This is what the decades of scholarly endeavour since Perry Miller reinvigorated the study of Edwards have confirmed. The greatness and continuing significance of Miller's work is that it demonstrated that Edwards had something to say to America – and, indeed, the rest of the world. Building on what has come since, we are now able to insist that what Edwards had to say was explicitly and irreducibly theological. It might not – should not – be 'Sinners ...', but if we are to hear Edwards' voice it will be a sermon.

---

[62] Joseph Haroutunian's fine book *Piety vs Moralism: The Passing of the New England Theology* (New York: Harper & Row, 1970), first published in 1930, shows great insight into both the greatness of Edwards' theology, and what was lost in the tradition that came after him.

2
A Vision of Glory: Edwards' Quest for God's Fundamental Purpose

Asserting that Edwards is a specifically Reformed theologian, as I did at the end of the previous chapter, is likely to bring to mind the doctrine of predestination. I will have something to say in my final chapter about the idea that this doctrine is the defining point of Reformed theology, but for now reflection upon predestination may provide a useful route into the subject matter of this one. If it is asserted that God has determined all things towards an appointed end, it is not unreasonable to ask what that end might be. God is not fundamentally inscrutable; the doctrine of revelation and particularly the narratives of the life of Jesus determine that point. Knowing something of who God is, we could at least expect to know the sorts of things He would intend in His fundamental act of creating the world.[1] Indeed, a teleological view of creation, asserting that a fundamental reason could be given for God's decision that there should be something other than an eternity of His own perfection, was a commonplace amongst the Reformed orthodox theologians of the seventeenth century from whom Jonathan Edwards learnt much of his theology.[2]

The answer given by these writers to the question of the ultimate purpose of creation was very simple: God creates for the promotion and display of His own glory. This often stood as a simple assertion that was neither argued for nor discussed.[3] Edwards, by contrast, saw the many difficulties

---

[1] Fundamental in the temporal sense, that all else followed on this. I am not, at this point, making any claims about the logical priority between creation and redemption.

[2] On which see Chapter 1, pp. 14–16, and particularly the note on p. 14 concerning terminology.

[3] For example: '... he has determined to show forth the glory of his

inherent in such a view, and wrestled with these problems throughout his life. This process of reflection can be seen in the *Miscellanies*, the theological notebooks he kept almost throughout his adult life, which provide a constant insight into what he was thinking about.[4] The results can be seen in the first of the posthumously published *Two Dissertations*, the *Dissertation Concerning the End for Which God Created the World*, or *End of Creation* as it is usually now known.[5]

The place to begin, perhaps, is in reflection on the question, rather than the various proposed answers. Why, asks Edwards, with the orthodox before him, did God create the world? He is not, in asking this question, making an implicit statement about the ordering of the works of creation and redemption in the divine plan, for he is certainly numbered amongst those who would insist that

---

power, wisdom, and goodness in the creation and preservation of all things' (Wollebius IV.1.2.). (Beardslee's translation in *Reformed Dogmatics*, p. 50); 'He has by an unchangeable counsel and purpose specified and resolved on the things that were to come into being outwith Himself in time, together with their causes, operations and circumstances and the manner in which they are bound to be made and to exist, for proof of His glory' (Heidegger V.4; quoted by Heppe, p. 137). Examples could be multiplied, but see especially Barth, *CD* II/2, pp. 128–9, where Barth identifies a primal divine decision to display glory as fundamental to both supralapsarian and infralapsarian schemes, and *CD* II/1, p. 643 where the definition of the *gloria Dei* is 'the self-revealing sum of all divine perfections ... the emerging, self-expressing, and self-manifesting reality of all that God is ... ' – and this definition is followed by the assertion: 'Many of the older theologians understood the *gloria Dei* in this way.' Also, Hans Urs von Balthasar, *The Glory of the Lord: a Theological Aesthetics Vol. VI: The Old Covenant*, pp. 25–6 and n. 11 (p. 26), where Balthasar discusses, albeit briefly, the medieval scholastic heritage which informed Reformed discussions.

[4] The most convenient source is currently a chapter in: Harvey G. Townsend (ed.), *The Philosophy of Jonathan Edwards from his Private Notebooks*, University of Oregon Monographs Studies in Philosophy no. 2 (Eugene, OR: University of Oregon, 1955), pp. 126–53. Thomas Schafer is editing the complete collection for Yale, and this will be the definitive edition when complete. The first volume, covering *Miscellanies a–500*, is *YE13*.

[5] This can be found in *YE8*, pp. 403–536.

God's prior purpose is to redeem.[6] Edwards' question is rather why God should do anything at all: He is entirely sufficient in Himself, as Father, Son and Holy Spirit, perfect in His own Triune life, so what purpose is served for Him in bringing into being the legions of angels, the expanses of the universe, and the sinful race of human beings?[7]

Creation, according to Christian theology,[8] is wholly given its being by God; it is *ex nihilo*, out of nothing. Its being, however, is genuinely other than God. Pantheist accounts, which identify God with the world, and panentheist accounts, which place the world in God as a part of God, have always been resisted by the Church.[9] However, the world also depends for its being on God; aseity (the ability to exist without being upheld by another) and necessary being are divine perfections, not given to creature or creation. It is this combination of dependency

[6] This will become clear in my discussions of *End of Creation* below, so one example here should suffice: Edwards describes the crucifixion of Christ as '... as it were the cause of all the decrees, the greatest of all decreed events, and that on which all other decreed events depend as their main foundation' (*Miscellanies* 762; as yet unpublished, but an (edited) text may be found in *BT2*, p. 528). The 'decreed events' here certainly include creation. In passing, let me merely highlight that, in contrast to his favoured dogmatics text (that of Turretin), Edwards is numbered on the side of the supralapsarians. That he should adopt this logically rigorous position and seek to answer the question of the justice of the scheme, rather than embracing the infralapsarian attempt to evade the full force of the logic of predestinarian doctrine, is characteristic. His account of these questions will be explored in chapter 4 below.

[7] This question is heavily nuanced, of course, by the particular account of God's aseity that is adopted, and I will discuss this issue in some detail below.

[8] For important recent restatements of the Christian doctrine of creation, see Barth, *CD* III/1; Langdon Gilkey, *Maker of Heaven and Earth: The Christian Doctrine of Creation in the Light of Modern Knowledge* (London: University Press of America, 1959); Colin E. Gunton (ed.), *The Doctrine of Creation: Essays in Dogmatics, History and Philosophy* (Edinburgh: T&T Clark, 1997); Colin E. Gunton, *The Triune Creator: A Historical and Systematic Study* (Edinburgh: Edinburgh University Press, 1998); W. Pannenberg, *Systematic Theology* vol. 2 (tr. G. W. Bromiley) (Grand Rapids, MI: Eerdmans, 1994), pp. 1–174.

[9] I will discuss in chapter 3 below how successfully Edwards' own understanding of the immediacy of God's relationship with creation preserves this note of genuine otherness.

and yet genuine otherness that the assertion that creation is 'out of nothing' seeks to protect.[10]

At this point, my purposes demand that a somewhat artificial division be made between what may be termed the 'how?' and the 'why?' questions concerning creation.[11] The 'how?' question – the account of the relationship between God and His world, between eternity and time – is one I will explore in the next chapter, where I will consider Edwards' idiosyncratic account of creaturely identity and agency. Edwards will not accept any account of any freedom, including God's own freedom, that embraces 'liberty of indifference', which means that there must be a reason, a motive, for every action. Confronted with the decision to create, then, we may – indeed must – ask: why? What is it in God that makes this decision appropriately perfect or beautiful, whereas the converse would have been less so?

As so often in seeking to answer theological questions, there is a very narrow course to be steered here between two dangers: the need is to discover an adequate reason for God to create the universe, without making God's own fulfilment dependent upon the creation. Although there is no explicit statement of these two dangers in Edwards' works, throughout his discussions he can be seen to be attempting to find this middle course. Without any apparent awareness of the patristic discussions, he does this by the same theological method: invoking the doctrine of the Trinity to explain both God's self-sufficiency and the genuinely other nature of the creation.[12]

---

[10]   On this, see R. W. Jenson, 'Aspects of a Doctrine of Creation' in Gunton (ed.), *Creation*, pp. 17–28.

[11]   This division may be regarded as defensible particularly given Edwards' supralapsarianism: the question of God's purposes for the world is clearly separate, and prior, to the question of God's relationship with the world, according to this scheme. John H. Gerstner finds this division in Edwards: 'Jonathan Edwards was surely interested in the creation, but he was far more concerned with what happened behind the creation scene.' *Rational Biblical Theology* vol. 2, p. 189.

[12]   See F. Young, ' "Creatio ex Nihilo": a context for the emergence of the Christian Doctrine of Creation', *Scottish Journal of Theology* 44 (1991) pp. 139–51; and Gerhard May, *Creatio ex Nihilo: The Doctrine of Creation out of Nothing in Early Christian Thought* (tr. A. S. Worrall) (Edinburgh: T&T Clark, 1994).

There is a distinction made regularly in the history of Christian theology between those things that God cannot be God without doing, and those things that He merely chooses to do. The standard application of this distinction relates to God's decision to create: it is of the nature of God to beget the Son (and to spirate the Spirit); He could not be who He is without so doing.[13] By contrast, it is merely God's good pleasure to create. He could have not done so, and His perfection would not have been altered or lessened in any way.

The importance of this for the idea of aseity concerns the possibility within a Trinitarian account of God of seeing an inner dynamism to the divine life. If God's perfections must find exercise – as Edwards will argue – then there is a need either for this or for creation. If God is love, then He must have an object for His love, and without a doctrine of the Trinity that means He must create in order to be able to love. Thus, a non-trinitarian account would have to make creation necessary to God's existence at this point. This will become clearer as I consider Edwards' struggles with the issue, to which I now turn.

The Development of Edwards' Position in the *Miscellanies*

Edwards' *Miscellanies* show an interesting process of development towards the mature statement in *End of Creation*, which will illuminate certain themes in that work. In analysing the latter, then, I intend to start by exploring Edwards' journey to that point. The discovery and close reading of the *Miscellanies* have been among the most

---

[13] 'He does not have this freedom in respect of His being God. God cannot not be God ... His freedom or aseity in respect of Himself consists in His freedom, not determined by anything but Himself, to be God, and this means to be the Father of the Son. A freedom to be able not to be this would be an abrogation of His freedom.' (Barth, *CD* I/1, p. 434). For the same point in Edwards – although not in connection with Trinitarian doctrine – see my discussion of *The Freedom of the Will* in chapter 4 below, pp. 151–7.

significant features of Edwards scholarship over the past few years, providing great insight into how his thought holds together, and illuminating references to many theological issues not dealt with in any of the published works. This has led, however, to a mistaken regard for these notes. They cannot be considered as Edwards' final word on any subject, but must rather be seen as his 'rough workings'. These books are the place where he jotted down interesting ideas that he felt the need to think more about; where he sketched new statements of arguments to see if they worked. I hope, then, that as well as illuminating what Edwards was about in the *End of Creation*, this section will also illustrate the provisional nature of *Miscellanies* entries.

The journey begins with entries written during Edwards' brief pastorate in New York. In entry *gg*[14] (1722–3), he argues that a universe without immortal intelligent beings would profit God nothing – He 'could neither receive good himself nor communicate good'.[15] This is picked up in *kk*, where it is argued that religion (rather than social morality) must be the chief business of humanity.

In entry *tt* (1722–3) Edwards addresses the question of the usefulness of devotion. He argues against the suggestion that an excessive practice of devotion reduces a person's usefulness to the common good of the universe, and so is inappropriate. If, Edwards claims, the common good is the highest good, then the universe as a whole can have no purpose. Taking an illustration, he points out that the parts of a clock work together to turn the hands to provide purpose by reference to something outside itself. The lesser creatures exist for the greater, until at last humanity is reached – who can have usefulness and purpose only outside the connected whole that is the creation, and so only in reference to the Creator: 'He was undoubtedly made to glorify the Creator, so that devotion must be his highest end.'[16] This finds a particularly

[14] The *Miscellanies* contain two alphabetical series before the main numeric series starts, numbered *a–z* and *aa–zz*. Entry *gg* is, therefore, the thirty-first entry (as *j* and *v* are missing from the first alphabetical series).
[15] *YE13*, p. 185.
[16] *YE13*, p. 190.

attractive presentation in entry 3, where 'Happiness is the end of creation ... because creation had as good not be as not rejoice in its being.'[17] Again, creation exists to glorify God (this, a position which Edwards will later reach by careful argument, is here simply asserted, presumably as a result of the Reformed heritage already discussed), which is to say creation exists to rejoice at the glory God has displayed.

Up to this point, Edwards has assumed the creation, and asked about its purpose. In *Miscellanies* 87 (Nov.–Dec. 1723), the question is raised of why God should create at all; why He desires to make known His attributes – His 'power, wisdom, etc.' The answer given is that, of all God's attributes, goodness contains within itself the desire for its own display. One may be wise without desiring to display wisdom, one may (indeed, perhaps can only) be just without desiring to display justice – but goodness includes the desire for the opportunity of its own exercise. Therefore God created the world in order to be good to it, that is, in order to make intelligent beings happy. Happiness is the perception of excellency, so the world is created that angels and humanity may see God's perfections and rejoice in the sight. Entry 92, written at a similar time, is a response to Rev. 4:11, 'For thy pleasure they are and were created.' How so? asks Edwards, if human (and, presumably, angelic, although he makes little of it) happiness is the end of creation. The answer is simply that God enjoys making others happy.

Thus far, Edwards' theology is heart-warming but dangerous – a danger he recognises. The above is very close to making God's own happiness dependent on creation. If God is good, and that goodness includes the inclination to exercise itself, to communicate happiness, then God cannot be fully Himself without exercising that desire – without, given what Edwards has offered so far, creating. That is to say, in the language of the distinctions offered earlier, that creation is at this point apparently necessary for God to be Himself. This danger is addressed

17 *YE13*, p. 199.

in entry 96, where it is argued that perfect goodness desires to communicate perfect happiness, which means happiness equal to the happiness enjoyed by the communicator. Hence God's perfect goodness must find its fulfilment in an 'equal' – this is offered as proof of the doctrine of the Trinity.[18] In entry 104, Edwards realises that now, according to his earlier accounts, God has no reason to create: 'the Father's begetting of the Son is a complete communication of all his happiness, and so an eternal, adequate and infinite exercise of perfect goodness ....'[19] The problem is created by Edwards' embracing of Trinitarian doctrine, and it is to that doctrine he turns for an answer: the Son also has the desire to communicate Himself, to be good to another – and this other is the Church, which is said to be the completeness of Christ (Eph. 1:23). The corollaries to this include the insistence that the Son created the world and the Son was the Person who revealed Himself in the Old Testament theophanies, both of which are standard positions for Edwards.[20]

This is brilliant, but still fails. To the first question raised: why is the response to the Father not an adequate exercise of the Son's goodness? Edwards suggests that the Son did not take the initiative in the relationship, and so has a desire to communicate Himself on His own account.[21] This, of course, leaves Edwards in precisely the position he was before: now the Son's fulfilment depends on the creation, so God still needs the world. Edwards, however, seems not to see either this difficulty or any solution to it, as he is

---

[18] The word 'proof' here needs care: Edwards is not, at this point, operating as a natural theologian; rather, he is arguing on the basis of the biblical revelation about God (perfect goodness, for example) that this demands God to be understood in a Trinitarian way. Careful analysis of his concept of 'goodness' might also demonstrate that it is based on fundamentally biblical ideas, adding further weight to this point. The Trinitarian argument Edwards uses here will be of significance when I come to offer comparisons of his understanding with modern writings on hell in chapter 6 below, pp. 235–8.

[19] YE13, p. 272.

[20] See my discussion of the *History of the Work of Redemption* in chapter 3, pp. 115–19 for a discussion of the implications of these positions.

[21] The Spirit is mentioned several times in the *Miscellanies* entry under discussion, but the references are not integral to the line I am tracing.

silent on the subject for nearly four years, until a spate of entries begins with 271, in late 1726. If God is not to need the world, His act of creation must be for His own sake. It is this idea that Edwards begins to discuss here, again using his Trinitarian apparatus; he apparently recognises that to speak of God making 'himself his end' sounds dangerously like ascribing selfishness to God, and so proposes God making His Son His end. Once again, the language is beautiful: 'It perhaps was thus: God created the world for his Son, that he might prepare a spouse or bride for him to bestow his love upon; so that the mutual joys between this bride and bridegroom are the end of the creation.' Once again, the problem is God's dependence on the world for His own fulfilment, as the 'joys' of the Son are not complete without His creaturely Bride.

In entry 243[22] Edwards adopts a different angle of approach and first proposes a separation: to communicate goodness is indeed an ultimate end, an end in and of itself worthy of God, but so is the display of God's glory. That is, for God to be glorified is not a part of His communication of happiness, but something separate but equally worthy to be God's motive.[23] Edwards is led to this, according to this entry, by passages of Scripture: Jn. 17, 12:28, Is. 42:8, 48:11 'and many other such'. It is not a solution to the problem I have raised, but prompts a new line of thinking about God's glory as an ultimate end. Just four entries later (entry 247), we find analysis and definition of this concept: 'For God to glorify himself is to discover himself in his works or, to communicate himself in his works ... in his acts *ad extra* to act worthy of himself, or to act excellently ... the glory of God is the shining forth of his perfections; and the world was created that they might shine forth ....'[24]

This is perhaps an appropriate point to pause for some preliminary reflections. Edwards has introduced various

---

[22] According to Schafer's dating, 271 precedes 243 and 247. See *YE13*, Table 2, facing p. 90.

[23] At this point, Edwards' departure from Reformed orthodoxy becomes significant, although he will later find in Mastricht the way to resolve this. See below.

[24] *YE13*, pp. 360–1.

possibilities for God's ultimate purpose in creating the world, which all overlap to some extent: the exercise of God's goodness; the communication of God's happiness; the display of God's glory. These begin as simple suggestions but are quickly developed as Edwards sees problems and solutions. In particular, an awareness of both the threat to God's aseity implied by making Him somehow dependent on the creation, and an acute awareness of the impropriety of making God's motives somehow selfish are addressed, if not totally solved, by a conscious invocation of Trinitarian doctrine. In this, Edwards has laid the foundations of his approach: what will follow will essentially be an analysis of the nature of, and relationships between, goodness, communication, and glory in a Trinitarian context in an attempt to avoid both the charge of selfishness and the threat to aseity.[25] With this map in place, I return to the historical analysis.

In entry 332 (late 1728[26]) the beginnings of an answer to the threat to God's aseity start to become apparent: the language chosen now is that of communication, but what is new is an analysis of God's fulfilment: 'It don't make God the happier to be praised, but it is a becoming and condecent and worthy thing for infinite and supreme excellency to shine forth: 'tis not his happiness but his excellency so to do.'[27] This is a key advance, in that here it is appropriate for God to create, rather than in some sense necessary. With this insight, creation is finally something appropriate and beautiful for God to do, but not something necessary for His perfection. A hint of a second theme is also present: 'the communication of himself to their understandings is his glory, and the communication of himself with respect to their wills, the enjoying faculty, is their

[25] Although, as I have indicated above, Edwards is following the same line as the Fathers took, it seems he is doing it without any conscious borrowings from patristic theology.
[26] There is a misprint in Schafer's table of dates: under '1726 Sept'. The confusing entry '331–314' appears; as p. 84 of the introduction makes clear, this should read '311–314'.
[27] YE13, p. 410.

happiness.'[28] This language will turn out to be of great importance later.

A year later, in late 1729 and early 1730, Edwards produced three entries (445, 448 and 461) which take these thoughts further. Entry 445 is a long analysis of the exercise of goodness and the display of glory as joint ultimate ends. Goodness must be exercised for its own sake, or it is not goodness, in distinction from every other attribute which is glorified. Edwards invokes the example of justice, and the argument he had used previously: God can be just without ever acting justly – so long as He never acts unjustly; God cannot be good without ever acting in a good way. Entry 461 continues this theme, arguing on the basis of Scripture that 'God delighteth in the creatures' happiness in a sense that he doth not do in their misery.'[29] This, surely, is a significant statement, and Edwards takes it further: 'The glory of God cannot be considered as the proper end of God's acts of justice.'[30] God acts justly because He is just, although He might have had in mind the glorifying of Himself when He gave Himself occasion to act justly. God enjoys His creatures' happiness, and God enjoys their knowledge of, and delight in, His perfections. The latter demands the display of those perfections, and so may involve (in the case of justice) suffering for some creatures, but this is a bad thing, an inappropriate thing, in itself, although outweighed by the good of God's perfection being seen in the final analysis. There is little need to draw attention to how far we are from caricatures of Edwards' God as 'the cosmic sadist' at this point.

Miscellanies 448 takes up Trinitarian analysis once again: God's internal self-glorification occurs in two ways: in knowing Himself in His own perfect idea, the Son, and in flowing forth in love and delight for Himself – the Spirit. Correspondingly, His glory is externalised in two ways: being known by His creatures and being loved and enjoyed by His creatures. In this, the fullness consists in

28 *YE13*, p. 410.
29 *YE13*, p. 502.
30 *YE13*, p. 502.

God's delight in giving to His creatures; He cannot receive anything from them. All His communication of glory is an overflow of the dynamics of His own intra-Trinitarian life. God is given nothing by creation, so His aseity is preserved, but God enjoys giving something to the creation, and so He creates.

In entry 547, Edwards brings in another necessary complication to this story: the reality of history. Providence, Edwards asserts, has a goal, which will be reached at the end of the world. At that point, it will have been necessary for each moment in history to have happened, or 'providence never would have ordered them. The world never would have been in such a state.'[31] Edwards actually uses this as a proof of the survival of intelligent beings, as their memories are all that remain of the intermediate states of history. This corollary is in danger of being inconsistent with Edwards' own metaphysics, which ascribes existence to reality in the mind of God, and history to the sequential nature of that reality,[32] but the attempt to account for the fact of history is significant, and will become a part of Edwards' final position.

Entry 553 is also important, as in it Edwards pulls together much of what has gone before, and makes a further move: the removal of goodness from its prime place amongst the attributes. All divine attributes, Edwards now argues, are exercised only because of creation, and 'it is fit that the divine attributes should have exercise'.[33] This is not because God needs to exercise his perfections, but because He delights to. In fact, God exercises His perfections internally, in that 'He infinitely loves and delights in Himself', and this contains the external exercise, but is not precisely the same. Hence, it is appropriate for God to give Himself opportunity to externalise His perfections – that is, to create.

And this, broadly, remains Edwards' settled position

31 Townsend, *Philosophy*, p. 135.
32 On this see chapter 3 below, pp. 111–12.
33 Townsend, *Philosophy*, p. 136.

until the burst of activity that accompanied his desire to publish his conclusions in *End of Creation*. Entries 581 and 586 reiterate that all things God creates are for His own purposes. There are three entries in the 600s that show Edwards trying to refine his language to avoid any weakening of aseity. These deserve some comment. Entry 662 uses the language of appropriateness once again: 'It was meet that His attributes and perfections should be expressed.'[34] Entry 679 asserts that God does not need creatures, but would be less happy if His desire to display His own goodness were frustrated, a point which is refined still further in entry 699: 'God don't seek His own glory for any happiness He receives by it, as men are gratified in having their excellencies gazed at ... but God seeks the display of His own glory as a thing in itself excellent.'[35] This is a theme Edwards develops elsewhere:[36] God, in putting Himself first, is not being selfish, in that it is appropriate for all things – including God – to put God first.

One further entry from around this time is interesting in this connection. In entry 681[37] Edwards links the gift of happiness to creatures with their (eschatological) being in God, so as to essay a link between God's self-glorification and God's gift of happiness to His creatures. The saints are indeed 'exalted to glorious dignity' and to 'fellowship' and even 'union' with God Himself,[38] but 'care is taken' (by God, we presume) that this is not their own glory, but that it comes to them as they are 'in a person that is God'. Edwards' conclusion is full of admiration for the systematic cleverness of this arrangement: 'Thus wisely hath God ordered all things for his own glory that however great & marvelous the exercises of his grace & love & condescension are to the creature, yet he alone may be

[34] Townsend, *Philosophy*, p. 138.
[35] Townsend, *Philosophy*, p. 139.
[36] For example, the notion of consent to 'being-in-general' (i.e. God) in *True Virtue*; see *YE8*, p. 540 and *passim*.
[37] Thus far published only in the Dwight edition of Edwards' *Works* in 1830; the quotations above all come from the fourth page of Thomas Schafer's transcript of the entry.
[38] Edwards will even say that the saints are given to be 'in some respects divine in glory and happiness'!

exalted & that he may be all in all.'[39] Here, Edwards discovers, almost in passing, is a way to talk about God's gift of goodness as another aspect of His act of self-glorification.

Following this, there is a gap of over three hundred entries without reference to the question of the end of creation.[40] Then, beginning with 1066, a spurt of entries occurs representing the creative effort Edwards put into systematising his thoughts for publication in *End of Creation*. Rather than analysing all these before turning to that statement, I will next address the published work, and make reference to *Miscellanies* entries where relevant.[41]

Edwards' Mature Position in the *End of Creation*

Concerning the End for which God Created the World is the first of two dissertations Edwards was preparing for publication on his death.[42] It is a characteristically careful attempt to answer a question which, as the foregoing will have made abundantly clear, Edwards had been thinking about throughout his life. In offering a reading of it, one important hermeneutical point must be made: as Paul Ramsey, the modern editor of the *Two Dissertations*, makes

---

[39] The grammatical idiosyncrasies and (particularly) the lack of punctuation, are characteristic of Edwards' unpublished notebooks. The editors of *YE* are (quite rightly) silently tidying up the English as they publish, but in the absence of their authoritative edition, I have chosen to reproduce it as exactly as possible.

[40] Although the ideas that Edwards had been developing do arise in passing in other contexts. To cite merely one example, some relevant comments may be found in *Miscellanies* 864 (as yet unpublished, but an adequate text may be found in *BT2*, pp. 511–14), discussing the moral government of the world.

[41] It is perhaps worth noting that Edwards does make occasional reference in the *Miscellanies* to other works that have clearly influenced him as he was preparing to write *End of Creation*. Apart from the obvious Biblical interest (see, for instance, entries 1080 and 1081), Edwards transcribes a passage from Ramsay's *Philosophical Principles of Religion* that clearly influences, or at least supports, Edwards' own argument in entry 1253 (see particularly p. 5 of the Schafer transcript), and also a series of quotations from Thomas Goodwin in entries 1275 and 1277a.

[42] The companion volume is *True Virtue*; both may be found in *YE8*.

clear they should be read together, not apart.[43] This is more of an issue, perhaps, in the interpretation of the second dissertation, *True Virtue* (as Ramsey's examples show[44]), but will also affect a reading of the first dissertation in important ways, as I hope to demonstrate. This section, then, will contain a (necessarily[45]) full exposition of *End of Creation* coupled with a briefer reading of *True Virtue* to make Edwards' final account of the teleology of creation clear.

End of Creation begins with an introduction defining terms and setting forth axioms, in which Edwards is concerned to make distinction between a 'chief end', an 'ultimate end' and a 'subordinate end'.[46] Starting with the last, a subordinate end is something sought for the sake of something else – the example is offered of buying a medicine, not because of a desire to own it, but because of a desire to regain health.[47] An ultimate end, by contrast, is sought purely for its own sake. Clearly, there may be a chain of subordinate ends leading to the one ultimate end, and a thing may be both an ultimate end and a subordinate end, sought partially for its own account and partially for the sake of something else.[48] Contrasting with both of these is a chief end, which is the thing 'most valued'. This is not the same as an ultimate end; a person may have several ultimate ends – things valued for themselves – but only

---

[43] *YE8*, pp. 5–6. *Miscellanies* 1208 (which is published in an edited form in both Townsend (pp. 140–9) and the *Miscellaneous Remarks*) demonstrates this point quite well. It is headed 'END of the CREATION. GLORY OF GOD Nature of REDEMPTION. SATISFACTION OF CHRIST Nature of TRUE VERTUE & RELIGION', which might be considered an ambitious programme for one notebook entry! The contents, however, demonstrate the close linkage between the theses of the *Two Dissertations* in Edwards' mind.

[44] *YE8*, p. 6 n. 5.

[45] Necessary because there is so little attention paid to this Dissertation in the secondary literature. McClymond has a chapter on the work (*Encounters*, pp. 50–64); Jenson's account (*America's Theologian*, pp. 38–43) is characteristically insightful, although brief; and Gerstner makes occasional comments throughout his *Rational Biblical Theology*. Apart from these, very little has been published.

[46] *YE8*, pp. 405–15. A note in the *Miscellanies* between entries 1355 and 1356 shows Edwards working on these ideas.

[47] *YE8*, p. 405.

[48] *YE8*, p. 406.

one will be the chief end. On the basis of these distinctions, Edwards makes a series of comments concerning purposefulness, which lead in to a discussion of God's aims and goals in creating the world. Edwards suggests that if there is only one ultimate end this may therefore be termed the 'supreme end'.[49] He indicates here that he will show this to be the case with God, although as yet no argument for this position is offered.[50] The act of creation is directed towards this supreme end, although God having created, a number of other ultimate ends (which Edwards terms 'consequential ultimate ends') come into view. It is pleasing to God to act justly, for instance, and so this is an end in itself after the fact of creation, but not the reason for creating. All God's works will clearly be governed by His supreme end, but any given act of God may also be governed by consequential ultimate ends as well.[51] Any general work of providence, however, will be governed by God's original ultimate end. Finally in this section, Edwards raises the possibility of multiple original ultimate ends in God, and although he has already indicated that he will argue that this is not the case, the position may not yet be assumed.[52]

Thus far, Edwards has merely clarified the question he is asking: what is (are) God's supreme end(s) in creating the world? He begins his answer with a chapter entitled 'What Reason Teaches'.[53] He does so, he explains, because he is engaged in apologetic work, and so must begin with reason to meet objections based on reason. In the first section of this chapter, six general dictates of reason are offered:[54]

1. God's aseity.
2. That anything presupposed by God's work cannot be its end (e.g. God's own existence).

[49] *YE8*, p. 410.
[50] *YE8*, p. 410.
[51] *YE8*, p. 413.
[52] *YE8*, pp. 414–15.
[53] *YE8*, pp. 417–63.
[54] *YE8*, pp. 419–27.

3. The most valuable thing attainable by creation must be God's end.
4. Hence, if possible, God will be His own end in creating, so that God's self-revelation is an appropriate end.
5. Whatever is valuable in itself, which can be shown to be God's purpose in creation, must be an ultimate end.
6. Therefore, any valuable thing resulting from God's creation can be assumed to be an ultimate end.

On the basis of this, the second section of the chapter asks what good things are the consequence of creation.[55] Four are listed. Firstly, the exercise of God's attributes is valuable in itself: if God delights in His attributes, then He will delight in their display. Secondly, it is more valuable if these perfections are not just exercised but seen to be exercised, and so God's perfection is known by other beings. Thirdly, this is again more valuable if His perfections are not just seen and known, but loved and delighted in. Finally, God's fullness of perfections, beauty and happiness is capable of communication, and this is also valuable in itself. So, Edwards asserts, 'it was [God's] last end, that there might be a glorious and abundant emanation of his infinite fullness of good *ad extra*, or without himself, and the disposition to communicate himself or diffuse his own *fullness*, which we must conceive of being originally in God as a perfection of his nature, was what moved him to create the world.'[56]

The fourth thesis of the first section in this chapter had suggested that, if possible, God should be His own end in creating. Edwards' third section of this second chapter[57] is devoted to demonstrating that, in each of the four points made above, this is precisely what God is doing. The first three points are trivial: God's love of His own perfections

---

[55]   *YE8*, pp. 428–35.
[56]   *YE8*, pp. 433–4. These arguments may be seen developing in *Miscellanies* 1182 (Townsend, *Philosophy*, p. 140).
[57]   *YE8*, pp. 436–44.

naturally implies that He values their display, and their being known and loved. The fourth end, the communication or emanation of God's fullness, is more difficult. Edwards starts by drawing a distinction between love in general, which is God's disposition to love, and love in a strict sense, which presupposes an object to be loved. Given this, it is God's delight in His own glory which causes Him to communicate and diffuse it. The Church is called the 'fullness' and the 'glory' of Christ, so the Church is God's end in creating: 'His exercising his goodness, and gratifying his benevolence to them in particular, may be the spring of all God's proceedings through the universe.'[58] But God Himself must be the ultimate end: the Church can only be a consequential end. This is explained by reference to the communications that God makes: God communicates divine knowledge, but the creature's knowledge of God is simply participation in God's knowledge of Himself. God communicates virtue and holiness, and the creature participates in God's own moral excellency. God communicates happiness, and the creature, rejoicing in who God is, is participating in God's own joy in Himself. In all of this, the concept of participation, the Church being in Christ and the Spirit being in each particular Christian, is clearly key. Because, in Edwards' soteriology, the Church participates in the divine life,[59] in making the Church His end God is making Himself His end. The more we participate in these perfections, the closer we draw to God: 'The image is more and more perfect, and so the good that is in the creature comes forever nearer and nearer to an identity with that which is in God.'[60] This is

---

[58] *YE8*, p. 440; see also *Miscellanies* 952 (in the continuation, which occurs after entry 954 in the manuscript; p. 10 of Schafer's transcript) '... the churches of Christ (for whose sakes chiefly all heaven & earth is made) ...' Robert Jenson makes the same point in a recent essay: 'The church is responsible for the world in the elementary sense that were it not for the church there would be no world.' Jenson, 'The Church's Responsibility for the World' in Carl E. Braaten and Robert W. Jenson (eds), *The Two Cities of God: The Church's Responsibility for the Earthly City* (Grand Rapids, MI: Eerdmans, 1997), pp. 1–10; p. 1.

[59] On this point see chapter 5 below.

[60] *YE8*, p. 443.

movement towards a fulfilment of Christ's own prayer recorded in John 17, as we share the unity He has with His Father, 'being,' in Edwards' words, 'as it were, one with God'.[61]

So in each of the ends postulated in the second section, God makes Himself His own ultimate end. Edwards' position is now basically in place; in the last section of this chapter he turns to objections to what has come before.[62] Firstly, the objection that this impairs God's aseity – that He is apparently here fulfilling a lack within Himself. Edwards answers that God's pleasure is pleasure in Himself, which nothing can hinder, so his happiness is genuinely independent. Aseity is threatened by any account that assumes that there is a reason God created the world, and, by making God His own end, Edwards is as far from threatening it as any other account can be.[63] The second objection is that God is selfish, if He acts as He is presented here. Edwards here invokes his metaphysics: God's self-regard is regard to being in general, and so in God 'selfishness' and 'unselfishness' are meaningless terms, or at least they have the same definition. Because of this, God's interests exactly coincide with the interests of the whole, and God's self-regard causes him to regard the interests of the creature.[64] Thirdly, Edwards anticipates that his account will lead to accusations that God is ignoble, in that He should not be interested in seeing Himself applauded. Once again, the identity of God's being with being-in-general provides a response: love of self and love of all (i.e. true virtue) are not distinguished, so love of self is virtuous, not ignoble. A second response asserts that it is not unworthy of God to value the opinions

[61] *YE8*, p. 443.
[62] *YE8*, pp. 445–63.
[63] *YE8*, pp. 445–50. Edwards does not here identify the traditional distinction between necessary and appropriate acts of God that I have been using to expound his theology, but the underlying concept seems to be present, if not articulated. He teaches it expressly in a sermon, *The Excellency of Christ* (*BT2*, pp. 680–9), where he says '[Christ's] proceeding from the Father, in his eternal generation or filiation, argues no proper dependence on the *will* of the Father; for that proceeding was natural and *necessary*, and not arbitrary' (p. 682; italics original).
[64] *YE8*, pp. 450–3. See further my discussion of *True Virtue* below.

of His creatures, because of His 'infinite grace and condescension.'[65] Finally, if esteem is deserved it is not ignoble to
value it.[66] The last objection Edwards deals with is the
suggestion that this account diminishes the grace of God,
and hence the obligation to gratitude placed on the
creature. Once again, Edwards resorts to his metaphysical
position to insist that God's glory and the creature's good
are not distinct: 'God in seeking his glory, therein seeks the
good of his creatures: because the emanation of his glory
implies the communicated excellency and happiness of his
creature.'[67]

Edwards turns in his second chapter to consider 'What
is to be learned from Holy Scriptures concerning God's last
end in the creation of the world'.[68] Firstly, Scripture is
constantly clear that God makes Himself His end – He
is both the 'first efficient cause' and the 'last final cause' of
all things; this is the meaning of 'Alpha and Omega'
language, as well as the teaching of many texts.[69] Having
established this initial position, Edwards outlines the
exegetical principles he will be adopting in examining it in
more detail – in particular, in asking in what sense God
makes Himself His end.[70]

The first group of principles insists that those things that
are spoken of most frequently and most generally as God's
purpose are most likely to be His ultimate end.[71] Then
Edwards proceeds to explain the theological basis of the
exegesis he will perform. The moral (i.e. 'spiritual', in
current usage) world, he asserts, is the reason for the rest of
creation to exist, so whatever is spoken of as the end of the
moral creation may be assumed to be the end of all
creation.[72] The purpose of a thing may be inferred from its
use, and providence is the description of the use of

---

[65] YE8, p. 457.
[66] YE8, pp. 453–8.
[67] YE8, pp. 458–63; quotation from p. 459.
[68] Chapter title; YE8, p. 465.
[69] YE8, pp. 467–8.
[70] YE8, pp. 469–74.
[71] Positions 1–3; pp. 469–70.
[72] Position 4; pp. 470–1. See chapter 3 below for a discussion of this
doctrine of creation.

creation, so the aim of God's works of providence will be the end of creation, particularly as they are applied to the moral realm.[73] Again, theologically, the moral world is made for that part of it that is good,[74] so the purpose of this part may be seen to be the purpose of all creation. On the basis of this, Edwards makes a series of more precise assertions: that which defines the goodness of the moral world,[75] that which makes this goodness admirable, and that which is the reason for the commendation of pious people in the Scripture, can each be regarded as the chief end of all creation. These prepare the way for the final exegetical position: Jesus Christ is both the head and goal of the moral world, and the chief pattern of piety, so whatever He sought as His great purpose is the chief end of God in creating.[76]

Edwards' purpose in offering these exegetical positions would seem to be twofold: to narrow the question asked, from a general one about creation to a more specific one about the Church and, particularly, Jesus Christ; and to widen the available evidence, since Scripture speaks far more of the Church (including, of course, in Edwards' terms, Israel) and of Christ than it does about general questions. In the next few sections, Edwards goes on to offer, on the basis of these principles, a series of answers, drawn from Scripture, to the question of God's ultimate end in creating, before working theologically with these answers to demonstrate their coherence with each other, and with the positions reached by means of reason in the earlier chapter.

Applying these principles to Scripture, then, will offer various possible answers concerning God's ultimate end in His work. Firstly, God's 'glory'[77] is regularly described as

---

[73] Positions 5–6; p. 471.
[74] Recalling Jenson's phrase in n. 58 above, it is the *Church* that is the reason for creation, not merely humanity in general.
[75] I.e. the ethical commands of Scripture.
[76] Position 12; *YE8*, p. 474.
[77] At this point Edwards simply uses the word. His discussion of its meaning will follow later.

God's ultimate purpose – it is the purpose of the Church, and what Christ sought as His highest end.[78] Again, God's 'Name' and 'praise' are both spoken of in Scripture in significant places[79] as the purpose of God's actions. Finally, picking up a theme which I have noted as important in the development of his position, Edwards still insists that the exercise of God's goodness is appropriate in itself in a way that the exercise of His justice is not:

> According to Scripture, communicating good to the creatures is what is in itself pleasing to God: and that this is not merely subordinately agreeable, and esteemed valuable on account of its relation to a further end, as it is in executing justice in punishing the sins of men; which God is inclined to as fit and necessary in certain cases, and on account of the good ends attained by it: but what God is inclined to on its own account, and what he delights in simply and ultimately.[80]

So Edwards finds 'glory', 'Name', 'praise' and 'communicating goodness' as appropriate ultimate ends for God, according to Scripture. Before discussing their interrelation, he offers a brief exposition of what Scripture means when speaking of God's 'glory' and 'Name'. The etymology of *kavod* in Hebrew carries the idea of weightiness or greatness, sometimes just possessed, sometimes in their display. 'Glory', then, refers firstly to the internal greatness, majesty, excellency and dignity possessed by (or inherent in) a person, and the satisfaction or happiness that this produces. Secondly, it denotes this internal glory in its display, or visible exhibition. Applied to God this means the display of His goodness and grace, particularly in the gift of salvation in Jesus Christ.[81] But, Edwards insists, it

---

[78] *YE8*, pp. 475–92.
[79] E.g. the various events surrounding the Exodus are said to be 'for the sake of God's name': (p. 494), referring to 2 Sam. 7:23; Ps. 106:8; Is. 63:12.
[80] *YE8*, p. 503.
[81] *YE8*, pp. 518–21; a footnote to this section (p. 518 n. 5) comments on Rom. 9: 22–3 in the following terms: 'In the 22nd verse where the Apostle

means more than this: not just the exhibition of God's goodness and fullness, but their communication.[82] Thirdly, 'glory' can mean the apprehension, and hence knowledge, of displayed glory.[83] Fourthly, it may also be a synonym for 'praise' – the creature's delight in, and celebration of, God's glory.[84] Finally here, Edwards indicates that 'Name' is virtually synonymous with 'glory' in the Scriptures.

So, Edwards has gathered up 'glory', 'Name', 'praise', and the communication of God's goodness into one multi-faceted concept involving God's perfections, and particularly His mercy and grace, being displayed, known, rejoiced in and communicated. Thus what Scripture teaches concerning God's ultimate end in creating the world is shown to be coincident with the results of the investigation into 'what reason teaches'. The final section makes explicit the unity of God's ultimate end, and suggests that the 'most common and most apt' name for it is 'the glory of God'.[85]

This has been demonstrated biblically, in that the term 'glory' will cover all these areas in its scriptural use.

---

speaks of God's making known the power of his wrath, saith he, "God willing to show his wrath, and make his power known." But in verse 23rd (sic) when he comes to speak of mercy, he saith, "That he might make known the riches of his glory, on the vessels of mercy."' This, in passing, suggests that Ramsey's desire to link God's glory with God's wisdom, power, justice and goodness (YE8, p. 514 n. 7) is misconstrued: glory has properly to do with mercy and goodness in a way it does not with justice and power, at least in Edwards' thought.

[82] 'The word "glory," as applied to God or Christ, sometimes evidently signifies the communications of God's fullness, and means much the same thing with God's abundant and exceeding goodness and grace' (p. 518).

[83] YE8, pp. 521–2.

[84] YE8, pp. 522–3.

[85] YE8, p. 526. Edwards had reached this position early in the spurt of entries in the Miscellanies that show him beginning to work up to writing this dissertation. Entry 1066, for example, (Townsend, Philosophy, p. 139) begins by asserting that language seems to lack a term that is adequate for God's ultimate purpose ('a proper general word to express the supreme end of the creation'). However, having further identified the problem as the need for a word which will cover both God's self-glorification and His self-communication, Edwards finally asserts that both these are described as 'God's being glorified' in Scripture. Again, in entries 1082, 1084 and 1092 (all unpublished), Edwards can be seen working at the different senses that the word 'glory' bears in the Scriptures.

Edwards will now demonstrate it theologically; these different components 'are all but the emanation of God's glory; or the exceeding brightness and fullness of that divinity diffused, overflowing, and as it were enlarged; or in one word [*sic*!] existing *ad extra*'.[86] The demonstration is achieved by what I take to be a Trinitarian argument, although at no point in the final version of the text is it explicitly so. Edwards argues that 'God's internal glory, as it is in God, is either in his understanding or will.'[87] His glory in the former is His self-knowledge; in the latter His holiness and happiness. Now, the psychological analogies of the Trinity are a part of Edwards' heritage, and in his *Essay on the Trinity*[88] Edwards explicitly identifies the Son with God's perfect knowledge of Himself in His understanding and the Spirit with God's perfect delight in Himself in His will, a passage he invokes when talking about the end of creation in *Miscellanies* 679, if not in the final work. It is surely not unreasonable, then, to see Edwards offering a Trinitarian account of God's glory here.[89]

Such a reading is supported by a number of the *Miscellanies* entries that Edwards writes as he is gathering his material for the *End of Creation*, where we have a repeated insistence on the parallel between the twofold external going forth that Edwards sums up with the word 'glory' and the twofold internal going forth of the Father's substance which is the generation of the Son and the procession of the Spirit.[90] These entries are actually rather repetitive, with the same basic argument being presented

[86] *YE8*, p. 527.
[87] *YE8*, p. 528.
[88] In Helm (ed.), *Treatise*, pp. 99–131.
[89] The pervasiveness of psychological analogies in the tradition may even permit an assumption that Edwards expected his readers to recognise Trinitarian references here without any explicit mention. Jenson's comment perhaps makes the point: 'And yet all this language [concerning the glory of God] is in fact christology, though only tentatively so': (*America's Theologian*, p. 41.)
[90] This may be found in entries 1082, 1151, 1218 and 1266a. Of these, only the parts of 1218 that are in Townsend (*Philosophy*, pp. 149–52) are published in any convenient source.

in slightly different words each time. The flowing out of God's glory is twofold, consisting in the communication of knowledge to the creature and the communication of love to the creature. These correspond[91] to the internal begetting of the Son, or Logos, or Wisdom, of God, and proceeding of the Spirit, or Love, of God. In entry 1082 these are described as 'only a second proceeding of the same persons; their going forth *ad extra* as before they proceded [*sic*] *ad intra*'.

Why is this Trinitarian conception not explicit in the final text? It is difficult to know, of course, but I suspect that Edwards decided that his Trinitarian theology needed spelling out in a work devoted to that purpose, and that until he had done that a piecemeal use of his distinctive categories would merely cause confusion. Particularly with the *Essay on the Trinity* also in hand,[92] Edwards may have decided to leave the doctrinal connections in the *End of Creation* implicit, with the intention of spelling them out when he came to write his projected statement of the whole of Christian theology.

This repetition works because Edwards sees all God's glory and perfections as summed up in the perfection of knowledge in His understanding and the perfections of virtue and happiness in His will:

> The whole of God's internal good or glory, is in these three things, viz. his infinite knowledge; his infinite virtue or holiness, and his infinite joy and happiness. Indeed, there are a great many attributes in God, according to our way of conceiving or talking of them: but all may be reduced to these; or to the degree, circumstances and relations of these .... And therefore

---

[91] In entry 1082 'answer'; in 1151 'are agreeable to' or are 'correspondant to'; in 1218, again, 'are agreeable to'; in 1266a 'are answerable to'. Too much should not be read into the precise wording of *Miscellanies* entries, however; Edwards was here recording his thoughts for private use, not seeking an exact statement to communicate them to the public.

[92] See Helm, *Treatise*, pp. 99–131 for this text.

the external glory of God consists in the communication of these.[93]

The creature who knows God is participating in God's
perfect knowledge of Himself, and so the display
of God's perfections is equivalent to the communication
of His knowledge. Equally, the creature who loves and
delights in God is the recipient of the communication of
His happiness and joy. True holiness is nothing but
superlative love for God's beauty, so the creature who
loves God is also participating in God's holiness, and so
is the recipient of the communication of God's holiness.
The underlying Trinitarian conception suggests that
participation in the Son and Spirit is what is intended,[94]
and thus that notions of the indwelling Spirit and
salvation as participation in the Son are not far from the
surface. Further, Edwards argues, our creation in
the image of God, as having both knowledge and will,
means that the distinctions in the overall concept of glory
are suited for our appropriation, not just God's gift. Thus
the end of creation is one: 'God's internal glory or
fullness extant externally, or existing in its emanation.'[95]
   Edwards has one final point to make: he has argued
earlier that it is fitting for God to make Himself His end,
but this overflow of glory appears to be directed towards
the good of the creature. The response offered is a reiteration of the central concepts of communication and
participation: the creature's knowledge, love and joy are
God's own knowledge, love and joy given (communicated)

---

[93] *YE8,* p. 528; it is worthy of notice that in this passage Edwards has
succeeded in gathering up the whole tradition of discourse about the
attributes of God into an overarching Trinitarian framework. Edwards
makes the same point in his *Essay on the Trinity,* as I shall discuss later. See
further my comparison of Edwards with Barth on the divine perfections
at the end of this chapter.
[94] 'Thus that which proceeds from God *ad extra* is agreable [*sic*] to the
twofold subsistences which proceed from him *ad intra* which is the Son &
the holy Spirit the Son being the Idea of God or the knowledge of God &
the holy Ghost which is the love of God and joy in God': *Miscellanies*
1218.
[95] *YE8,* p. 531.

to the creature, and then returned to God. A lengthy quotation is perhaps useful here:

> In the creature's knowing, esteeming, loving, rejoicing in, and praising God, the glory of God is both exhibited and acknowledged; his fullness is received and returned. Here is both an *emanation* and *remanation*. The refulgence shines upon and into the creature, and is reflected back to the luminary. The beams of glory come from God, and are something of God, and are refunded back again to their original. So that the whole is *of* God, and *in* God, and *to* God; and God is the beginning, middle and end in this affair.[96]

Once again, the language seems to demand Trinitarian interpretation, but that is not the key point. God, in communicating Himself to the creature, is known, loved, rejoiced in – is, in short, glorified. So God is, in a sense, His own end in creation. But implicit in this is a stricter sense in which this is true. It warrants another quotation, if only because the position is surprising, found so far west of the Danube:

> God's respect to the creature's good, and his respect to himself ... are united in one, as the happiness of the creature aimed at is happiness in union with himself. The creature is no further happy with this happiness which God makes his ultimate end than he becomes one with God. The more happiness the greater union: when the happiness is perfect, the union is perfect. And as the happiness will be increasing to eternity, the union will become more and more strict and perfect; nearer and more like to that between God the Father and the Son; who are so united that their interest is perfectly one ... in this view, the creature must be looked upon as united to God in an infinite strictness.[97]

---

96 *YE8*, pp. 531; italics orginal.
97 *YE8*, pp. 533–4.

In common with Eastern Orthodox thought, Edwards was prepared to see salvation as *theosis*, being made one with God. Everything that has gone before has, in fact, presupposed this position, but still, perhaps, it is a shock. Nonetheless, with this in place the account is coherent and consistent. God's first purpose is to share His own life, and so His fullness overflows to creatures that they may be drawn in to the eternal life of God. An image Edwards used very early on in his quest, in *Miscellanies* 271 (1726) which I have already quoted,[98] and returned to repeatedly, recurs once again at the end of this text, as the 'one flesh' union between husband and wife becomes a type of the final union between Christ and His Church. An earlier statement is more attractive, if less careful, so it is perhaps fitting to end my exposition by quoting once more from the *Miscellanies*:

> The end of the creation of God was to provide a spouse for his Son Jesus Christ that might enjoy him & on whom he might pour forth his love, & the end of all things in providence are to make way for the exceeding expressions of Christ's love to his spouse & for her exceeding close & intimate union with & high & glorious enjoyment of him.[99]

Only now it is not just the love of the Son, but the mutual love, knowledge and holiness of the Trinity that is given to the Church.

The argument of this dissertation will be central to my account of Edwards' theology, and it is not well known, so I have spelt it out at very great length. The process of exploring the adequacy of this account will be the burden

[98] P. 39
[99] *Miscellanies* 710, appendix (thus-far published only in the Dwight edition of 1830; my quotation is taken from Schafer's transcript). This image is recurrent in Edwards' writings. Just a few entries later in the *Miscellanies*, it appears again: 'There was [supply 'as'] it were an eternal society or family in the Godhead in the Trinity of persons it seems to be Gods [*sic*] design to admit the church into the divine family as his sons wife ...' (entry 741, again, published only in Dwight).

of all that is to follow, and addressed finally in my conclusions in chapter 7, but some initial remarks may usefully be
made here.

Firstly, Ramsey, in his editorial notes on the text,
constantly raises the issue of a suspicion of Neoplatonism,
particularly in regard to the language of 'emanation'.[100] His
response is to seek to use textual analysis to demonstrate
that this is not what Edwards meant; how successful this
may be is a question I leave to others, because my
contention is that a neoplatonic reading of Edwards is
simply inconceivable, if my Trinitarian reading is accepted.
The Fathers, after all, avoided platonising emanationisms
precisely by asserting the doctrine of the Trinity.[101]

Secondly, concerns about morality may be raised. Is God
not, despite all Edwards' arguments to the contrary,
painted as simply selfish here? The objection has apparent
force, in that there is little in *End of Creation* to defend
against such charges[102]– but then it is only one of *Two
Dissertations*. An understanding of the account of virtue
Edwards offers in *True Virtue* will be sufficient to answer
this charge.

The second dissertation has been much more widely
received and read than the first, a fact which Ramsey
suggests has skewed many interpretations.[103] Nevertheless, this familiarity, and the fact that it is less central to
my purposes, will enable me to offer a briefer reading of the
second work. Edwards' concern is to analyse virtue; it is, he
asserts, simply beauty in the moral realm,[104] so the question
becomes one of analysis of beauty. This is a task Edwards
attempted early in his career, in the *Notes on the Mind*,[105]
where he had argued that 'all beauty consists in similarness,
or identity of relation'[106] – that is, that proportion,

[100] See *YE8*, p. 433 n. 5; and footnotes later taking the same theme forward.
[101] On this, see Jenson in Gunton, *Creation*.
[102] Although there are hints which become more obvious when the work
is read with the conclusions of *True Virtue* in mind.
[103] *YE8*, pp. 5–6.
[104] *YE8*, p. 539.
[105] *YE6*, pp. 332–93; begun in 1723 (see Anderson's Introduction in *YE6*,
pp. 313–31).
[106] *YE6*, p. 334.

symmetry and harmony are the essence of the quality we call beauty or excellence. Edwards returns to this same point in the posthumously published work, and expands it: true virtue is '*general* beauty', that is 'beautiful in a comprehensive view as it is in itself, and as related to everything that it stands in connection with'.[107] So, stated baldly, true virtue is 'love to Being in general'.[108]

'Love' can be analysed into 'love of benevolence', which desires good for its objects regardless of their worth, and 'love of complacence', which delights in the beauty of its object. The object of virtuous love is not beauty or gratitude, since these would make virtue its own object, a meaningless position. So the object of virtue must be 'Being, simply considered'[109] – which is to say Being-in-general. So, virtue may now be analysed. It will produce love to any individual being, but only so long as that is not in conflict with a higher love – love for Being-in-general. In particular, a being that is opposed to Being-in-general will be opposed and hated by the truly virtuous heart. Thus the strength of benevolence that the truly virtuous person will feel for any given being can be determined: it will first be proportional to the 'degree of *existence*' of that being, and next to the virtue it has – if my primary concern is towards Being-in-general, then I will, as a result of that concern (which is simply virtue), value another being that shares such a concern more than I would if it did not.

Following this philosophical analysis Edwards turns (again – this is the second of two works) to explicitly theological considerations. God has infinitely more being than the whole creation together, so love for 'Being-in-general' is simply love for God. Human virtue, then, is wholly composed of love for God, and other loves – of spouse, family, country, animal creation – are virtuous to the extent that they are a part of this love. To the extent that they are raised above this love, they are simply and

[107] *YE8*, p. 540.
[108] *YE8*, p. 541.
[109] *YE8*, p. 544.

precisely idolatry, which is not virtuous. A truly virtuous mind, however, seeks the promotion of God's glory above all other things, the position reached in the first dissertation.

God's virtue has the same definition, so it 'must consist primarily in *love to himself*'. This is, however, immediately – and crucially – defined as 'the mutual love and friendship which subsists eternally and necessarily between the several persons of the Godhead'.[110] The corollary is obvious: God's love to created beings is, as *End of Creation* demonstrated, entirely dependent on His love to Himself. Edwards' position is now complete, and the remainder (and greater part) of the dissertation is an analysis of this position, and a demonstration that systems of ethics that do not make love to God their foundation must be defective.

This, then, is virtue – an entirely theological account, as may have been expected. Are God's motives, according to the first dissertation, selfish or virtuous on these grounds? The immediate answer is both, since in God self-love and love to Being-in-general coincide exactly, but Edwards' account of this introduced the crucial nuance: God's self-love is not the self-love of some arbitrary deity, but of the Triune God of the Christian gospel. It is a love of eternal mutual self-giving, not of selfish solipsism. Once again, the doctrine of the Trinity is central to understanding Edwards' logic – and it is invoked explicitly this time. Selfishness cannot be an issue with this doctrine in place.

On the basis of all this, the question may be put again to the first dissertation: even if God's self-regard is not selfish, it presents a danger for Christian devotion; after all, if God makes His own life His end in all His works, one wonders why human beings should be interested;

---

[110] *YE8*, p. 557; italics original. A precursor of this position can be seen in *Miscellanies* 1077 (Townsend, *Philosophy*, p. 184), where the fact that God is 'as it were, the sum of all being' means that His holiness 'consists mainly and summarily in his infinite regard or love to himself'.

if God's love is not love *for us*, there is little relevance in discussing it.

Jenson[111] suggests that Edwards recognised this danger and also its converse: describing God as making His creatures His end, and so making God simply an excuse for our selfishness. The answer he finds in the dissertation is surely correct: that, through the logic of his metaphysics (the discussion of God as 'Being-in-general' in *True Virtue*), Edwards cuts through the dichotomy: God, in making Himself His own end, makes us His end, and vice-versa. This is clear in a passage I have already quoted: 'God's respect to the creature's good, and his respect to himself ... are united in one, as the happiness of the creature aimed at is happiness in union with himself.'[112] The *theosis* doctrine, made possible only by the adoption (albeit *sub voce*) of Trinitarian discourse, offers Edwards a way through this difficulty.

The Glory of God: A Historical and Systematic Comparison

The remainder of this chapter will be taken up with comparisons designed to demonstrate what is particularly distinctive about Edwards' account. I have already indicated that the bare assertion, 'God created for His own glory', was common amongst the Reformed orthodox; detailed descriptions of what is meant by 'the glory of God' are less common.[113] One exception, however, stands out, and is key: Petrus van Mastricht, in his *Theoretico-Practica Theologia*, treats at some length of glory – the same work that Edwards describes in a letter as 'for divinity in general,

---

[111] Jenson, *America's Theologian*, pp. 38–9.
[112] *YE8*, p. 533. See also *Miscellanies* 681, which I have discussed above on pp. 43–4.
[113] Turretin, for instance, does not treat the subject at all in his third topic, 'On the One and Triune God'; the same may be said of Wollebius in I.1, 'The Essence of God'. Heppe, in his synopsis, lists glory alongside majesty, perfection and blessedness as the final content of all God's attributes: V.43 (p. 104).

doctrine, practice and controversy; or as a universal system
of divinity ... much better than Turretin, or any other book
in the world, excepting the Bible, in my opinion'.[114] Barth,
whose knowledge of Reformed orthodoxy is enviable by
any standards, follows Mastricht on this issue in his account
of the divine perfections, commenting: 'So far as I can see,
he alone among the Reformed orthodox attempted a
detailed examination and presentation of the concept of the
gloria Dei in a way that does justice to all the biblical statements and references.'[115] My exploration of Edwards'
doctrine of glory must start here.

The dogmatic section of van Mastricht's chapter on the
majesty and glory of God spells out what glory means in a
fourfold development.[116] Firstly, God's glory is His infinite
eminence of being and perfections. This perfection
naturally shines, however, and so God's glory must also
include in its definition the brilliance of His perfections and
eminence. If this brilliance shines out, it will inevitably be
recognised, and so the recognition of this eminence, called
God's face, is the third part. And these three together –
eminence, brilliance and recognition, make up the internal
glory of God, which is co-eternal with Him.

Mastricht's derivation of God's glory is not yet
complete, however. Fourthly and finally, glorification – the
reception and manifestation of internal glory – must be
included. This includes eternal acts of glorification internal
to the Trinity. It also includes the glorification of God by
the recognition and praise of His internal glory in creation
– not just the direct praise of angels and human beings,
but also the recognition of God's glory in His works –
in the gospel, in providence, and so on. These should
prompt worship and praise from the intelligent creation,
as it recognises God's omnipotence, omniscience and
inexhaustible goodness.

The similarity to Edwards' account is evident, but so

---

[114] Letter of 15 Jan. 1746/7 to Joseph Bellamy, *YE16*, pp. 216–18; the
quotation is from p. 217.
[115] *CD* II/1, p. 649.
[116] Van Mastricht, *Theoretico-Practica Theologia* II.22.3–10.

also are the moves that Edwards made. Whilst ideas of overflow and participation are implicit in Mastricht, they have none of the prominence that Edwards was to give to them. This is perhaps explained by the second dissimilarity: in van Mastricht Edwards would have found little or none of the Trinitarian grammar that is so crucial to his mature statement. It is this move, understanding that the word 'God', spoken in Christian discourse, demands Trinitarian content, and working out what that means consistently, that is distinctive to Edwards. Van Mastricht leaves the reader with the feeling that God's glory is seen across a gap – an infinite qualitative distance; a feeling that God remains outside the world He has created, looking in, and perhaps occasionally reaching in, but not intimately involved. Edwards' consciously Trinitarian language offers the possibility of speaking of God as simultaneously other than, and involved with, His world: speaking of God giving not just a vision, but genuinely Himself to His creatures, and calling His creatures to share in the fullness of joy that is His own life. This is the heart of Edwards' advance.

A second suggestive comparison may be made with Karl Barth, a theologian also within the Reformed tradition, and who also learnt from van Mastricht on this subject. Barth's account of the divine perfections is found in *CD* II/1, pp. 322–677, and is split into three (unequal) sections: an introduction to the divine perfections; an account of the perfections of the divine loving; and an account of the perfections of the divine freedom. The basic definition of the reality of God that Barth is working with here, 'the One who loves in freedom', is itself a Trinitarian formula,[117] and so he, like Edwards, can be seen to be attempting to gather up all the language concerning God's attributes that is found in the tradition into a more basic (and indeed credal) form. Language of divine glory occurs at the beginning and the end of this account, indicating the importance of this language for Barth.

---

[117] As is made clear by a phrase very early on in this section: ' Since God is Father, Son and Holy Ghost, i.e., loves in freedom . . .': (*CD* II/1, p. 323).

The initial section on 'The Perfections of God'[118] uses the word 'glory' to sum up the fullness and the overflow of all the divine perfections. Barth's concern is to find a way to insist (as theologians have almost always sought to insist and, according to Barth, almost always failed to insist) that God's perfections are genuinely His, essentially and immanently, and so our knowledge of them is knowledge of God Himself.

Barth's whole discussion of the divine perfections ends with a subsection on 'The Eternity and Glory of God' which serves to bring together all that has gone before.[119] Barth's first definition of glory follows Biblical usage: 'God's glory is His dignity and right not only to maintain, but to prove and declare, to denote and almost as it were to make Himself conspicuous and everywhere apparent as the One He is.'[120] In developing this, Barth follows Reformed orthodoxy: 'It is the self-revealing sum of all divine perfections. It is the fullness of God's deity, the emerging, self-expressing and self manifesting reality of all that God is. It is God's being in so far as this is in itself a being which declares itself.'[121] This is spelt out in a fourfold account which follows van Mastricht, and a discussion of the category of beauty, which Barth will not make central, but regards as important. Finally, Barth insists that it is proper to God's glory that it should become known: 'It belongs to the essence of the glory of God not to be *gloria* alone but to become *glorificatio*.'[122]

What is striking when this account is placed alongside Edwards' is the similarity: not just the categories of communication and overflow adopted from van Mastricht, but the use of the concept of beauty, and the attempt to bring all this language into a Trinitarian framework. There is no evidence that Barth had any knowledge of Edwards' work, but one cannot help thinking that he would have recognised a kindred spirit in at least some areas. This is

[118] *CD* II/1, pp. 322–50.
[119] *CD* II/1, pp. 608–77.
[120] *CD* II/1, p. 641.
[121] *CD* II/1, p. 643.
[122] *CD* II/1, p. 667.

not, perhaps, surprising: Barth and Edwards stood in the same, Reformed, tradition, although both (Barth probably more so) modified it in new and creative ways.

Beyond the similarity, however, differences present themselves. The first of these, I suggest, is that Edwards is more thoroughly Trinitarian in his discussion of the divine perfections than is Barth. To demonstrate this, I will explore briefly Barth's attempts to avoid nominalism in this area: in his first section on the divine perfections, Barth points to the theological relevance of the nominalism–realism debate, and suggests that it turns on this doctrine.[123] The classic form of this debate occurred in later medieval theology, but the question there addressed, concerning the status of universals, is a perennial one.

Universals are words that describe generic concepts. The fact that I can name objects of different sizes, shapes, materials and colours all as chairs suggests that I have a concept of 'chairness' which I am able to apply generally. The fact that someone else who I have never met gives the same objects the same name suggests that she and I share a concept of 'chairness'. One way of accounting for this is to suggest that the concept of 'chairness' is a real thing to which we both have access; this is realism. Alternatively, it could be argued that it is just a cultural and linguistic artefact that we share this concept, and so universals do not exist, but are just convenient names for our mental construct. This is nominalism. In relation to chairs the point might be trivial, but in relation to goodness or beauty it becomes of great importance: is an action wrong, or a work of art beautiful, because there is an external standard against which it may be judged, or is it just a majority opinion? In particular, in relation to God, is there a standard of goodness external to God and constraining Him to act in certain ways, or do we just call an action 'good' because it is a word that applies to what God does? If the former, how do we defend the genocide that God ordered Israel to commit in the book of Joshua? If the latter,

---

[123] *CD* II/1, pp. 325–35.

how do we account for our sense that these actions, rather than others, are difficult things to ascribe to God?

There are two basic errors to be avoided here. The extreme nominalist error, which Barth charges to Eunomius, Occam, Biel and Schleiermacher, is to view the divine perfections as in no sense divine, merely projections of human qualities on to a divine Being who Himself (the temptation at this point to write 'itself' is almost overpowering) is nothing but naked being.[124] The opposite, realist, error is to make God's perfections substantial so that they are independent entities within, or even above, the being of God. Against this Barth insists that there is no 'second, alien divinity in God'[125] and that 'There are not first of all power, goodness, knowledge, will, etc. in general, and then in particular God also as one of the subjects to whom all these things accrue as a predicate.'[126]

The mainstream of theological history, according to Barth, lies between these two, but is still flawed. Citing thinkers ranging from Irenaeus and John of Damascus to Thomas, Calvin and the Reformed orthodox, Barth recognised a desire to identify the divine perfections economically rather than immanently with God, that is, to make knowledge of the perfections part of the accommodation of God to our understandings, denying that they are part of God's knowledge of Himself.[127] Thus there is a nominalistic tendency present, what Barth calls a 'partial nominalism',[128] which, he contends, must also be resisted.

The way forward Barth offers depends first on a recognition of the fundamental basis of the doctrine of God. The problem is one form of that of the One and the Many, and so calls for Trinitarian resolution: '... the fact that the idea of God was not determined by the doctrine of the Trinity, but that the latter was shaped by a general conception of God ... was now avenged at the most sensitive spot ... the idea of the divine simplicity was necessarily exalted to

---

[124] CD II/1, p. 327.
[125] CD II/1, p. 331.
[126] CD II/1, p. 334.
[127] CD II/1, pp. 327–30.
[128] CD II/1, p. 330.

the all-controlling principle, the idol, which, devouring everything concrete, stands behind all these formulae ...'.[129] Following this, Barth offers three 'explanatory propositions' in order to protect a correct statement.[130] Firstly, the diversity of the divine perfections belongs to the being of the one God, and not to any second divine nature. Secondly, this diversity is a diversity of God's simple being – 'In God multiplicity, individuality and diversity do not stand in any contradiction to unity.'[131] Thirdly, this diversity of perfections is immanent and not merely economic.

Barth's fundamental insight – that the underlying problem here is a failure, throughout the tradition, to be rigorously Trinitarian whenever God is spoken of – is certainly sound. And the three propositions he advances are certainly adequate to the problem, if they can be held to constantly. My concern with the formulation, however, is the lack of any obvious connection between the fundamental insight and the propositions. If this really is a question of Trinitarian discourse, should it not be possible to derive those propositions which are necessary to an adequate statement from Trinitarian doctrine? Put another way, Barth proceeds by laying down boundary conditions. If it were possible, would not an answer formulated in Trinitarian terms that could be shown to lie within these boundary conditions be preferable? My contention here is that Jonathan Edwards offers just such an answer.

As so often, seemingly, with Edwards, it is a position offered in passing, *en route* to an answer to a different question. In a passage in the *Essay on the Trinity*, Edwards says this:

> It is a maxim amongst divines that everything that is in God is God which must be understood of real

---

[129] *CD* II/1, p. 329; it is perhaps worth noting (particularly in view of my use of it in chapter 6 below) that Barth certainly does not reject the doctrine of divine simplicity, but argues that it be understood aright, citing (p. 329) Augustine's phrases, *multiplex simplicitas* and *simplex multiplicitas*.
[130] *CD* II/1, pp. 330–35.
[131] *CD* II/1, p. 332.

attributes and not of meer [*sic*] modalities. If a man should tell me that the immutability of God is God, or that the omnipresence of God and authority of God, is God, I should not be able to think of any rational meaning of what he said .... But if it be meant that the *real* attributes of God, viz. His understanding and love are God, then what we have said may in some measure explain how it is so, for deity subsists in them distinctly; so they are distinct Divine persons.[132]

This dense passage contains several surprising features. Firstly, Edwards is uncompromising in his commitment to a serious Trinitarianism: the only available referents for the word 'God' are the 'distinct Divine persons'. The residue of a common 'essence' which was so pervasive in Western theological discourse is wholly absent, and Edwards claims to be unable to think of 'any rational meaning' behind the standard language that describes the essence.[133] Secondly, however, his approach is clearly that of a child of Augustine: the Trinity of the mind, the mind knowing itself/God and the mind loving itself/God is straight from the master's work, and so he does not fall into this century's characteristic error of assuming that the language of persons must have meant three minds, three knowledges and three wills, rather than three Persons with one perfect will and so on. So, and thirdly, Edwards makes a striking move: the Father's perfections are only and precisely the Son and the Spirit. As noted earlier in this chapter, this is not an isolated statement, but occurs in *End of Creation* as well. With these passages in view, even Edwards' adoption of the classical language of the Reformed tradition in *Religious Affections* seems loaded:

> ... there are two kinds of attributes in God, according to our way of conceiving him, his moral attributes, which

[132] Helm (ed.), *Treatise*, p. 119; my italics.
[133] The practice of discussing the attributes of God under the locus of the One God and so identifying them with God's essence was pervasive throughout scholasticisms both before and after the Reformation.

are summed up in his holiness, and his natural attributes, of strength, knowledge, etc. that constitute the greatness of God; so there is a two-fold image of God in man, his moral or spiritual image, which is his holiness ... and God's natural image, consisting in men's reason and understanding, his natural ability, and dominion .... [134]

There is, then, in Edwards a move to subsume the doctrine of the divine perfections under the doctrine of the Trinity.[135] In this move we see that he takes with full seriousness the warnings in the tradition (that Barth claims the tradition itself was unable to heed) that the perfections of God are truly the being of God – the position Barth is arguing for – and offers a way of understanding it built on the doctrine of the Trinity, gathering all the perfections of God up into the Son and the Spirit. Let me immediately say that this is radical within the tradition. The Athanasian Creed after all, asserts that Father, Son and Spirit are alike all wise, yet there are not three that are all wise, but one, and even in Barth the assertion that the perfections belong to the one essence of God remains.[136] Yet once the move (resisted by Augustine) from psychological analogies to psychological accounts[137] had been made, Edwards' further move is an obvious one.

---

[134] YE2, p. 256; this passage is certainly less clear than those in the *Essay on the Trinity* and *End of Creation*, and it may be that Edwards moved away from traditional language towards the end of his life (a difficult contention to prove, since no more accurate date than later than 1727 has been offered for the *Essay* to the best of my knowledge – see Helm, *Treatise*, p. 5). However, reference may be made once again to the pervasiveness of the psychological analogies in the tradition, which would support a Trinitarian reading of this passage.
[135] Edwards' 'Outline of "A Rational Account" ' – a note indicating how he intended to arrange his projected Summa – is very brief, and too much should not be read in to it, but the line 'Trinity, and God's attributes' surely lends support to my reading. YE6, p. 396.
[136] CD II/1, pp. 322–50 *passim*.
[137] By 'psychological accounts' I mean the attempt to project the analogies found in the mind of humanity back into the life of God. With Augustine's psychological analogies in place, this is an obvious move, invited by the Biblical language of *Logos* – rationality, idea – and Wisdom (and indeed Love, if Augustine's identification of the Spirit with Love is accepted). This is particularly the case if the Puritan faculty psychology is adopted – although to what extent this was derived from this sort of Trinitarian account is an historical question I am not competent to answer.

Obvious it may be, but is it valid? Given that the patristic doctrine never intended to suggest three centres of knowledge and will in its language of Three Persons,[138] the question becomes one of appropriation and perichoresis. Edwards is essentially seeking to appropriate different perfections of the divine *phusis* to particular *hypostases*. To the best of my knowledge, this is a move unique in the tradition, a radical extension of the doctrine of appropriation (which classically refers to the external acts of the Trinity). I suspect that, provided the doctrine of perichoresis is remembered and asserted, a form of this move could be developed that would not damage Trinitarian theology in any fundamental way, but Edwards did not live to do this, and it is impossible to say how he would have aligned these ideas with his broader Trinitarian theology, or indeed whether questions like those raised above would have led him to abandon them. He offers, however, the beginnings of a way to formalise what Barth merely asserts: that only by a thoroughgoing re-appropriation of the fundamentally Trinitarian nature of Christian theism can a satisfactory doctrine of the divine perfections be offered; which is almost to say that this is the only route to a satisfactory doctrine of God, within the Reformed tradition, given the centrality of the discussion of the divine perfections within the doctrine of God in most Reformed dogmatics.

So, a comparison with Barth demonstrates both a common inheritance in the Reformed tradition and the strength of Edwards' Trinitarian reworking, but a third comparison may be made, and one that is perhaps more interesting for a study of Edwards: apparently Barth is not

[138] On this see G. L. Prestige, *God in Patristic Thought* (London: SPCK, 1952), pp. 242–64, especially pp. 263–4, where a passage of Ps.-Cyril which John of Damascus incorporated into *The Orthodox Faith* is referred to: 'There is ... one ousia, one goodness, one power, one will, one energy, one authority; one and identical; not three similar to each other, but a single identical motion of the three hypostases ... the Father, the Son, and the Holy Spirit are in every respect one entity, save for ingeneracy and generation and procession.' Prestige argues that this is a summary of the position held by the Greek Fathers from Origen, citing Athanasius and the Cappadocians in particular.

prepared to let this language of glory take centre stage when he comes to discuss the 'end of creation'. Rather, he returns to his basic statement concerning God, 'the One who loves in freedom', and so brings the doctrine of election into the doctrine of God in order to speak of those God is free to love.[139]

This bare assertion needs some care, however, since Barth's whole account of the divine perfections has been an attempt to spell out the content of the statement 'the One who loves in freedom', and the language of glory lies at the beginning and end of that attempt. For Edwards, language of glory is language of God's primal decision, whereas for Barth language of glory is a description of God's nature. God's primal decision, by contrast, which is definitive of who God is, is the decree of election, which is both an inner-Trinitarian event (Jesus Christ, elected and electing) and a movement outward in loving freedom to the creation.

Once again however, care is needed: this primal decision, for Barth, is God's self-definition and so this must be what gives content to the doctrine of the divine perfections – and the language of glory is the summary of these perfections. The conclusion is surprising, but difficult to avoid, that Barth could have spoken of divine glorification as God's primal decision without materially changing his doctrine. Indeed, when we read the account of the divine election of grace, language of glory is often present.[140]

This is a difficult place to reach. A comparison with Barth has found more similarities than differences, and yet it is undeniable that Edwards' theology and Barth's feel very different. A second modern comparison will perhaps suggest a reason for this difference. Hans Urs von Balthasar, who was a friend of Karl Barth as well as a significant Roman Catholic theologian, places categories of beauty and glory right at the centre of his thought. Once

[139] *CD* II/2, pp. 3–93.
[140] A glance at the index to *CD* II/2 will perhaps make this point best, but see especially pp. 169–70, where election is explicitly identified with the overflowing of God's inner glory.

again, there is no evidence that von Balthasar ever read Edwards, but echoes can be heard.

Von Balthasar's *The Glory of the Lord*[141] is the first part of a (massive) trilogy, but has thus far been seen as the most significant of his writings. In it, he attempts to restore aesthetics to its place within theological thought, arguing that the beautiful should find its place alongside the good and the true as the appropriate object of Christian discourse.[142] It would be impossible to do justice to the sweep of von Balthasar's thought in a few paragraphs here, but the key discussion of the last two volumes of this work will highlight the point I am interested to make. These volumes present a powerful and original biblical theology, vol. 6 on *The Old Covenant* and vol. 7 on *The New Covenant*. In them, von Balthasar shows the disintegration of the old notion of divine glory during and after the exile, which established the possibility for a radically new concept, gathering up the broken pieces and re-forging them in a hitherto inconceivable way.

The Old Testament records a journey out of paganism, a journey from an unreflective vision of what 'glory' might mean to the verge of a new and unlooked-for possibility. The fundamental basis for this journey is God's revelation, but that also provides the most intractable problem: God's glory, as it is perceived by His people, is marked above all by dialectic, not to say contradiction. Whichever way the subject is looked at, we are forced to speak of both 'knowing and not knowing', 'seeing and not seeing', of a 'dazzling darkness'.[143] This is because the divine glory spoken of in the Scripture is itself an attempt by the Hebrew theologians who were the redactors of the biblical books to make sense of the apparently incompatible witnesses to God's revelation that are contained in the earlier traditions.[144]

---

[141] Hans Urs von Balthasar, *The Glory of the Lord: A Theological Aesthetics* (7 vols) tr. Erasmo Leiva-Merikakis; ed. Joseph Fessio and John Riches (Edinburgh: T&T Clark, 1982–9).
[142] Von Balthasar, *Glory*, vol. I, p. 9.
[143] All titles of sections taken from *Glory*, vol. VI, pp. 37–41.
[144] So, for example, *Glory*, vol. VI, p. 53.

God's glory attains its most concrete form in the creature, particularly the human creature, created in God's image, and in the covenant-history of Israel. In both creation and covenant God is active in giving His creatures space; but the creatures use that space to reject God. Now one of von Balthasar's basic commitments comes into play: this history is not merely history, but, as Biblical history, has a decisive and distinctive shape as that which reveals God's revelation, God's glory.[145] This commitment, however, poses a problem: the revelation of God's glory under this scheme is overwhelmingly a story of God's rejection, of the breaking of His covenant and the apostasy of His people. The prophets provide glimpses of what obedience should be, but still, the history is one of disobedience, and so the liturgy of the Lamentations has a peculiar place in that history: here Israel prays as the people from whom the Lord has departed, and so the prayers end not with affirmation, but with question – 'Or hast thou utterly rejected us? Art thou exceedingly angry with us?'[146]

At this point, von Balthasar turns to consider Job, who knows this experience of being forsaken by God. In his case, however, it is not a result of unfaithfulness, and so Job allows the question to be asked: could it be that God's glory will be revealed even in the destruction of His temple, in the exile and shame of His people? Could there be a new way of conceiving God's glory that will gather up the shattered remains? The vocation of the anonymous prophet whose words are recorded in Isaiah 40–55 is to give an affirmative answer to such questions.

The literature dating from after the return of the exiles (in which von Balthasar includes Trito-Isaiah and Daniel, and those books usually regarded as apocryphal by Protestant churches) demonstrates the attempt of an abandoned people to rediscover God's glory in their own situation, with the *shekinah* gone from the temple, the king

---

[145] This is the content of von Balthasar's *argumentum ex prophetia* in the concluding pages of *Glory*, vol. VI, for example.

[146] Lamentations 5:22, so von Balthasar, *Glory*, vol. VI, p. 280; some modern translations turn these questions into statements, but the Hebrew at least admits the standard reading.

gone from the land, and the Word gone from the prophets. There are three parallel attempts: a renewed prophecy, seeking to predict the immediate coming of the messianic glory of God; a retreat into the mysticism of apocalyptic, which discounted the historical experience of God's people as something shadowy and irrelevant; and a wisdom tradition seeking glory in all of creation and in danger of syncretism.[147] These attempts were doomed to failure, but were necessary to show the impossibility of the synthesis of the fragments that were all that was left of the vision of God's glory.

Turning to the New Testament, von Balthasar sees all these fragments gathered up, and the old prophetic tradition renewed for the last time, in the person of John the Baptist.[148] This gathering up, however, is only for the purposes of handing over, and it is Jesus, the Incarnate Son, who is the final revelation of the astonishing synthesis of His glory that is the final and decisive determinant of what it means to be God. Political messianism finds its fulfilment in the Suffering Servant; the unveiling of that which is truly apocalyptic happens not in war in the heavens, but in the humble death on the tree; the wisdom of the world is confronted with God's foolishness. In Jesus, all the old expectations of what 'glory' should have meant are fulfilled, but they are transformed in their fulfilling. Von Balthasar can speak for himself on this point:

> What God's glory in its good truth is, was to be revealed in Jesus Christ, and ultimately in his absolute obedience of Cross and Hell. The unique ray of the divine majesty of love is to become visible from the unique momentum of this event, establishing the norm for everything that can lay claim to the predicate 'glorious', at whatever distance and periphery it may be. From here sentence and judgement are passed on everything that calls itself δοξα [Glory] in the sphere of

---

[147] Listed in summary in *Glory*, vol. VI, p. 303, and discussed at some length in the pages afterwards.
[148] *Glory*, vol. VII, pp. 40–54.

creation .... Inasmuch as the central event, Christ's
obedience unto death, is no myth but the final self-
revelation of God in history, all other glory is
'demythologised' by it ....[149]

Biblical language of glory includes, perhaps even centres
on, that of the fourth gospel, and so the cross must be seen
as the fundamental locus of God's self-glorification. This
dimension, clearly present in Barth's account of election, is
in Edwards' *End of Creation* notable by its absence. I have
claimed in this chapter that a vision of glory was at the
heart of Edwards' theology; but within the Christian
tradition a 'theology of glory' has been the object of sharp
criticism. Luther made the point with characteristic
strength at Heidelberg: 'That person does not deserve to be
called a theologian who looks upon the invisible things of
God as though they were clearly perceptible in those things
which actually happened. He deserves to be called a
theologian, however, who comprehends the visible and
manifest things of God seen through suffering and the
cross.'[150] The language is harsh, but my account of
Edwards' theology thus far makes it appropriate: under
this condition, does Edwards 'deserve to be called a
theologian'? In examining the outworking of his concept of
divine self-glorification throughout his theological scheme,
I hope to offer an answer to that question.

---

[149] *Glory*, vol. VII, p. 243.
[150] Luther, *Heidelberg Disputation*, Thesis 20, in *Works* (ed. Helmut H.
Lehmann) vol. 31, *The Career of the Reformer I*, p. 40.

3
The Glory of Creation

In 1755, three years before Edwards died, an earthquake devastated Lisbon in Portugal. Many were killed by falling buildings; many more by fires started by votive candles in the churches. Tragedy, as always, was news, and if in those days there were no newspaper columnists to pontificate, commentary in sermon and tract discussed the causes and meanings of the event. Two radically different responses can be traced in the literature: preachers announcing God's warning to an ungodly people, and philosophers discussing the natural processes that make such things happen.[1] Voltaire, in perhaps the most famous literary response, *Candide*, satirises both approaches, as the philosopher Pangloss is found amongst the ruins of Lisbon discussing the marvellous contrivance of the flow of underground lava, and is then burnt as a heretic by Jesuits who see an *auto da fe* as the obvious response to the disaster. These differing responses demonstrate the shift in the understanding of the natural world that was close to the heart of the Enlightenment. For the older, 'medieval' view, the world was comprehensible morally, reflecting the goodness and authority of its Creator. An earthquake, then, was a sign of God's displeasure, and the appropriate response was to call the people to repentance and a new seriousness in religion, lest something worse befall. For the coming 'modern' way of thinking, the world was to be understood by the use of mathematics, the language in which the physical laws of nature are expressed. Moral questions were not relevant; stones could not, after all, be held responsible for their movements.

The Puritanism that Edwards inherited had made much of the older world view in its understanding of creation. Examples abound of attempts to hear God speaking

---

[1] On this see T. D. Kendrick, *The Lisbon Earthquake* (London: Methuen, 1956).

through the course of nature and the events of history. Indeed, the whole self-understanding of New England Puritanism was built on such a reading of history, centred as it was around pictures of the American colonies as the 'city on the hill', the New Israel trekking into the Wilderness to learn true religion before triumphantly returning to the old world to establish godliness there also.[2] Edwards engaged in these Puritan games of tracing the outcome of Biblical prophecies in the history of his own day, and of seeking providential words from God in the events of nature, with enthusiasm, and part of the purpose of this chapter is to ask whether these practices were, in the final analysis, simply pre-Enlightenment anachronisms, or whether the suggestion that Edwards recast Puritan theology in a form that could stand up to its Enlightened (cultured?) despisers can be supported even in these most 'medieval' areas of his thought. In a time of great intellectual change, did Edwards' theology merely avoid that change, or engage with it?

Alongside this cultural challenge, Edwards placed his own, theological, constraints on his attempts to state a doctrine of creation. If (as the previous chapter has argued) God's act of self-glorification is the heart of everything that happens, then, he must show that the creation and its history glorify God. There is no room here for a gnostic religion that ignores or derides the world, and sees God's purposes only in the history of the Church; not just the heavens, as the psalmist insists, but every created being and every moment of created history must declare the glory of God, or Edwards' account as described in the previous chapter cannot be accepted. The purpose – the end – of creation in its entirety and in its detail is to give glory to God through promoting the knowledge and love of God in His intelligent creatures. If any part of creation, or any moment of history, is not able to serve this end, then it has no reason to be – and so God would not have created it.

Without doubt, Edwards rose to this challenge: *Images*

---

[2] See chapter 1.

and Shadows of Divine Things[3] shows him finding 'sermons in stones' as ardently as any sixteenth-century Puritan (or playwright!); and the *Notes on the Apocalypse*[4] demonstrate the parallel attempt to read contemporary history into the Biblical narrative. These are merely the two clearest examples of a recurrent practice: again and again in his writings Edwards sought to uncover the moral meaning that his teleological commitments told him must be present in God's creation.[5] However, as indicated in the first chapter, Edwards was not simply a Puritan anachronism. He had read Locke and Newton, and grasped with considerable insight what their discoveries might mean for Christian theology. It seems likely, then, that Edwards was able to offer such robust accounts of the moral meaning of creation only because he had found a genuinely Enlightened way of so doing.

If the distinction between moral and mathematical rationalities with which I began is accurate, then already Edwards appears to be unusual: he will not fit into this either–or, but rather insists that the world is comprehensible both physically and morally.[6] Following his early reading of Newton, Edwards produced a cluster of writings on the borders of natural science and metaphysics – borders which were not so

---

[3] *YE11*, pp. 49–142; the two subtitles that Edwards attached to this notebook perhaps make the point even more forcefully: 'The Book of Nature and Common Providence' and 'The Language and Lessons of Nature'; see *YE11*, p. 50.

[4] *YE5*, pp. 95–305. This volume is edited by S. J. Stein, who appears to feel the need to apologise in his introduction for Edwards' practices in this direction: 'The book of Revelation fascinated Jonathan Edwards ... a fact that has been a source of bewilderment and embarrassment to some students of American thought .... This volume does not promise to raise Edwards' intellectual or religious stock ...': *YE5*, p. 1.

[5] Throughout this chapter, I will be speaking of moral and teleological dimensions of creation as interchangeable; whilst this need not always be the case, it is within the terms of Edwards' thought as outlined in the last chapter.

[6] This attempt was common enough in the day; Kendrick describes many clergy who wanted to speak of God working through the physical order, even as it was described by the new natural science. There is little evidence, however, that any of them were aware of the philosophical questions such a practice raised. The final position available within this simple morphology, denying both forms of comprehensibility, is characteristic of late (or post-) modernity, of course.

sharply drawn in his day – which assert the physical rationality of the created order, and that in mathematical terms, but
deny the underlying picture of a 'world-machine'.[7] If this
position can be successfully held, then it makes possible an
account of creation that permits moral rationality whilst
accepting natural science; an account of creation, that is, in
which the creation itself can still be a locus for God's self-
glorifcation. Edwards attempted to give content to this by an
appropriation of the tradition of typological exegesis, a move
that will form the subject of the latter part of this chapter.
I will begin, however, by exploring the metaphysics Edwards
developed in response to Newton.

Edwards' Metaphysics, or 'Calvinism and Hobbes'

The recognition of the importance of his early reading of
Locke and Newton has been central to the recent revival
of interest in Edwards.[8] In the present context, with
Edwards' Enlightenment credentials in question, it is
difficult to overstate the importance of Locke and, particularly, Newton for the nascent Enlightenment. To cite
merely two examples: lists of the 'greatest men in history'
which inevitably featured Newton and Locke, and then
added either Bacon or Leibniz abounded; again, in
referring to Newton, 'the adjectives "divine" and
"immortal" became virtually compulsory'.[9] This given, a
credible restatement of Reformed theology, particularly in
the anglophone world, would have to take seriously these
two thinkers.

Edwards' interaction with Locke is well known and has
been extensively commented on, at least in relation to his

---

[7] Such 'theistic Newtonianism' was not an unusual position amongst
early readers of Newton. See Peter Gay, *The Enlightenment: An
Interpretation*, vol. 2: *The Science of Freedom* (London: W. W. Norton, 1977
but originally published 1969) pp. 140–5 for some indications of the rise
and decline of the movement; also Anderson's comments in *YE6*, p. 58, for
the direct influence on Edwards.

[8] See my comments on this in chapter 1.

[9] Gay, *Enlightenment*, pp. 130–1.

religious psychology in defence of the Awakening.[10] His reading of Newton, whilst regularly noticed, has occasioned less theological interest.[11] Whilst (self-confessedly) not a mathematician, Edwards read Newton with alertness, and his metaphysics could be considered to start from a slight ambivalence in Newton's writings, the refusal to speculate on the nature of gravitational attraction – famously, 'I frame no hypotheses.' As a result of this the philosopher Leibniz argued that Newton was in danger of reintroducing mystery into science, and so returning to the obscurantism that masqueraded as piety in the Middle Ages. He went so far as to claim that Newton had 'converted the physical career of the world into a perpetual miracle ...'.[12] The young Jonathan Edwards, with a very different purpose in view from the Enlighteners, seized on the same point in his scientific writings in order to prove Leibniz's charge to be precisely true. Gravity, and indeed the preservation of all bodies in existence moment by moment, was nothing other than an immediate action of God. Here, Edwards recognised, along with other theistic Newtonians,[13] was an adequate answer to the then popular materialism that derived from Hobbes.

The refutation of materialism was seen by many in the early eighteenth century to be a pressing apologetic task, and Edwards gave himself to it in his early writings.[14] 'Substance' (*substantia*) was a philosophical term inherited from the medievals to describe whatever it was that gave concrete reality to existing things. Thus, a horse is real in a way that a picture or a dream of a horse is not, because it is

---

[10] Beginning, at least in the recent renewal of interest, with Perry Miller's study; I will discuss this further in chapter 4 below when I consider Edwards' account of conversion.

[11] The only significant account to sustain a recognition of Newton's influence that I am aware of is, once again, Jenson, *America's Theologian*, see especially pp. 23–30.

[12] Gay, *Enlightenment*, p. 143.

[13] Notably Richard Bentley; see Anderson's footnote in YE6, p. 234 n. 5.

[14] For a fuller account of the following history, see Anderson's Introduction to YE6, pp. 1–143, and especially pp. 52–136. The present discussion owes much to Anderson, whose work will, I suspect, prove to be near-definitive.

substantial. The English philosopher Thomas Hobbes had asserted that matter was the only genuine substance,[15] but this could not be accepted, as doing so would involve either denying reality to God and the angels, or claiming that they were material beings, neither of which was acceptable. The failure of medieval scholastic accounts of substance was everywhere accepted, however, and the rising popularity of atomism (the old Greek idea that everything is composed of tiny particles arranged in different patterns) made materialist accounts seem attractive. The reactions were various, but generally based on some form of dualism. That matter was substance went uncontested (the influence of atomism), but attempts were made to prove that it was not the only reality. Descartes, for example, sought to demonstrate the separate realities of the body and the mind.[16] An alternative approach sought to demonstrate that the existence of matter was contingent, and so that matter was not genuinely substantial, but a result of some more basic substance. An example of this approach would be argument of the Cambridge Platonist Henry More that the basis of matter is infinite necessary space.[17]

However, both these approaches have problems, which centre on the issue of causation. If causation is held to operate only within a substance-world, then the mental and spiritual world can have no effect upon the material world, and its separate reality is of little relevance. God or other spirits can have no effect upon the physical realm, and even the human soul or mind cannot affect its body.[18]

---

[15] According to *Leviathan* I.4, 'incorporeal substance' is merely an 'insignificant sound', like 'round quadrangle'.

[16] Descartes, *Meditations* 6.

[17] See Copleston's *History of Philosophy* vol. V, p. 64. More was a significant influence on Edwards, and some similarities in thought can be discovered: YE6, p. 54.

[18] The 'Two Clocks' theory of Geulincx, a Dutch Cartesian, is a good example. Consider two clocks, wound up and set so that one strikes the hour when the other shows it. The two events are simultaneous, determined and unconnected. So it is, according to this theory, with body and soul, which have been so ordered by God that a volitional impulse to lift my left arm is co-incident with the physical movement of my arm, but has no causal effect upon that movement. See Russell's *History of Western Philosophy*, pp. 583–4.

If, by contrast, causation operates across substance-worlds, then the one undoubted philosophical success of the day, the discovery of regular universal scientific laws, is placed in jeopardy, as the movements of material bodies no longer form a closed system. Faced with this dilemma, English philosophy found a different route, not so much around the problem as away from it altogether: the empiricism of Locke and Newton ceased to build physics on the problematic basis of metaphysics, and sought to build it on observation instead. The world-machine was seen to work; and whether one could explain why or not, one could describe the laws by which it operates.[19] This way forward, of course, is an open invitation to return to materialism: belief in the 'world-machine', does not prevent belief in 'spiritual substance', just so long as it has no effect on matter, including our own bodies. So Bishop Berkeley, who saw all this with uncommon clarity: 'Matter once allow'd, I defy any man to prove that God is not matter.'[20]

Against this background, Edwards begins his analysis of matter in a short work entitled *Of Atoms*.[21] The essence of an atom, he argues, is not size but solidity, as any body that cannot be broken is, by definition, atomic. A body cannot be broken if it is perfectly uniform, since at no point is it weaker than at any other, so applied force will result in its breaking at every point simultaneously, and so total annihilation, or no fracture at all. Edwards believed annihilation through applied force to be an absurdity, and so suggested atoms are preserved by an infinite power, which is to say an immediate action of God. The eleventh corollary to this discussion asserts that 'it follows that the certain unknown substance, which philosophers used to think subsisted by itself, and stood underneath and kept up solidity and all other properties, which they used to say

[19] The success of this programme was sufficient to delay the widespread acceptance of Hume's recognition that observation is a basis at least as problematic as metaphysics. The failure of the Kantian project to find an answer to this is at least a part of the cause of the widespread disruptions in modernity in recent years.

[20] *Works*, vol. 1, p. 77.

[21] *YE6*, pp. 208–18.

it was impossible for a man to have an idea of, is ... nothing but the Deity acting in that particular manner in those parts of space where he thinks fit.'[22]

So, Edwards points out, the so-called 'laws of nature' are merely descriptions of God's usual ways of acting – causation, after all, by supposition of the materialists themselves, has its roots in substance. This argument will also serve as a proof of God's existence – or rather (Edwards is careful in his choice of words) a proof of 'the being, infinite power, and omnipresence of God'.[23] Edwards' next attempt at sustained natural philosophy, *Of Being*,[24] returns to the attempt to demonstrate the being of God, with an interesting version of the ontological argument, one of the standard philosophical arguments for the existence of God. The classic statement of this argument is in Anselm's *Proslogium*, and proceeds by identifying God with the greatest thing of which we can conceive. Existence is then asserted to be a good, such that a thing that exists is greater than the same thing only imagined. Thus it is impossible to think that God, under this definition, does not exist. The history of debate over this argument indicates that it is both suggestive and equally problematic. Edwards' version is rather different, however:

It is impossible for us to conceive of absolute nothingness, asserts Edwards; indeed, such a state would be the basic contradiction, since it is in relation to non-being that we demonstrate all other contradictions.[25] So, since nothing, or non-being, is a contradiction, something,

---

[22] *YE6*, p. 215. For a discussion of the influence of More and Locke on Edwards' argument at this point see Anderson's Introduction pp. 63–6.

[23] Corol. 7, p. 214.

[24] *YE6*, pp. 202–7; again, Anderson's discussion is illuminating, pp. 68–75.

[25] 'Absolute nothing is the aggregate of all the absurd contradictions in the world, a state wherein there is neither body, nor spirit, nor space: neither empty space nor full space, neither little nor great, ... neither infinitely great space nor finite space, nor a mathematical point ... a state wherein every proposition in Euclid is not true, nor any of those self-evident maxims by which they are demonstrated; and all other eternal truths are neither true nor false' (*YE6*, p. 206).

or 'being' must exist eternally. (As an afterthought, Edwards proposes a second demonstration of this position, arguing that the question 'can absolute nothing be?' is itself a contradiction, since the being of anything is incompatible with a state of absolute nothingness.[26]) Thus Edwards attempts to demonstrate the existence not of the greatest conceivable being, as is traditional in the ontological argument, but simply that of being. Existence exists; to assert otherwise is meaningless. Edwards seemed both to be impressed by this argument, and to be unsatisfied by his statements of it, as he tried several times during his life to restate it in a better form. In *Miscellanies* 650, he offers a construction turning on the assertion: '... if anyone says there may be nothing he supposes at the same time that nothing has a being ...'. In *Miscellanies* 880 he attempts a more carefully logical version:[27]

> There is a reason to be given why God should have a Being. The reason is because there is no other way. There is nothing else supposable, to be put with the Being of God as the other part of the disjunction. If there be it is absolute and universal Nothing. A supposition of something is a supposition of the being of God ... God is the sum of all being and there is no being without his being ... But there is no such thing supposable, as an absolute universal nothing. We talk nonsense when we suppose any such thing ....

Edwards' various attempts to state this argument perhaps suggest that he was not entirely happy with it. Its validity is not really an issue here, but the point is not so ridiculous as it might at first sight seem: 'no-thing' is a relational term, even if that relation is one of negation. It is meaningless without a prior concept (and hence, in Edwards' terms, existence) of 'thing'. Perhaps a (thoroughly Edwardsian) mathematical illustration will help: in a recent article on the nature of zero, Ian Stewart comments: ' "Nothing" is –

---

[26] *YE6*, p. 207.
[27] Both these *Miscellanies* entries can be found in Townsend, *Philosophy*.

well, nothing. A void. Total absence of thingness. Zero, however, is definitely a thing. It is a number. It is, in fact, the number you get when you count your oranges and you haven't got any.'[28] According to Edwards, 'nothing' is just as much a thing as 'zero' is a number, the ontology of the non-existent oranges is just as real as their quantity.

This argument, if it works at all, must work equally well at all times and places, so 'being' must be eternal (or at least omnitemporaneous; Edwards seems to assume that the latter implies the former) and omnipresent.[29] So, just as *Of Atoms* argued for the existence of that which is omnipresent and omnipotent, *Of Being* argues for being which is omnipresent and eternal. All that remains, as with any attempted proof of the existence of God, is the identification of what has been proved with God who is Father, Son and Holy Spirit. The distance remaining is perhaps best indicated by quoting the assertion that Edwards makes at this point: 'Space is God.'[30]

The remainder of *Of Being* dates from some time later, and elaborates arguments which Edwards first introduces in a *Miscellanies* entry:[31] 'We know that there was being from eternity', Edwards begins, 'and this being must be intelligent.' Must, because existence depends on being known. The reasons offered in the *Miscellanies* entry are elaborated in the latter part of *Of Being*, where the example of a universe without intelligent beings is offered: 'I demand in what respect this world has a being, but only in the divine consciousness. Certainly in no respect. There would be figures and magnitudes, and motions and proportions – but where? Where else but in the Almighty's knowledge.'[32] The same reasoning will apply, he goes on to suggest, to colours and sounds and temperatures. Hence,

---

[28] Ian Stewart, 'Zero, Zilch and Zip', *New Scientist* 2131 (25 April 1998) pp. 41–4.
[29] *YE6*, p. 202.
[30] *YE6*, p. 203.
[31] *YE13*, p. 188; for dating details see Anderson's Introduction to *YE6*, and, for a summary of the results, Schafer's Table of Dates in *YE13*, pp. 91–109.
[32] *YE6*, p. 204.

all existence is only in being perceived: *esse est percipi* ('to be is to be perceived').[33]

Anderson, in his discussion of Edwards' philosophical development, argues that Edwards reaches this position (*esse est percipi*) through reflection on two early assumptions:[34] firstly, that religion was the highest purpose of the universe (an early position in the discussion of teleology I outlined in the previous chapter); and secondly that the essence of religion was knowledge of God. Of particular note is *Miscellanies gg*[35] where Edwards argues that the universe must have a purpose, and that purpose is the religion of intelligent beings – so that the role of the intelligent creation in glorifying God is the teleological focus of creation. Add to this Edwards' constant assumption (to be explored later in this chapter) that God may be known through appropriate contemplation of the creation, and the position that the creation exists in order to be known by intelligent beings is secure.

Edwards' interest in this sort of metaphysics seems to have declined, but one can imagine how the position would develop if built on his mature account of the purpose of creation. Firstly, the creatures' knowledge of God is participation in God's own knowledge of Himself, so Edwards would have been able to incorporate God's own knowledge of creation as a key point in the argument, a move that is clearly necessary if the argument is to work. Secondly, it is not just the creatures' knowledge of creation that is its purpose (i.e. that brings God glory), it is also the creatures' delight in creation, and so Edwards' assertion that to be is to be known would have to become 'to be is to be known and loved' (*esse est percipi et amari*) – a position offering significant possibilities of developing a relational ontology similar to those current in theological discussions of this century, and built finally on Trinitarian grounds.

I left Edwards' version of the ontological argument in *Of*

---

[33] I will address the obvious, and much-discussed, similarities with Berkeley below. The Latin phrase is a standard slogan to describe philosophical positions of this sort.
[34] *YE6*, pp. 77–80.
[35] *YE13*, p. 185.

Being with the unpromising assertion, 'Space is God'. A way forward from here is now available. 'Space' – the substratum wherein things 'move and have their being', where the possibility of existence is available – is indeed God. To be precise, it is the mind of God, apart from whose knowledge nothing can exist.[36] Material things are objective, are other than each other, because God knows them to be so, because that is how God thinks of them, and His faithfulness is the only guarantor (and the only one needed) of that. In the more developed form of this metaphysics I have postulated, the creation exists through being known and loved by God, and so the Father holds the creation in being through His Son and His Spirit. Edwards, it seems, opened the possibility for a post-Newtonian restatement of the orthodox doctrine of creation first developed by Irenaeus. Leibniz's accusation – that Newton made the 'career of the world into a perpetual miracle' – seems abundantly justified, as do the fears that presumably lay behind it, that Newton's thought might be used by some in the Church to oppose, rather than support, the nascent Enlightenment in its rejection of theistic religion (although, as will be clear, only a Trinitarian theism may be urged here).

The serious question raised by this account is the nature of material reality: for too much of Christian history, the attitude to matter that the Gnostics learnt from Greek philosophy has prevailed, and material being has been denigrated, if not actually regarded as necessarily evil. The credal confession of the 'resurrection of the body' is a check on this tendency, but is also in constant danger of being replaced by a belief in the immortality of the soul. An idealist philosophy such as Edwards' would seem at first sight to be in particular danger of falling into this trap. Edwards does not. He clearly and unambiguously asserts the goodness of created material reality, and it is in fact precisely his so-called idealism that enables him to do this.

---

[36] A similar argument, based on more recent science, can be found in T. F. Torrance, *Space, Time and Incarnation* (Edinburgh: T&T Clark, 1997). See particularly p. 12.

'To be without the body', he insists at one point, whilst considering the intermediate state between death and resurrection, 'is in it self [sic] an evil because tis a want of that which the soul of man naturally inclines to and desires ...'.[37] This relies on the critique of the Enlightenment: for the Enlightened, the fundamental ontological and noetic distinction lay between spirit and matter. This given, it is incontrovertible that God is spirit, and so the natural tendency for any (Enlightened) theist is to denigrate matter. Even for a non-theist, the heights of human achievement are spiritual (art, for instance), and so the same temptation is present.

Edwards, however, has cut through this dualism, and returned to the fundamental ontological insight of Irenaeus and Athanasius: the only relevant ontological distinction that can be made is between Creature and Creator. In an (unpublished) *Miscellanies* entry, number 777, Edwards discusses the progressive nature of heaven's joys (I will return to his celebration of temporality later in this chapter, but in passing this is further evidence for the ontological points I am making, as temporality tends in the tradition to be classed with materiality as marks of ontological provisionality). His argument begins with a rousing assertion that the relevant ontological gap is between creatures and the Creator, as he insists that only Christ fully knows God, and that all other creatures depend on 'means or ... manifestations or signs held forth'. The fundamental sign is, of course, the Incarnate One who bridges the gap, but my point in mentioning this argument is to notice what Edwards will not say: it is not our material natures that prevent us knowing God fully, or even our sin; it is our being as creatures. The same assertion of an ontological, and thus a noetic gap between creature and Creator occurs in a much later entry, *Miscellanies* 1358, where Edwards asserts that '... we can have no other proper manifestations of the divine nature, but by some effects of it: for we cant [sic] immediately look upon and behold God & see what he is intuitively.' Even Scripture, according to Edwards, is only a testimony to God's works: 'The word

---

[37] *Miscellanies* 644 (as yet unpublished).

declares, but the works are the proper evidence of what is declared.' He goes on to insist that we can know God through His mighty works: creation, providence, redemption, regeneration, final judgement, and others. These, however, are all works attributed to Christ in the Scriptures, and so again, we know God only through Christ, because the ontological gap is between creature and Creator, not the Enlightenment dualism of matter and spirit.

It is perhaps appropriate at this point to step back and survey the argument so far. Edwards developed a metaphysical system which found not just gravitation, as Leibniz feared, but the very solidity, reality, and permanence of the physical world to be 'merely' thoughts in the mind of God.[38] In doing so, he answered a central question of the philosophy of the day, concerning the nature of 'substance', the thing which 'stood underneath and kept up solidity and all other properties ...'.[39] Edwards argued that, in these terms, the only proper substance is God, who alone can give permanence and reality to the world. Any other answer will eventually insist on something else that is *a se*, that can exist of itself without reference to God.[40] Edwards' answer, then, is surely the only appropriately Christian answer if the question is framed in these terms, and shows that it is precisely this Christian answer that can avoid the denigration of matter. More than this, however: by making the movement of bodies under Newton's physics 'a perpetual miracle', Edwards does establish the possibility of a natural science that is not inimical to moral meaning in creation, and hence to teleology.

Edwards made a third early assault on ontological questions, one that he did sustain into his later life, in the various entries in the *Notes on the Mind*.[41] This begins with

[38] 'Merely' in the old sense of 'purely', of course, with no implication of any lack. What could be a greater basis of being than to be known and loved by God?
[39] *YE6,* p. 215.
[40] That is to say, any other answer will finally deny the key Christian affirmation that God created *ex nihilo* – out of nothing.
[41] Found in *YE6*, pp. 311–93.

an aesthetic analysis of the nature of 'excellency': 'One alone, without any reference to any more, cannot be excellent; for in such a case there can be no manner of relation no way, and therefore, no such thing as consent.'[42] Beauty consists only in relationship; one alone *cannot* be excellent.[43] All excellency consists in relational categories such as harmony, symmetry and proportion. Edwards analyses this in relation to the physical world, exploring how all physical beauty is reducible to such categories,[44] but this seems to be all by way of preamble; the decisive move comes with the assertion: 'Spiritual harmonies are of a vastly larger extent; i.e., the proportions are vastly oftener redoubled, and respect more beings, and require a vastly larger view to comprehend them, as some simple notes do more affect one who has not a comprehensive understanding of music.'[45]

Why should beauty be defined by harmonious relations, in either the spiritual or the physical realm? The answer comes through a terse statement of a surprising move, a return to ontology: 'Being, if we examine it narrowly, is nothing else but proportion.' The explanation of this is only slightly less gnomic: '... when one being is inconsistent with another being, then being is contradicted. But contradiction to being is intolerable to perceiving being, and the consent to being most pleasing.'[46] There is a return to the centrality of perception here, but with a volitional element added to it. From this Edwards develops his basic statement of aesthetics: excellency is being's consent to being, and degrees of excellency are consent to wider and wider circles of being. True excellency – that is, true beauty, or true virtue – is being's consent to being-in-general, which is to say (as was made clear in the previous chapter) being's consent to God.

So it is that one alone cannot be excellent; one alone

---

[42] YE6, p. 337.
[43] This early position reappears in *True Virtue*, as the analysis in the previous chapter demonstrated.
[44] YE6, pp. 332–6.
[45] YE6, p. 336.
[46] YE6, p. 336.

cannot be in relation, and so cannot consent to anything. Were God, even, to be a perfect monad, alone, it would be meaningless to speak of His beauty, excellency or moral perfection. Once again,[47] Edwards refuses to find the answer to God's need for relationship in creation; rather it is in being Father, Son and Holy Spirit that God is truly God: 'We have shewn that one alone cannot be excellent .... Therefore, if God is excellent, there must be plurality in God.'[48] This is a very similar move to the one that I indicated was open to him from his earlier writings: if, as Edwards has claimed, being is merely proportion, or relation, then love becomes an ontological category to set alongside knowledge. Edwards here reaches a genuinely relational ontology through introducing the volitional or affective aspect of reality alongside the cognitive aspect that he had been working with previously; *esse est percipi et amari* or *percipere et amare*; the knowledge and love of God are definitive of all created existence.

It is perhaps now appropriate to refer briefly to the most famous, or perhaps notorious, aspect of Edwards' doctrine of creation: the idea of 'continuous creation'. This is a fixed position, found in an early *Miscellanies* entry,[49] and present still in *Original Sin*, finished the year before Edwards' death.[50] It should now be clear that this idea, and the accompanying one of an occasionalist account of causation,[51] are merely consequences of prior commitments to the positions outlined above. Existence is, for

---

[47] See the previous chapter.

[48] *Miscellanies* 117; *YE13*, p. 284.

[49] 'Tis certain with me that the world exists anew every moment, that the existence of things every moment ceases and is every moment renewed': entry 125[a]; *YE13*, p. 288.

[50] 'God's upholding created substance, or causing its existence in each successive moment, is altogether equivalent to an *immediate production out of nothing*, at each moment, because its existence at this moment is not merely in part from God, but wholly from him, and not in any part, or degree, from its antecedent existence': *YE3*, p. 402, italics original.

[51] 'Indeed, in natural things means of effects in metaphysical strictness are not proper cause of the effects, but only occasions. God produces all effects': *Miscellanies* 629 (as yet unpublished). The previous sentence suggests that in saying, 'God produces all effects', Edwards is thinking specifically of the Spirit of God.

created realities, the condition of being present to the mind of God. Without trying to divine Edwards' underlying conception of the nature of God's eternity, this position nevertheless surely demands that Edwards says what he does about continuous creation: for God to think of the beginning of a creature and to think of the continued existence of a creature are not radically different divine acts in the way that creating a material substance-world, and sustaining it, are. This is an interesting result, as the American Reformed tradition that looks back to Edwards has tended to assume that this doctrine of continuous creation is a minor aberration in the account which can be discarded at will.[52] Rather, as the discussion above should have demonstrated, it is an inescapable result of basic metaphysical commitments. If the universe is to give glory to God the way Edwards sees it doing, it must be possible to describe it as created 'anew each moment'.

Having said this, it is important to realise that Edwards' various comments on continuous creation, at least in works he prepared for publication, speak of providence as being 'equivalent to' continuous creation, rather than insisting on the actual truth of that theory.[53] Edwards' concern can perhaps be seen in the context of this chapter to be a polemical insistence on the radically dependent nature of creation, attacking the assumptions of matter that is itself *a se* (that is, that does not need God to exist) or a 'world-machine' that, having been set going by God, does not need His upholding to continue. Perhaps Edwards goes too far

---

[52] Gerstner, *Rational Biblical Theology*, vol. 2, 189–202, offers sufficient testimony for this point. Gerstner himself does attempt to link the idea of continuous creation with Edwards' metaphysics, but does not appear to have observed the closeness of connection for which I am arguing.

[53] The statement in *Original Sin*, cited in n. 50 above, makes this point effectively, as does *Miscellanies* 1358 (in Townsend, *Philosophy*, p. 262): '[U]pholding the world in being, and creating of it, are not properly distinct works; for tis manifest, that ... creating of the world is but the beginning of upholding it, if I may so say; the beginning to give the world a supported and dependent existence: and preservation is only continuing to give it such a supported existence.' This interpretation is further supported by the various statements of the idea of continuous creation amongst the Reformed Orthodox; see Heppe, *Reformed Dogmatics*, pp. 251–63 and especially pp. 257–8.

in the other direction, but his concern to speak strongly against these prevalent positions is surely understandable.[54]

Thus far in this chapter I have outlined Edwards' early metaphysical explorations. Although these apparently originated in reflection on Newton, I have indicated that a commitment to the teleological positions outlined in the previous chapter is basic to their developed and lasting forms, notably idealism and the idea of a 'continuous creation'. Thus Edwards' account of the being of creation depended upon his understanding of its purpose – on, that is, God's self-glorification. Further, his attempts to find a different basis for Newtonian physics allowed him, to the extent that they are successful, to continue to hold a teleological view of creation in an Enlightened and modern intellectual context. Thus the possibility of creation reflecting its purpose is established. I will go on to explore how creation reflects its purpose, according to Edwards, in considering his creative reapplications of the idea of typology, but before that a brief excursus comparing the idealistic metaphysics thus far uncovered with those of Berkeley will prove instructive.

Edwards' similarity with Berkeley has often been noticed and commented upon, but attempts to prove dependence are generally considered to have failed, thus far.[55] Rather, a common theistic reappropriation of the ideas of such philosophers as Locke, Malebranche and Bayle is assumed.[56] Berkeley's idealism[57] begins in a

---

[54]   In stressing the considered nature of the comments in works offered for publication, it is perhaps also possible to notice a shift through time. The most outspoken assertions of the literal truth of the idea of continuous creation are all early – *Miscellanies* 125 and 346, and *YE6*, p. 241. The more careful statements are later – *Miscellanies* 1039 and 1358, and *Original Sin* (see above). Theologically, it is tempting to link this shift to Edwards' awakening interest in the Trinitarian mediation of creation (discussed in the previous chapter), but the textual evidence is too scarce to make this anything more than a speculation.
[55]   See *YE6*, p. 76 n. 3 for a useful bibliography of the debate.
[56]   On this see Morris, *Young*, pp. 137–9; 257.
[57]   Following the opinion of most commentators, I will take the *Principles of Human Knowledge* (*Works* II, pp. 19–113) as the basic expression of Berkeley's philosophy, making reference to other works only when they offer clearer statements of a particular position. Basic secondary works include G. J. Warnock, *Berkeley* (Harmondsworth: Penguin, 1953) and David Berman, *George Berkeley: Idealism and the Man* (Oxford: Clarendon Press, 1994).

response to Locke on the question of 'material substance'. Locke had asserted that the knowledge of the external world comes to us only by sensations; the causes of these sensations are the 'powers' that objects possess to cause them, which he called 'qualities'. He then proceeded to divide these into secondary qualities, which cause a sensation in the mind of the beholder but bear no relation to the nature of the object itself, and primary qualities, which are attached to the substance of the object.[58] Berkeley objects that this distinction, although it has a long history in philosophy prior to Locke, is confused and meaningless: either all qualities are present only in the mind or all are possessed by the 'substance' of the object.[59] Berkeley proceeds to demolish the concept of 'substance', asking simply how we can know of its existence: Locke had admitted that it cannot be observed, as only the sensations caused by qualities can be observed.[60] Neither can it be argued for on the basis of the existence of sensations, since it is clear that (through memory or imagination) we can generate sensations in our minds of things that are not there.[61] So it is simply a supposition; albeit a necessary one, according to Locke, to account for the order and regularity of the world: a certain appearance, smell, taste, and feel coincide in my experience at regular intervals, and I call the combination an orange; does this not imply that there is some thing that causes this particular collection of sensations? No, says Berkeley, this may be accounted for entirely by the goodness of God.[62] All admit God to be the Creator of the world, why suppose that He has created numberless beings without any purpose to their existence?[63] His clinching argument relies on a presupposition: assuming,

[58] *Essay* II.i–viii. (All references to Locke are to his major philosophical work, the *Essay Concerning Human Understanding*. Unless the contrary is indicated, the references apply to all the various editions Locke published).
[59] *Principles* 9–15 (*Works* II, pp. 44–7); the arguments are more forcefully stated in the first of the *Three Dialogues* (*Works* II, pp. 187–94).
[60] *Principles* 4–6 (*Works* II, pp. 42–3).
[61] *Principles* 18 (*Works* II, p. 48).
[62] *Principles* 30–33 (*Works* II, pp. 53–4).
[63] *Principles* 19 (*Works* II, p. 49).

as Berkeley does, that only volitional beings (i.e. spirits) can properly be said to 'cause' anything, to speak of substance causing sensations is meaningless.[64]

So, no material substance exists. What does exist is a world of spirits causing sensations in themselves and each other. The orderliness and regularity of our experience of the world as other than us (in comparison to, say, a dream) is a gift of the good God; the laws of nature, for example, are not descriptions of physical cause and effect – a meaningless term – but evidences of the faithfulness and constancy of God.[65]

With this, admittedly brief, overview of Berkeley's philosophy in place, a comparison with Edwards may be made. The similarities are obvious and striking, but certainly the suggestion that most can be accounted for by a common response to Locke seems plausible: Locke's conception of primary and secondary qualities is without doubt confused, and once this is criticised his discussion of substance is clearly vulnerable. What is more interesting is the difference between Edwards and Berkeley; the obvious initial point concerns the relational and aesthetic note that Edwards introduces to his account with the *Notes on the Mind*, which is wholly lacking in Berkeley. This points to an underlying difference that is of the greatest moment: the thoroughly Trinitarian nature of Edwards' account. Not that Berkeley disbelieved in the Trinity – he was an Anglican bishop, after all – but in his philosophical writings he speaks of God without thinking of God as Trinity, and so the doctrine has no significance in his account of the matters under discussion.

This difference serves to rescue Edwards in some measure from a criticism that has been made recently of both these thinkers, that they insist on the immediacy of God's dealings with creation.[66] The relationality of

---

[64] *Principles* 19 (*Works* II, p. 49).

[65] *Principles* 65–66 (*Works* II, pp. 69–70).

[66] This criticism has particularly been made by Colin Gunton in a number of places – see, for example, 'The End of Causality' in Gunton (ed.), *Creation*, pp. 78–9; Professor Gunton's point, that a doctrine of creation must speak of mediation, but mediation through Son and Spirit, rather than any created (or eternal) forms, archetypes or substances, is well made; my concern here is to suggest that Edwards has more of such a doctrine than Gunton gives him credit for.

Edwards' account provides an illustration of the first point of response to this criticism: with Berkeley, one can get the sense that God preserves each creature individually in His thoughts; Edwards' stress on relationship means that God is seen as preserving the creation as a whole, and each creature in its place within the whole. Already the immediacy, although still present, is of a different, and perhaps less vicious, form to that found in Berkeley;[67] there is some attempt to rescue the internal coherence of the creation that the old scholastic idea of second causes had preserved. But this argument can be taken further: for both Edwards and Berkeley, existence is finally in being known by God, but for Edwards this is, as I have argued, a category of Christological participation.[68] Again, as Edwards develops his ontology in the *Notes on the Mind*, 'consent' or love becomes an important category: if to be is to be known and loved by God, then in Edwards' terms, created ontology is the gift of the Father through His Son and His Spirit.[69]

Unfortunately, interest in Edwards' idealism has largely been limited to the philosophical community, and so the implicit Trinitarianism of the account has seemingly been overlooked. It perhaps becomes more obvious when placed alongside Edwards' more direct statements about the work of creation. John H. Gerstner has provided abundant textual evidence spanning Edwards' adult life to

[67] An illustration will perhaps help: There is a sense in the creation account in Gen. 1:1–2:3 that the whole is greater than the sum of its parts – not only is each part of creation pronounced 'good' in its own particularity, but the whole brought together is declared to be 'very good'. My suggestion is that Edwards' account of creation, with its awareness of relationality, is equipped to account for this text, whereas Berkeley's is not so equipped.

[68] As will become clear in my discussion of *History of the Work of Redemption* (pp. 115–19 below), this Christological participation is firmly rooted in the gospel narrative. The same could not be said of Edwards' account of the role of the Spirit, which remains slightly idealistic, and to this extent Gunton's criticism retains force.

[69] This latter move is explicit in the *Notes on the Mind*, 45, where Edwards first argues that 'the personal Holy Spirit' is God's 'infinite beauty, and this is God's infinite consent to being in general', and then goes on to insist that 'his love to the creature is ... the communication of himself ... his Holy Spirit': *YE6*, p. 364.

show that he regularly spoke of God creating the world through His Son and His Spirit.[70] My argument is simply that these passages ought to be allowed to interpret his idealism; there are, as I have indicated, several suggestions that the idealist language of knowledge and love is implicitly Trinitarian, and occasional passages where it is explicitly so. I have argued in the previous chapter that he regularly uses the language of God's knowledge and God's love to speak of the Son and the Spirit, and that such language was natural within the tradition. There seems little doubt, then, that Edwards is saying the same thing in his more philosophical statements of idealism as he is in his explicit references to Trinitarian agency in creation and providence.

That Edwards never drew these threads together in the way that I have suggested is natural, is only to say that he never wrote the major dogmatic system that he had in mind, an observation that is hardly novel! Nevertheless, Edwards has two regular ways of describing God's relationship with His creation: in terms of his idealism; and as explicit Trinitarian agency. In a writer like Edwards, who seamlessly combined philosophy and theology and would certainly not admit a gap, it is natural to assume not only that these two can be reconciled, but that in his own mind they were. This given, and with the evidence I have offered for reading the idealist language in Trinitarian terms, the combination I

---

[70] *Rational Biblical Theology*, vol. 2, 189–202, and especially pp. 189–90 and 198–9. A few of Gerstner's citations will give the flavour: '[H]ere is a consultation of the Persons of the Trinity about the Creation of man for every Person had his particular and distinct concern in it as well as in the Redemption of men. The Father employed the Son and the Holy Ghost on this work' (*Blank Bible* on Gen. 1:26). 'Therefore both the beginning of the world and the end of the world are by Christ for both are subject to the great purposes of the work redemption. He is therefore both the Creator and the Judge of the world . . . the alpha and the omega' (*Blank Bible* on Eph. 3:9). 'It was made especially the Holy Spirit's work to bring the world to its beauty and perfection out of the chaos; for the beauty of the world is a communication of God's beauty: (*Miscellanies* 293). This last quotation also demonstrates my point that Edwards did not separate idealist language and Biblical language when speaking of creation. Gerstner does not mention *Miscellanies* 1349, although it makes the point as clearly as any text: '. . . tis manifest by the Scripture, that the world was made by the Holy Ghost or Spirit of God, as well as by the Son of God . . .'.

have suggested seems the obvious one. In his later works, at least, Edwards appears to be working with a concept of Trinitarian mediation, couched in Augustinian language.

This section has been something of an extended excursus; I began the chapter by indicating that Edwards' context demanded that he find an intellectually satisfying 'theistic Newtonianism' before he could begin to assert any teleological content to the being of creation. That his idealism (so-called) is appropriately Newtonian was established by the earlier parts of the section; that it is appropriately theistic, in the fullest Christian sense, has been the burden of the latter discussions. The result is the claim that Edwards offers an account of creation that could, in principle, allow him to assert the presence of moral meaning – teleology – in a way that could provide a basis for natural science, and so was appropriate to the early modernity that formed his intellectual context. The remaining question is whether, and how, Edwards actually sees God as glorifying Himself through the created order. Hobbes had insisted that all true knowledge of creation was either natural history or political history;[71] the remainder of this chapter will be devoted to exploring the tool Edwards uses to uncover God's self-revelation in both these spheres – the exegetical method of typology.

Typology and the Meaning of Creation

Typological exegesis has its roots in the earliest days of the Church, where it was eagerly adopted and honed as a Christological hermeneutic with which to appropriate the Old Testament as Christian scripture.[72] Although varieties

---

[71] *Leviathan*, I.9.
[72] For the early history of typology, see Leonhard Goppelt, *Typos: The Typological Interpretation of the Old Testament in the New* (tr. Donald H. Madvig) (Grand Rapids, MI: Eerdmans, 1982) for Biblical background; Jean Daniélou, *From Shadows to Reality: Studies in the Biblical Typology of the Fathers* (tr. Wulstan Hibberd) (London: Burns & Oates, 1960), the classic text on patristic usage; K. J. Woollcombe, 'The Biblical Origins and Patristic Development of Typology' in G. W. H. Lampe and K. J. Woollcombe (eds), *Essays on Typology* (London: SCM Press, 1957), pp. 39–75, for a briefer overview of both aspects.

of typological and spiritualising exegesis can be found throughout the history of the Church,[73] the immediate background to Edwards' use of this method was the Reformed re-appropriation of typology which occurred in the wake of the attempted rejection of all forms of allegorising by the first Reformers. Lowance[74] does a fine job of tracing Edwards' Puritan inheritance, but there was also an inheritance from the continental Reformed Orthodox, and he could have found typology used freely in standard theology texts, Wollebius and Turretin for instance. It is no surprise, then, that Edwards adopted a typological method of exegesis; nor is it particularly relevant to my concerns in this chapter. What is both surprising and interesting, however, is Edwards' appropriation of typology as a method of finding meaning and coherence in the created order and the course of human history.

The centrality of typology to Edwards' interpretations of Scripture has often been noted,[75] as has his extension of typology to the natural and historical realms.[76] What is perhaps less often seen, but crucial to my purposes, is the motivation behind this extension of typology; perhaps because the attention that has been given to this subject has usually, thus far, come from students of American

[73] See James S. Preus, *From Shadow to Promise: Old Testament Interpretation from Augustine to the Young Luther* (Cambridge, MA: Harvard University Press, 1969).
[74] Mason I. Lowance, *The Language of Canaan: Metaphor and Symbol in New England from the Puritans to the Transcendentalists* (London: Harvard University Press, 1980).
[75] In discussing Edwards' *Notes on Scripture*, its modern editor, Stephen J. Stein, asserts that it 'documents his consuming interest in typology' (*YE15*, p. 2). He goes on to say, 'The collective result of his exegesis is a scriptural organon with the typological principle at its foundation, a system composed of Biblical themes that Edwards regarded as central to Christianity ...' (*YE15*, p. 3). Wilson H. Kimnach, who is editing Edwards' sermons, calls him an 'ardent practitioner' of typology (*YE10*, p. 228) and an 'avid typologist' (*YE10*, p. 229).
[76] On this see *YE10*, pp. 230–6; *YE11, passim*. (This volume contains Edwards' texts on typology; close attention to both the texts and the excellent introductory material by Wallace E. Anderson and Mason I. Lowance is invaluable in discussion of this subject): *Miscellanies* 119 (*YE13*, p. 285) and 362 (*YE13*, pp. 434–5); Perry Miller's edition of, and Introduction to, *Images and Shadows of Divine Things* (New Haven, CT: Yale University Press, 1948).

literature, Edwards' purpose has been given less attention than the path that he paved for Emerson *et al.* [77] Edwards argues thus:

> ... the whole outward creation, which is but the shadows of beings, is so made as to represent spiritual things ... it's agreeable to God's wisdom that it should be so, that the inferior and shadowy parts of his works should be made to represent those things that are more real and excellent ... the highest parts of his work .... Thus God glorifies himself and instructs the minds he has made.[78]

The physical world is created and ordered to reflect and to show forth the spiritual world – God, and His relationships with His creatures – so that, through knowing God, we will glorify Him. Thus, typology, too, is made to serve the overarching teleological concern.

In order to explore this extension of typology to other areas it is, unsurprisingly, necessary to be aware of the key features of typology in its original, exegetical, form. As already noted, this stretches right back to the Scriptural writers themselves – indeed, some writers see typology used even within the Old Testament, as the prophets employ stories from the Torah in original ways to speak of what will happen to Israel.[79] This prophetic typology is perhaps best illustrated by an example, which I will borrow from Daniélou.[80] The return of the exiles that is prophesied in Isaiah 40–55 is spoken of repeatedly as a typological fulfilment of the Exodus story. God's people have completed their 'hard service' (40:2); and He will once again lead His people out (40:11). The comparison is at

---

[77] See, for example, Lowance, *Language*.
[78] *Miscellanies* 362 (*YE13*, p. 434).
[79] For instance, see Daniélou, *From Shadows*, pp. 12–13, for typologies of paradise in Hosea, Ezekiel, Amos, Micah and Isaiah; pp. 70–3 for flood typologies in Isaiah and the Psalms; and particularly pp. 153–7 for typologies of the Exodus throughout the later Old Testament writings, but preeminently in Is. 40–55.
[80] Daniélou, *From Shadows*, pp. 155–6.

times explicit: the God who 'made a way through the sea, a path through the mighty waters', is now 'making a way in the desert, and streams in the wasteland' (43:16, 19). Again, memories of the first Exodus are invoked with the command to come out in 48:20–21. But typology is more than simple repetition; God is doing greater things, repeating with elaborations what He has done in the past: 'This is what the LORD says – he who made a way through the sea, a path through the mighty waters, who drew out the chariots and horses, the army and reinforcements together . . . . "Forget the former things; do not dwell on the past. See, I am doing a new thing! . . . I am making a way in the desert . . .".' Whereas the first Exodus was remembered by the use of unleavened bread, because the people fled without time to bake properly (Ex. 12:39), now God says, 'Depart, depart from there . . . but you will not leave in haste or flight . . .' (Is. 52:11–12). Jeremiah completes the picture: this new salvation will replace the Exodus in the minds of all people: 'The days are coming . . . when people will no longer say, "As surely as the LORD lives, who brought the people up out of Egypt," but they will say "As surely as the LORD lives, who brought the descendants of Israel out of the land of the north . . ." ' (Jer. 23:7–8); and there will be a new covenant attached to the new Exodus, written not on tablets of stone but on human hearts (31:31–3).

Old Testament prophetic typology, then, looked forward to mighty acts of God that repeated what had gone before in a more significant and more 'spiritual' way.[81] It is this background that is taken and developed by the New Testament writers to provide the texts which are the foundation of Christian typological exegesis.[82] The key difference is that whereas Old Testament typology looked

[81] More spiritual in that (for example) the new covenant was to be written in hearts, not on stones.
[82] Typological exegesis was, of course, practised and developed in the intertestamental period and in Judaism of the New Testament period (Philo is particularly relevant here), but such developments are not important for my current purposes. See Goppelt, *Typos*, pp. 23–58 for some details.

forward, seeking to discern the contours of a coming act of God through a retelling of what had gone before, New Testament typology looks backward, showing how every act of God in the past found its true meaning and true fulfilment in Jesus Christ. Whether it is the Matthean tradition of seeking correspondences to events in the life of Christ,[83] or Johannine sacramental typology,[84] the New Testament exegesis of the Old often depends on a new, but still typological, hermeneutic.[85]

Most writers who discuss the subject are very concerned to distinguish 'typology' from 'allegory'. At times this distinction can feel like little more than 'types are interpretations I accept, allegories are those I do not', but there is a legitimate basis to it. When the (unquestionably allegorical) Old Testament interpretation of Philo is compared to that of the New Testament and the early Fathers (particularly Irenaeus), a difference in approach is clear: Philo moves 'upwards', from a historical to a 'spiritual' sense; Irenaeus moves forwards, from a historical prefiguration to its historical fulfilment – and, crucially, finds every fulfilment in the person of Jesus Christ. Two characteristics thus distinguish the legitimate (because Biblical) typological method from the illegitimate allegorical one: historicity – or perhaps better, eschatological nature – and Christocentricity.[86]

Passing over 1500 years of history in a somewhat cavalier way, we can see that the typology that Jonathan Edwards inherited only just managed to keep hold of these distinctives. Samuel Mather's standard manual, *Figures or Types of the Old Testament*, certainly insisted on them in its definition,[87] but respected works could break either rule (although seemingly

---

[83] E.g. Mt. 2:15–18; 3:14–16; 12:17–21; 27:9–10.

[84] See Daniélou, *From Shadows*, pp. 160–1.

[85] Old Testament stories as types of the spiritual life of the Christian also feature (just) in the New Testament – 2 Pet. 2 provides one example. This form of typology becomes very significant in the Fathers.

[86] This statement is an oversimplification, although adequate for my purposes. For more complicated assessments, see Daniélou, *From Shadows*, pp. 287–8 and Woollcombe, 'Origins', p. 75.

[87] 'A Type is some outward or sensible thing ordained of God under the Old Testament, to represent and hold forth something of Christ in the New': quoted in *YE11*, p. 27; see also Lowance, *Language*, pp. 74–88.

not both). So, central to the self-understanding of the New England Puritans was the typological assertion that they were the New Israel, and so the attempt to apply the Old Testament typologically not to 'hold forth something of Christ', but to find prophecies of their own lives.[88] Equally, Puritanism on both sides of the Atlantic found images of Christ's redemption in the ordinary things of life, not just the history of redemption recorded in Scripture.[89] There are even instances of both rules being ignored, of a thoroughgoing natural theology that sought to read God's will for the people directly from the events of nature.[90] The scene was set, then, for Edwards to reforge typology in ways that would serve his own theological purposes.

On the basis of the theology of creation described earlier in this chapter, Edwards was in a position to construct a doctrine of general revelation. If creation is not self-sufficient, but instead upheld and preserved by the knowledge and love of God, by Son and Spirit, then it is natural to assume that the world is morally and theologi-cally meaningful, that with the right hermeneutic God's revelation may be found in creation as well as in the pages of Scripture. Puritan developments in typology offered the necessary hermeneutic, which Edwards eagerly adopted. The various notebooks published under the title *Typological Writings* in the Yale Edition[91] demonstrate his abiding interest in this area, but traces can be found throughout the corpus[92] – 'natural typology' was a fixed and important part of Edwards' world-view.

---

[88] A number of illustrations of this, together with an analysis of its changing expression through time, may be found in Lowance, *Language*, pp. 57–61. For examples of Edwards doing something very like this, see *Miscellanies* 691 (on the Sabbath) and 694 (on baptism) (both as yet unpub-lished), where Edwards argues theological points by using a typological hermeneutic to interpret the Old Testament.

[89] The classic example, and a work Edwards used and respected, is John Flavel's *Husbandry Spiritualized*. See *YE11*, p. 23; Lowance, *Language*, pp. 69–72.

[90] Lowance, *Language*, pp. 63–7.

[91] *YE11*.

[92] See *YE10*, pp. 227–36, for a discussion of Edwards' use of typology in his preaching; the various entries headed 'Types' in the *Miscellanies*; or *YE8*, pp. 25–6, for the centrality of typology in Edwards' ethical theories.

Edwards' essays in this form of typology could be seen as just another pre-Enlightenment attempt to discover some form of general revelation. This doctrine has not had the best reputation amongst theologians in recent decades, with a resounding *Nein!* still echoing whenever it is mentioned.[93] In Edwards' own inheritance, the particular theory he advances would hardly have been mainstream, a fact he recognises when he candidly admits, 'I expect by very ridicule and contempt to be called a man of a very fruitful brain and copious fancy, but they are welcome to it. I am not ashamed to own that I believe the whole universe, heaven and earth, air and seas, and the divine constitution and history of the holy Scriptures, be full of the images of divine things ....'[94] However, this would be too facile a dismissal of Edwards' position, albeit one he invited; here, as elsewhere, his theories are integrated into his theological and philosophical commitments, and are coherent with the overall system he presents.

The key assertion, on which all Edwards' efforts in natural typology are based, is that the natural, physical world has been deliberately created in order to represent in its various parts spiritual realities. It is not just that gravitational attraction as the basis of the (Newtonian) universe is a good illustration of the role of love in the spiritual world; rather, God ordered the universe in that way in order to image forth love. Again, the gradual progress of spring as the sun approaches is 'a remarkable type' of the coming gradual approach of the kingdom of God, and Edwards spells out the various resemblances, which he clearly believed were arranged by God to be read off in this way, in some detail. This theory is at its clearest in

---

[93] *Nein!* was the title of a book by Karl Barth repudiating any form of natural theology. Edwards' caveats would presumably have gained Barth's approval however: 'The whole of Christian divinity depends upon divine revelation. For tho there are many truths concerning God and our duty to him, that are evident by the light of nature; yet not one truth is taught by the light of nature in that manner in which it is necessary for us to know it. For the knowledge of no truth in divinity is of any significance to us, any otherwise than it some way or other belongs to the gospel scheme, or has relation to Christ the Mediatour' *Miscellanies* 837.
[94] *YE11*, p. 152.

Miscellanies 362, which Edwards indicated would serve as a heading for his 'Types' notebook:[95]

> For indeed the whole outward creation, which is but the shadows of beings, is so made as to represent spiritual things. It might be demonstrated by the wonderful agreement in thousands of things, much of the same kind as is between the types of the Old Testament and their antitypes, and by spiritual things being so often and continually compared with them in the Word of God. And it's agreeable to God's wisdom that it should be so, that the inferior and shadowy parts of his works should be made to represent those things that are more real and excellent, spiritual and divine, to represent the things that immediately concern himself and the highest parts of his work. Spiritual things are the crown and glory, the head and soul, the very end and alpha and omega of all other works: what therefore can be more agreeable to wisdom, than that they should be so made as to shadow them forth?[96]

This paragraph is preceded by one showing the sun to be a type of the Trinity, and followed by a discussion of Biblical types, and a brief reference to an Augustinian image of the Trinity in the human mind. I have quoted at such length because several parts of this crucial definition are relevant to my argument. Firstly, it is clear how much the typological system depends on the metaphysics discussed in the earlier part of this chapter – not just the idealism, but also the relational nature of the world, are concepts that underlie Edwards' adoption of this interpretative method.[97] Secondly, the teleological note that has been my focus surfaces again here: 'spiritual things', things that 'immediately concern [God] himself', are the purpose, goal

---

[95] A reference to this entry was added next to the title – see *YE11*, p. 7.
[96] *YE13*, pp. 434–5.
[97] Anderson comments on this relationship in his Introduction to the 'Images' manuscript: *YE11*, pp. 13–20.

or 'end' of the material creation.[98] Later in the entry Edwards will say','Thus God glorifies himself and instructs the minds he has made.' Edwards is able to adopt typology because it is consonant with his prior commitments concerning the doctrine of creation, and he chooses to adopt it because it furthers his fundamental teleological vision. He also believed that this method of approaching nature is sanctioned by Biblical use, and he lists a number of examples – for instance, marriage as a type of Christ's love for the Church.[99] His typological hermeneutic, by which he sought to identify true types (ordered by God) from mere fanciful resemblances, was dependent on the assumption that he could 'learn the language of types' from these Scriptural examples.[100]

The content that Edwards finds in his types is also significant: the tradition had seen all the types of the Old Testament as finding their antitype in Christ, but Edwards' natural types extend further (although the 'Types of the Messiah' notebook demonstrates that Edwards remained committed to traditional Christological typology of the Old Testament).[101] Probably the best way to describe the complicated evidence is to say that Edwards saw creation as imaging redemption. The antitypes, although clustered around Christ and His work, also include such things as the sanctification of the saints, the temptation and destruction of the reprobate, and the wiles of the devils. All these, however, may be included under the general heading of the work of redemption, broadly considered. That this is an unsurprising result should be clear from a restatement: Edwards' great theme is the self-glorification, by means of self-communication, of God as the final end of all His actions; this self-glorification occurs especially in

---

[98] Again, Anderson notes this emphasis: *YE11*, pp. 9–10.

[99] 'Images' 5, 9, 12, 56 (*YE11*, pp. 52, 53, 54, 67).

[100] See 'Types' notebook, (*YE11*, p. 152), where Edwards uses the image of a 'language of types' himself; also 'Images' 156 (*YE11*, p. 106) where Edwards suggests that Scripture both tells us plainly what are the mysteries that are typified in the natural world, and teaches us to think typologically by the many examples it gives us.

[101] *YE11*, pp. 187–324.

the eternal joy – or death – of His intelligent (i.e. spiritual, in Edwards' terms) creatures; the physical creation serves this self-glorification. Therefore the created order exists for God to make known His will concerning salvation and perdition; this it does by being a mass of typological relationships with the 'higher' spiritual reality.

One final point is relevant here: physical type and spiritual antitype are connected by a relationship expressly thought of by God – that is to say, the connection is metaphysical; types are really related to their antitypes.[102] Reading a system like Edwards' it would be easy to assume that he is in some sense downplaying the importance of creation, but he is not. Creation is genuinely – metaphysically; objectively, to use Jenson's word – bound up with God's final purpose. Jenson again: 'Reality is a community of minds; and it is an actual community, that is, one engaged in communication .... The world of bodies is the *between* of their communication, the perspectival field in which persons can come together while each remaining an *other* from all the others ....'[103] Edwards' typological account of creation emphasises an aspect that is only implicit in the quotation: the world of bodies is also part of what enables God to fulfil His highest purpose of communicating with His creatures.[104]

There remains a weakness in the account as I have described it thus far, however: communication is a dynamic category, not a static one, as was clear in the discussion of God's self-communication in the previous chapter. In this context, that is to say that creation must be dynamic, not static, and that Edwards' system could not work without a theology of history.

The modern American theologian Hans Frei,[105] in

---

[102] Jenson makes the point well: 'Edwards' typologizing ... is not an arbitrary game or mere hangover from older exegetical method; since all things are thoughts in God's mind, their imaging references are precisely their objective connections': *America's Theologian*, pp. 48–9.

[103] Jenson, *America's Theologian*, p. 32.

[104] And as such is good, as I have already indicated Edwards insisted (pp. 88–9 above).

[105] See Hans W. Frei, *The Eclipse of Biblical Narrative: A Study in Eighteenth and Nineteenth Century Hermeneutics* (London: Yale University Press, 1974) pp. 6–8.

discussing how changing views of the Bible led to the failure of traditional typology, links this with changing views of history. Frei offers three elements that serve to define 'precritical realistic reading' of Scripture – which all, significantly, relate to the nature of history.[106] Firstly, all history-like narrative in Scripture was unreflectively assumed to describe true historical occurrences accurately. Secondly, typological exegesis was used to read a single narrative out of the Bible – a historical metanarrative. Thirdly, this metanarrative was assumed to embrace the whole world, and so readers were called to fit their own lives, and the lives they experienced in their own periods in history, into the story. The empiricism of Locke and Newton, and with them the Enlightenment, clearly offered a powerful challenge to each of these points: historical science, treating all texts as equal, and trusting the mute testimony of artefacts more than that of any text, would determine what was historical and what was not; the literary structure of the Scriptural texts would be determined by critical analysis, not by *a priori* theological commitments; and if a metanarrative was to be permitted, it would be the 'scientifically validated' one of the Enlighteners, not something found in ancient texts. Frei speaks of an increasing distance between the narrative as read and reality as it was understood, and a reversal in the direction of interpretation: no longer was the question how well my experience of the world fitted the Biblical narrative; rather, the Biblical narrative was judged on its relation to my experience.[107]

Described like this, there is much in Edwards that sounds pre-critical. This is perhaps unsurprising – he lived, after all, at the very start of this movement, when an unreflective preacher might have been able to continue in the old ways with some success, serenely unaware of the winds of change. But Edwards was not unreflective; Stephen J. Stein, in his introduction to the *Notes on Scripture*, demonstrates that in his exegesis Edwards was

---

[106] Frei, *Eclipse*, pp. 2–3.
[107] Frei, *Eclipse*, pp. 5–6.

very aware of the modern critical challenges, and often sought to combat one or another of them.[108] In part, the conflict was between two radically divergent ways of viewing the world – both Enlightened, in the sense of taking Newton and Locke seriously, but using the conclusions of Newton and Locke very differently. It is important to recognise this because a discussion from the perspective of Edwards of the points Frei makes will at times depend on a flat denial, but this is not an unreflective denial seeking to hold to the 'medieval' certainties; it is, rather, a denial based on a different way of being Enlightened and modern. An example would be Frei's third point, concerning metanarrative: with Edwards' account of creation, as described in the earlier part of this chapter, a Christological metanarrative can be simply insisted on as not just consonant with, but actually demanded by, an adequate description of the being of the world. (This is not to criticise Frei's penetrating analysis, of course, merely to point out that Edwards had resources to combat the general trends which Frei identifies.)

This given, Edwards could continue to seek this metanarrative in Scripture, and so to read the Bible as an overarching story into which the events of life are to be fitted, as Frei describes. That is to say, Edwards could continue, on the basis of his doctrine of creation, to offer a theology of history. His practice in this direction can be seen in a number of works, the *Notes on Scripture*[109] or the various works contained in the *Apocalyptic Writings*,[110] but it shows up most clearly in the *History of the Work of Redemption*.[111] This work, consisting of a series of thirty sermons on the text Isaiah 51:8, describes the progress of God's redemption as Edwards read it in Scripture from 'the fall of man to the end of the world'[112] and constitutes

---

[108] *YE15*, pp. 12–21. See also *Miscellanies* 851, 1172 and 1293, which each show Edwards reflecting carefully on his hermeneutic.
[109] *YE15*.
[110] *YE5*, particularly the *Notes on the Apocalypse*.
[111] *YE9*.
[112] The Doctrine of the whole discourse; see *YE9*, p. 116.

an overarching and breathtakingly ambitious theology of history.

Before analysing this work, it would be as well to gather some indications of Edwards' viewpoint from other texts. Perhaps the clearest proof that he had a theology of history is his conviction, already mentioned in the previous chapter, that history continues beyond the end of the world, into the lives of the saints in heaven: 'If the happiness of the creature be considered as it will be, in the whole of the creature's eternal duration, with all the infinity of its progress and infinite increase of nearness and union ...'.[113] Progress and increase continue in perfection (again, for Edwards, unlike so much Platonist-influenced theology, temporality is not a defect in the creature); there is nothing static about the joys of heaven, any more than there is about God's gift of Himself through the created order of the earth.[114]

Miscellanies 547[115] discusses the theology of history in relation to the teleological theme that I am pursuing. The 'goal of providence' will not be reached until the end of the world, insists Edwards, but all created providence is a necessary part of that goal. Each snapshot state of the world in history must be of relevance, or 'providence would never have ordered them. The world would never have been in such a state.' In the first corollary to this entry, Edwards argues that this proves the survival of created intelligences, as these intermediate states of the world exist only in the memory of such intelligences. This may seem slightly out of step with the metaphysics that I have described in this chapter, as an assertion could be made that history has genuine reality because it is eternally perceived and enjoyed by God,[116] but Edwards' point is

---

[113] From the *Dissertation Concerning the End for Which God Created the World*: *YE8,* pp. 533–4.

[114] Paul Ramsey, the editor of *YE8,* has collected the various references Edwards makes to heaven as a progressive state in his Appendix III: *YE8,* pp. 706–38.

[115] Townsend, *Philosophy,* pp. 135–6.

[116] Again, it is easier to hold this from Edwards' position than from Berkeley's, as the successive states of history could be described in terms of differing relationships between created objects. Relationships, it will be

that what God does is done so that His glory may be known and loved, and so there must be creatures to remember history and so to see God's glory therein displayed.[117] Nevertheless, the point stands: history has its own ontology, and if Edwards will use the word 'shadow', it is not the insubstantial illusion of Plato's cave. The world remains beautiful, but it is the sequential beauty of a piece of music (to borrow an image from Jenson[118]) rather than the static beauty of the 'still life'. The community of minds meeting harmoniously in dependent material reality is subject to change and movement – movement forward, to all eternity.

Here, once again, Edwards' rigorous Calvinism is of benefit.[119] If it is assumed that the fall was a mistake, never part of the plan, then the same is likely to be said of history. The turning of ages will become, as it did for Origen,[120] an unfortunate necessity to get back to the place where it all started. For Edwards, God's first and best thought was of change – the crucifixion of Christ being 'as it were the cause of all the decrees, the greatest of all decreed events, and that on which all other decreed events depend as their main foundation'.[121] The end of history is not its beginning; indeed, history has no 'end', in the sense of a static, immutable 'Omega point'. Rather, 'the end of history' still

---

remembered, are integral to Edwards' system, but not to that of Berkeley, as indeed Edwards states in this *Miscellanies* entry: '[T]he various successive states of the world do in conjunction or as connected in a scheme together attain God's great design.'

[117] '[T]here is nothing remains that can be supposed to be the thing reached or brought forth as the great thing aimed at in all that God had for so many ages been doing ... God ... has gained no knowledge ... by all that has happened. There remains no declarative glory of God nor any benefit to any other being.'

[118] *America's Theologian*, p. 35.

[119] Jenson makes the point, although his illustration is perhaps unfortunate: 'The division runs between those for whom Christ's atoning work is contingent to the sheer fact of sin, and those for whom the fact of sin is contingent to God's intent to redeem. Some cannot and some can join the ... carol that rejoices in Adam's sin, since otherwise "our Lady" would not have been "heaven's queen".' (p. 45) With all due deference to Professor Jenson's knowledge of the subject, I for one would be surprised to find the Puritan Edwards willing to refer to the Blessed Virgin as 'heaven's queen'!

[120] *De Principiis* 1.6.2.

[121] *Miscellanies* 762, corol. 2.

features temporal change, with the saints moving into closer and closer union with God for all eternity. History, very simply, is the necessary condition for the event of the overflow of God's glory, and as such can never come to an end. Given this, it is natural that Edwards should conceive of precisely the *history* of the work of redemption as a fitting subject for a major discourse – and a fitting title for his projected *Summa*.[122]

A problem raises its head, of course: a theology of history may very well speak of the necessity of Old Testament history for the Incarnation – indeed, may even claim that such 'salvation-history' is presupposed by the fact of personal conversion.[123] But what of the rise of Islam, the Reformation, or the European colonisation of the Americas? How are we to theologise concerning these? Three approaches seem possible: one may, with Augustine,[124] proffer general theories concerning the nature of human history and speculate as to how recent events might relate to such; one may, with the Puritan radicals and Fifth Monarchists of the English Civil War seek prophecies in Scripture that speak about the current day; or, most ambitiously, one could seek a hermeneutic with which to interpret history itself. Perhaps the feature that marks Edwards most clearly as an Enlightenment thinker is his confidence, not just in the rationality of the world, but in his ability to uncover that rationality; it is no surprise, then, to find Edwards adopting all three of these methods.

I have already discussed the theology of history that will underline the first. *Miscellanies* entry 547 can be seen in this light: creation has a teleology, so history must conform to that teleology. This, however, will not take us very far, and so Augustine's tale of two cities does

---

[122] Edwards' intention to write a 'body of divinity' under this title is indicated in a letter to the trustees of the College of New Jersey concerning the offer of the presidency of the college. For the text see *YE16*, pp. 725–30.
[123] Although Edwards would never have consented to such a de-objectifying of the drama of salvation. See chapter 4 below.
[124] In *The City of God*.

not presume to explain God's purpose in every detail of recorded history. The second road may travel further, and Edwards' copious *Notes on the Apocalypse* demonstrate his attempts to walk this way. These books, of all Edwards' writings, are perhaps the most foreign to the modern reader, but then the *modern* reader will not share Edwards' assumption that history is precisely the history of redemption, the unfolding action of God in revealing His glory through the salvation and eternal joy of His elect creatures. If we find it strange or even amusing to read Edwards' attempts to link the 'sixth vial' of Revelation 16:12 with the disruption of the flow of riches from the colonies to Roman Catholic monarchs in his own day,[125] then that may have as much to do with our own assumptions that God is powerless in history – paganism – or even that our salvation is out of, rather than through, 'secular' history – gnosticism – as with any primitivism on Edwards' part. The third route is the most dangerous, if potentially the most fruitful. Edwards' attempts in this direction involved a further extension of his typological hermeneutic to the events of history in order to show that these, too, could show forth Christ and His saving work, to God's glory. Indeed, if creation and its history are as Edwards has described them, then the events of history must show forth Christ because such events are essentially relationships that God thinks of, which is to say their being is Christologically grounded: 'Christ God-man is not only Mediatour between God and sinfull men but he acts as a middle person between all other persons & all intelligent beings.'[126] This is no sub-Hegelian logos-mysticism; Edwards, when speaking about Christ, is speaking of the One who was crucified under Pontius Pilate, not of any organising principle of the cosmos – or, better, he is speaking of the One who was crucified

[125] *YE5*, pp. 253–84.
[126] *Miscellanies* 781. The assertion is breathtakingly daring, but entirely in accord with Edwards' system.

under Pontius Pilate *as* the organising Person of the cosmos.[127]

I have had cause to comment earlier in this chapter that Edwards will admit no basic ontological distinction other than that between creature and Creator;[128] a further piece of evidence of this commitment will demonstrate just how seriously Edwards takes this theme of the work of Jesus Christ as that around which the universe is organised. A theology that had not been thoroughly emancipated from Greek or Enlightenment views would see the angels, as the inhabitants of heaven, as perfect and unchanging. Edwards will not. The elect angels are creatures as we are and so are in need of confirmation, and that confirmation comes only through the work of Jesus Christ. Briefly, Edwards argues that it was the awareness of the coming humiliation of Christ that caused the fallen angels to reject God's plans, as they regarded this as unworthy of the Son of God. So, it was appropriate that the test of the elect angels that confirmed their obedience was their submission to the man Jesus Christ as their King. They could do this only at the ascension, so it was only at the completion of the gospel plan that the elect angels were confirmed as elect.[129] It is not just the material creation that finds its history bound up in the life, death, resurrection, ascension and return of Jesus Christ; the heavens themselves depend on Him for their being.

The History of the Work of Redemption, then, describes the

---

[127] This is clear from the *History of the Work of Redemption*, which focuses on the events of the gospel narratives: 'And we are now come to the most remarkable article of time that ever was or ever will be. Though it was between thirty and forty years, yet more was done in it than had been done from the beginning of the world to that time. We have observed that all [things] that had been done before were only preparatory for what was done now, and it may be observed that all that was done before the beginning of time in the eternal counsels of God and that eternal transaction there was between the persons of the Trinity, chiefly respected this period': *YE9* p. 294.

[128] See pp. 89–90 above.

[129] *Miscellanies* 515 contains substantially this account, but most of the positions are common throughout the *Miscellanies*. Entry 938 in particular makes the same point: 'So it was in Christ God-man that the angels have found rest.'

history of the world through the hermeneutical key of Jesus Christ. All that happens before the Incarnation is preparatory for His mission, all that happens after is an outworking of what He has done. Edwards is concerned to demonstrate that at every point in history God is applying the salvation found in and through Jesus Christ to men and women. In the first section of the work,[130] Edwards discusses the history of the world from the Fall to the Incarnation. The proposition here is that this span of time 'is taken up in doing those things that were forerunners and earnests also of Christ's coming and working out redemption and work preparatory to it'. Whether God's mighty acts of liberation in Old Testament history, or the rise and fall of the ancient empires, or the actual redemption of individual Israelites – all history in this period was so ordered by God to provide the right conditions for the coming of Christ. But this is not the most striking feature of the discourse: Edwards also insists that the salvation that is wrought by God in these times is only through Christ – He is the one who stands in the place of the mediator, and so all God's actions are through Him. This is represented as a result of the judgement that followed the Fall: 'Henceforth, this lower world with all its concerns was as it were devolved upon the Son of God. For when man had sinned, God the Father would have no more to do with man immediately ... He would henceforth have no concern with man but only through a mediator.'[131]

A tension with Edwards' metaphysical thought will be apparent. I have argued that Edwards sees the act of creation as mediated by Son and Spirit; here there is the (implicit) suggestion that God acted immediately on the original creation. Once again, the provisional nature of the text must be taken into account: this is an unrevised sermon, which cannot be expected to state every point in the most careful manner. The suggestion is no more than implicit, and as it contradicts explicit statements made by Edwards in more carefully

[130] *YE9*, pp. 113–293.
[131] *YE9*, p. 131.

considered points,[132] we may assume that it was a slip of
phrasing that would have been eliminated had Edwards
lived to revise the text as he intended. The present point,
however, is to notice how thoroughly Christocentric
Edwards' account of history is: '... when we read in the
sacred history what God did from time to time towards
his church and people, and what he said to them, and
how he revealed himself to them, we are to understand
it especially of the second person of the Trinity.'[133]
Again, in speaking of the Exodus, Edwards insists
that 'this redemption was by Jesus Christ', arguing that
Christ appeared in the burning bush, that Christ was in
the pillar of cloud and fire, that Christ destroyed the
pursuing army in the Red Sea. This whole passage is a
remarkable example of the Christological hermeneutic
which informs Edwards' writing; not only is every
divine action ascribed specifically to Christ, but the
event as a whole is seen as a type of Christ's
redemption, and many of the details are linked to
prophecies and details of His life and work. So the
burning bush in its details is a type of the Incarnation
and passion of the Redeemer, the Red Sea a type of
baptism, and hence of salvation through being washed
in Christ's blood, and many other images and allusions
appear in between.[134] History in its grand sweep and its
apparently incidental details is ordered by God through

---

[132] 'All works of God are done by the Spirit, but in all works relating to
the world he acts as the Spirit of the Son .... So Christ can be called the
Author of both the old & new creation ...': *Miscellanies* 958 (unpublished).
[133] *YE9*, p. 131.
[134] *YE9*, pp. 175–7. Similar insistences can be found throughout the
Miscellanies. Entry 663, for instance, (as yet unpublished) accounts for
the salvation of the Old Testament saints by asserting that 'it was the Lord
Jesus Christ, the second Person of the Trinity, that was wont to appear &
to reveal himself to the people of God of old ...'. Again, in entry 691 (also
unpublished) he says that 'Christ himself came up on that day out of the
Red Sea with the children of Israel in the cloud and the fire': (§19, p. 15 of
Schafer transcript). The *Blank Bible* on Jn 1:18 is also significant: all the
theophanies throughout the Old Testament are types of the coming
Incarnation; Christ delighted to appear as a man because He delighted in
His coming Incarnation.

Christ to prepare for the greatest act of God in the humiliation of His Son.[135]

And this is the second of Edwards' three periods of history. It is, as he says, a 'very unequal division', since this 'second period is so much the greatest'.[136] It is, Edwards says, taken up with 'the purchase of redemption'.[137] Bracketing the question of the appropriateness of the mercantile metaphor, which will be properly considered in the next chapter, the central point that Edwards makes is that the gaining of redemption began on the morning of Incarnation, and was completed on the morning of resurrection. Nothing took place before this period, or after it, and the whole of this period – the whole of Christ's life – was taken up with the work.[138] Most of the discussion of this period in the sermon series is taken up with the nature of redemption, a subject that will be dealt with in the next chapter, so I will pass over this section without further comment.

The last, and for my purposes, perhaps the most interesting, of Edwards' divisions covers the time from the resurrection to the end of the world. For the greater part of this period there is no revealed interpretation of history, so Edwards was forced to interpret reported history – and the events of his own day[139] – using the hermeneutical tools that he had developed. His first sermon concerning this period is devoted to describing these tools for his listeners.[140] Firstly, he has a general theory of history which will shape his account, as this period is 'all taken up in bringing about the great effect or success of Christ's purpose'; secondly, he finds prophecies in Scripture relating to this period – those passages which speak of 'the

[135] In this work (which, it must be remembered, survives only in sermon-manuscript form, and not as the statement of Christian doctrine which Edwards had intended to produce) Edwards is vulnerable to the charge that he has little place for the Holy Spirit in his account of creation and its history.
[136] YE9, p. 127.
[137] YE9, p. 295.
[138] YE9, p. 295.
[139] Although this is more prevalent in the *Notes on the Apocalypse*.
[140] Sermon 18; YE9, pp. 344–56.

last days', 'the end of the world' and similar; and thirdly, within the discussion of Scripture, is an indication that history will be read typologically in order to produce his account. There are four successive events in the setting up of Christ's kingdom: the destruction of Jerusalem, of the Roman empire, of Antichrist (i.e. the papacy) and Christ's coming in glory. 'I would observe', says Edwards, 'that each of the three former of these is a lively image and type of the fourth and last ...'

Further details of Edwards' arguments in this section need not detain us; assuming that we are less convinced than he was that Biblical prophecies of the Antichrist refer to the papacy, there is little of interest in the content of his description of history, and the ingenuity of the method should already be clear. My analysis of the *History of the Work of Redemption* has sought to provide the data to establish that Edwards had a theology of history. It should be clear enough that he had theological resources to find meaning in historical events, and I indicated earlier that Edwards was concerned to find an ontology of history. Indeed, such a theory was necessary for history to fulfil its basic teleological purpose in his scheme. One final point is worthy of notice: in applying his typological categories to history as well as nature, he has linked the ontology of history with epistemology, and so the existence of historical events is real and is a result of their being media for communication.[141]

A summary seems in order. Edwards lived during the period when 'medieval' conceptions of the world as morally comprehensible were being displaced by 'modern' conceptions of the world as mathematically comprehensible. His own thought was an attempt to embrace the advances being made by natural science whilst holding on to the very robust doctrine of providence he inherited from the Puritan tradition. This, I have argued, he achieved by finding a Trinitarian idealist metaphysic that could

[141] Edwards' vision of the possibilities of mass media was thus not only two centuries earlier than that of his fellow Americans such as Bill Gates, but also considerably more audacious!

underpin Newtonian physics at least as well as the rational-
isms of the Enlightening philosophers. The way was open
for him, then, to offer an account of the moral, or teleological, meaning of creation. Edwards sought to do this
through a development of the old hermeneutical tool of
typology. Combined with his metaphysics, this becomes
not just an interpretative, but also an ontological, tool to
describe why and how creation – including history – has
meaning, and so to demonstrate that creation can fit into the
teleological scheme that I described in the previous chapter.
Simply, Edwards offered a way to reassert, whilst accepting and celebrating all the advances made by natural
science, that creation is the display and communication of
God's glory, just as it must be for Edwards' account
of God's purposes to work.

Finally, some interim conclusions: this account is certainly
coherent in its own terms, but is typology really able to bear
this amount of weight? The language, after all, seems alien to
the current generation of theologians,[142] but it could, I
suggest, be restated in more familiar language. For Edwards,
typology is a category – *the* category, perhaps – of mediated
communication. Because of this, in his metaphysical system,
it is also an ontological principle. But God's self-communication, in Edwards' idealist language, is only another way of
speaking of the Son. Creation, claims Edwards, with his
ontological typology, is a mode of God's self-communication
through His Son. And, because God's self-communication is
finally a participative category (as my previous chapter
explored), creation is a mode of God's self-giving through
His Son. For the moment, let us assume that all of Edwards'
typological identifications are wrong – and certainly many of
them are fanciful enough – still, was he not right
to assert the Christological basis of creation, noetically
and ontically, and to seek to give some content to that? I have
mentioned already the question of the lack of pneumatology

---

[142] Although perhaps not so alien as it was to recent generations, thanks
to the degree of rehabilitation brought about by (amongst others) Frei and
Daniélou.

in all this; perhaps the only other point of contention would be the assumption that content can be given. The *Nein!* still rings in our ears, after all.

For Edwards' system to work this content must be given. If God is not glorified by the being of creation, then creation has no reason to be. Edwards at least wants his natural theology to be Christian natural theology – of Christ, from Christ, through Christ – and even Barth was prepared to accept that there are 'true words which are not spoken in the Bible or the Church, but which have to be regarded as true in relation to the one Word of God, and therefore heard like this Word, and together with it', and indeed that 'Jesus Christ speak[s] through such words'.[143] Edwards thought he had a way of hearing those words, not a way apart from Jesus Christ, but a way built on the one Word he had heard, which he claimed could, if listened to, give the charism of interpretation necessary to hear the Word in these words too. If he was wrong in this, he was surely not wrong to insist that such words existed, that Jesus Christ gave Himself in creation and its history too, and indeed, that creation was nothing other than the network of such words, the structure of this divine self-giving.

Every structure, according to Jacques Derrida, has its 'point of presence', that 'transcendental signified' which serves to 'orient, balance, and organize the structure'.[144] Derrida is no fan of such 'points of presence', but let that pass; the question that will perhaps finally determine the value or otherwise of Edwards' doctrine of creation is this: where is that point of presence? If, as so often in 'Christian' accounts of history, it is an alien theory of history that is used to explain how the gospel story relates to the whole, then it must finally be discarded. But I have suggested throughout that this is not the case: the centre that gives coherence and meaning to the whole is precisely the gospel

---

[143] Barth, *CD* IV/3.1, p. 114.
[144] See Jacques Derrida, 'Structure, Sign and Play in the Discourse of the Human Sciences' in David Lodge (ed.), *Modern Criticism and Theory: A Reader* (London: Longman, 1988), pp. 108–23, and particularly pp. 109–10 for the point and quotations.

story. '[A]ll that was done . . . in the eternal counsels of God
. . . chiefly respected *this* period', says Edwards;[145] 'the sin
of crucifying Christ' is precisely 'that on which all other
decreed events depend on as their main foundation.'[146]
Robert Jenson, in a fascinating discussion of Augustine's
understanding of created time as *distentio* (distension),
suggests that the only route between idealism and atheism
is to insist that this *distentio* is the 'drama, the complex
energeia that the living God is'.[147] Edwards allows us to
specify this *distentio* in a daring way, with a Biblical text.
Time – creation, and its history – can be because, and only
because, the Son of God once cried '*Eloi, Eloi lama
sabachthani*'.[148]

I ended the previous chapter by borrowing a question
from Luther: does Edwards view God's glory through the
Cross? In his account of creation the answer is an
unambiguous 'yes'. There are rough edges and questions
in the scheme, unsurprisingly, as what would have been its
main statement was unwritten, but in this area Edwards'
account is broadly coherent and satisfying. Creation and its
history are ontologically dependent on, connected to, and
revelatory of, the gospel story. Perhaps this should not be
too surprising; it is a commonplace of Reformed theology
that God created in order to fulfil His prior purposes in
salvation and damnation, and Edwards' account of God's
self-glorification assumes this position. In this context, an
account of creation should be built and focused on the
gospel, but the majority of the tradition failed to be true to
itself on this point. Apart from the minor qualifications I

---

[145] *YE9*, p. 294.
[146] *Miscellanies* 762, corol. 2.
[147] 'Aspects of a Doctrine of Creation' in Gunton (ed.), *Creation*, pp. 17–28,
p. 27.
[148] Would Jesus have been crucified if humanity had not fallen? No doubt
Edwards would insist that it was inevitable that humanity should fall,
and so the question is a meaningless one. But one can imagine an answer
analogous to that the Fathers gave: distension would have been necessary
– Jenson's argument is that creation can have no being without it – but one
could posit a less vicious form of distension, a way for the Son to be
incarnate which did not lead to crucifixion. Clear echoes of the position of
John Duns Scotus can be heard here.

have noted, Edwards succeeded in linking creation to redemption theologically. The next chapter turns to ask how far he was able to speak of God's self-glorification in the work of redemption in an equally crucicentric way.

4
'God Glorified in the Work of Redemption'

In 1731, two years after his grandfather's death and his consequent elevation as Stoddard's successor, Edwards was invited to give the prestigious annual Public Lecture in Boston. Perry Miller has eloquently explained the reasons for regarding the sermon Edwards preached on that occasion as almost a personal manifesto.[1] This was Edwards' opportunity to set out his stall publicly: he had succeeded to a significant pulpit, and one regarded with suspicion by the Boston elite; he was, moreover, the grandson of 'Pope' Stoddard, who had made that Northampton pulpit a power base to rival those in Boston; there was every chance of the lecture being sponsored for publication, and so a lasting statement might be made. Edwards, now 28 years old, was presented with the opportunity to set out his principles, to take his own stand. The short title, the text and the doctrine of the address all demonstrate that God's self-glorification is central to Edwards' concerns in this manifesto: 'God glorified in man's dependence' was the title; 1 Corinthians 1:29–31, '... He that glorieth, let him glory in the Lord,' was the text; and the doctrine claimed, 'God is glorified in the work of redemption in this, that there appears in it so absolute and universal a dependence of the redeemed on him.'[2]

In teaching us to regard this lecture as definitive, however, Miller also set a fashion for seeing the second half of the short title as determinative of the content: it is 'man's dependence' that Edwards sought to insist on.[3] But a consideration of the text and doctrine surely tells against this, still more so a reading of the lecture. Having sought to prove his doctrine, Edwards immediately turns to its use in

---

[1] Miller, *Jonathan Edwards*, pp. 28–34.
[2] The lecture can be found in *BT2*, pp. 3–7, and the quotations on p. 3.
[3] Miller, *Jonathan Edwards*, pp. 28–34.

demonstrating God's wisdom: even 'man's emptiness and misery, his low, lost, and ruined state' become a means of serving God's glory. '[a]ll is of the Father, all through the Son, and all in the Holy Ghost' so the three Persons are equally glorified in this work, and any theology that lessens human dependence in any way – the target is clearly Arminianism – robs God of His glory.[4] Edwards is uncompromising in his assertions of God's sovereignty and glory. The dependence of humanity is a means to an end. The end is the glory of God.

In soteriology as well, then, Edwards saw God's self-glorification as fundamental. This chapter will seek to explore this theme, asking how he sees God as being glorified and whether here, too, the vision of God's self-glorification is crucicentric. Some structure must be proposed for the material; recognising that Edwards' Puritan heritage is at least as relevant here as elsewhere, I will seek to order it according to the pattern of the 'Golden Chain', working from God's decrees through the work of Christ to human response to God.

The Basis of Redemption: Election and Christology

There is a standard classification applied to Calvinist accounts of election, dividing them into supralapsarian and infralapsarian doctrines. The debate, which was important historically in the seventeenth century, concerns the order in which God decreed various things. Specifically, the question turned on whether the decree of election preceded or followed the decree to permit the Fall. If it preceded (was *supra lapsus*, before the Fall), then the assertion made was that God first decided to save some creatures and to reject others, and then created those creatures and allowed them to fall in order to bring about His will; if election followed the Fall (was *infra lapsus*, below the Fall) then for some inscrutable reason, having

---

[4] The point and quotations are all from the 'Use' section, *BT2*, pp. 6–7.

created humanity, God permitted the Fall, but afterwards determined to rescue some of His fallen creatures.

The great advantage of the former scheme is that it takes the centrality of Christ in Christian doctrine with due seriousness. Its great weakness, however, lies in the implicit doctrine of God, who is portrayed as creating a certain number of creatures with the fixed intention of condemning them to eternal punishment already in mind. The infralapsarian scheme, by contrast, seeks to avoid saying things that are unworthy of God but suggests that the incarnation and passion of His Son was not His first and best thought, but a response to prior events. Inasmuch as these events must also be decreed or permitted by God (this is a debate within Calvinism), what is given up here is far more than is gained, as there is inevitably a hiddenness about God under this account, something behind the gospel narrative that is more basic, and makes salvation necessary.[5]

On the basis of even this brief sketch, it should be plain that both supralapsarian and infralapsarian presentations of the doctrine of election have their flaws. To their credit, the Reformed theologians realised this. In the tradition that reached Edwards, supralapsarianism and infralapsarianism have something of the character of ideal types – Beza may be cited as an example of the one, and Turretin of the other, but there are many others who stand between these poles. Of particular note is Petrus van Mastricht, not only because his attempt to find a mediating position seems to be regarded as the most successful,[6] but also because Edwards speaks of van Mastricht's *Theoretico-Practica Theologia* as better than 'any other Book in the world, excepting the Bible'.[7] It is inappropriate, then, to ask if Edwards is 'a supralapsarian' or 'an infralapsarian' as if these two positions spanned the range of possibilities. The

---

[5] Perhaps the most penetrating discussion of the theological implications of the lapsarian debate is in Barth, *CD* II/2, pp. 127–45.

[6] Both Heppe (*Reformed Dogmatics*, p. 162) and Barth (*CD* II/2, pp. 132–3) choose van Mastricht's position to demonstrate the possibilities for mediation.

[7] Letter to Joseph Bellamy, 15 January 1746/7 *YE16*, p. 217.

tradition Edwards inherited from the end of the seventeenth century was exploring positions between the two, and discovering middle ground, and so it is there we should expect to find him.

A cluster of *Miscellanies* entries show Edwards' attempts to find this mediating position. In *Miscellanies* 700[8] the first move is made: 'God in the decree of election is justly to be considered as decreeing the creature's eternal happiness, antecedently to any foresight of good works, in a sense wherein he does not in reprobation decree the creature's eternal misery, antecedently to any foresight of sin.' There is an asymmetry between election and reprobation: God decrees to elect – to allow certain creatures to share His glory and happiness – with no other reason than His own love in view; in the decree of reprobation God has sinful creatures in view, and so this decree is necessarily infralapsarian – 'necessarily', because of positions Edwards explores in the next entry in this cluster. *Miscellanies* 704[9] is largely an explicit discussion of the notion of the ordering of the decrees. Decrees are, of course, not before or after one another in time – they are all alike God's decision from all eternity – but they may be logically, and this in two ways. Firstly, decrees that are means to ends can be regarded as consequent on the decree of the end that is in view; secondly, if one decree presupposes another, it may be regarded as dependent on the decree of the thing presupposed. So, God's decree to punish sinful creatures is consequent on both the decree to glorify Himself – the end to which this decree is a means – and the decree that (some) creatures will be sinful – the necessary basis for this decree. Hence, it is infralapsarian. Edwards will not, at this point, accept that glorifying His justice is an appropriate end for God; He rather glorifies His holiness and majesty by means of His justice: 'The considering of the glorifying of vindictive justice as a meer [i.e. pure, simple] end, has led to great misrepresentations, and undue and unhappy

---

[8] Not yet published in *YE*, but §57 of the *Miscellaneous Remarks Concerning the Divine Decrees* (*BT2*, p. 540) contains an adequate text.
[9] Not yet published in *YE*, but §58 of the *Miscellaneous Remarks Concerning the Divine Decrees* (*BT2*, pp. 540–2) contains an adequate text.

expressions about the decree of reprobation. Hence the glorifying of God's vindictive justice on such particular persons, has been considered as altogether prior in the decree to their sinfulness; yea, to their very beings . . .'[10] The textual evidence is clear; when he explicitly explores the ordering of the decrees, Edwards asserts the decree of reprobation to be infralapsarian.[11]

What of election? If Edwards' principles are applied strictly, this should be supralapsarian if it has no logical dependence on the decree of the Fall. Edwards is careful to distinguish two aspects: God's decision that some creatures should share His love is dependent only on God's ultimate end, here described as 'glorifying his love and communicating his goodness'. The decree that this should happen through God being merciful to undeserving creatures, by contrast, is logically dependent on the Fall. The fact of election is decreed *supra lapsus*; the form of election *infra lapsus*. The sterility of argument concerning Edwards' credentials as a supra- or infralapsarian should now be clear.

Gerstner actually quotes most of the passage I have been expounding as 'proof' of Edwards' infralapsarianism,[12] and even acknowledges that Edwards 'may seem to be supralapsarian with reference to the decree of election and infralapsarian with reference to the decree of reprobation.'[13] Gerstner argues, however, that in Edwards' view God's decree is to be generally gracious before the Fall, and to choose objects of His mercy *infra lapsus*. This is apparently not the case: Edwards argues on the basis of his metaphysics that God's election is creative ('. . . the glory of God's love, and the communication of his goodness . . . give both . . . being and happiness', *Miscellanies* 704), and so specific election precedes creation and Fall: 'hence the design to communicate and glorify his goodness and love

---

[10] *BT2*, pp. 540–2.
[11] The *Blank Bible* on Rom. 9:11–13 ('. . . Esau I have hated . . .') makes the same point, with a reference to Turretin, who was a noted proponent of the infralapsarian scheme.
[12] *Rational Biblical Theology*, vol. 2, pp. 152–6, 162.
[13] *Rational Biblical Theology*, vol. 2, p. 162.

eternally *to a certain number*, is to be considered as prior . . .
to their being and fall' (my italics). This metaphysical move
answers Turretin's first criticism of supralapsarianism, that
'a non-entity [i.e. a human being not yet created and not
yet fallen] cannot be the object of predestination'.[14] It also
raises a significant question: if this is the case, then are not
the elect created differently from the reprobate? If so, are
there not two ontologically different ways of being human?
I will return to these questions later in this chapter.

Gerstner is apparently so concerned to paint Edwards as
an infralapsarian because he is compounding the lapsarian
debate with another, admittedly linked, discussion. He
seeks to insist that Edwards would not think of God as the
author of sin, a point he claims Edwards saw the 'vital
importance of'. This is in some contrast to Robert Jenson's
presentation, where Edwards is numbered with those for
whom 'the fact of sin is contingent to God's intent to
redeem'.[15] In the context of my discussion, the question
becomes: is the Fall part of God's self-glorification, or is it
only the backdrop against which God carries out His
purposes?[16] This would seem to be an either-or question,
with a simple assertion of ignorance offering the only
mediating position, unlike the lapsarian debate, and is the
question that Gerstner links with that discussion.[17]

At this point, Gerstner's presentation is simply
confused. He shows that, for Edwards, evil is necessary to
God's schemes and hence part of the decree,[18] and quotes

---

[14]   *Inst. Elenc. Theol.* IV.9.9.
[15]   Gerstner, *Rational Biblical Theology*, vol. 2, p. 152; Jenson, *America's Theologian*, p. 45.
[16]   The latter position may be found in Turretin, for whom the purpose of
creation was '. . . the communication and (as it were) the spreading out
(*ekstasis*) of the power, wisdom and goodness of the Creator . . .' – not the
justice and mercy of God – '. . . But after sin had corrupted and disturbed
this order entirely, God . . . instituted the work of redemption for no other
end than to display more magnificently . . . the same attributes and with
them his mercy and justice.' The Fall was 'only the occasion and end from
which God began the counsel of salvation'. *Inst. Elenc. Theol.* IV.9.22.
[17]   Perhaps unhelpfully, as several infralapsarians who held God to have
decreed sin can be found in the tradition. For example, see Heidegger,
quoted in Heppe, *Reformed Dogmatics*, p. 146.
[18]   Gerstner, *Rational Biblical Theology*, vol. 2, pp. 148–9.

Edwards twice as asserting 'all the sins of men are foreordained and ordered by a wise providence',[19] and yet insists that Edwards will not see God as the 'author of sin' – without spelling out what might be involved in the last statement, which is not asserted by the others. This linguistic gymnastics seems to be aimed at insisting that God was just in decreeing sin – a point Edwards certainly wants to make (and which I shall discuss in Chapter 6), but which is not sufficiently made by insisting on the use of words like 'orderer' instead of 'author'.[20] Nevertheless, the *Miscellanies* entry Gerstner quotes will answer the question well enough: the crucifixion of Christ was a sin, yet this was God's first and best thought. Therefore God decrees sin, too, for the promotion of His glory. He is the 'author of sin' in any natural sense of that phrase – God thinks of sin, and determines that the world shall be with sin and evil, not without. How God can do this justly is a subsequent question, which should not be allowed to obscure Edwards' uncompromising answer to the first. Sin and evil, too, are part of God's act of self-glorification. So there is a sense in which Edwards must be described as uncompromisingly supralapsarian after all. Regardless of the place of the decree of reprobation, God's first thought is emphatically that He will redeem, not that He will create.[21]

Seven entries after the one Gerstner quotes in this connection, Edwards resumes his discussion of the election

---

[19] Both quotations on p. 150; the phrase is from §12 of the *Miscellaneous Observations Concerning the Divine Decrees* (*BT2*, p. 528), which is a much reduced version of *Miscellanies* 762, not yet published in any better form.

[20] That this is a common distinction in the tradition is not relevant; Edwards shows himself impatient of a similarly standard verbal distinction, between God's active decree and God's passive permission, in an unpublished notebook on the doctrines of grace (Beinecke Collection, Box 15, Folder 1205): 'What God permits, he *decrees* to permit. If it is no blemish to God to permit sin, then it is no blemish to him to [word crossed out] or intend to permit it ...' (p. 9 of the notebook; the emphasis is Edwards').

[21] This could be demonstrated from a multitude of *Miscellanies* entries, but one example will serve: 'The greatest work of God & the end of all other works, and all God's DECREES [are] contained in the Covenant of REDEMPTION' (entry 993, unpublished; this is the first sentence of the entry, and the capitalised words are those under which Edwards indexed the entry in his table).

of Christ. In *Miscellanies* 762 it is an assertion to prove
something else – God's decreeing of sin; in entry 769[22]
Edwards explores what it means to talk about the election
of Christ. God elects His Son to mediatorial office through
being joined to the man Christ Jesus; God elects this man to
mediatorial office through union with His Son, and thus
God elects the God-man, Jesus Christ the Lord to be the
'head of election and the pattern of all other election'. This
last phrase is expounded: election of other creatures
(angels and human beings) is contained in the election of
Christ. God chooses the elect to be in Christ,[23] and thus
they are elected to share the glory to which God has elected
Christ. Although not stated in this *Miscellanies* entry, this
seems an appropriate point to note that as well as
describing the object of election Christologically, Edwards
will apply the same logic to the subject of election. The God
who elects is not the abstract majesty that Barth suggests is
found so often in the Reformed tradition, but the Triune
Lord of the gospel story. Edwards repeatedly speaks of the
eternal counsels of the Trinity regarding God's purposes in
salvation.[24]

Edwards returns to this theme in *Miscellanies* 1245.[25]
What, he asks, does it mean to say (as Paul does in
Ephesians 1:4) that we are chosen 'in Christ'? It does not
mean that we are chosen because our belief in Christ is
foreseen, nor that we are chosen because His act of
atonement is foreseen. Again, it cannot mean that we are
elected to be in Christ (this is at least a clarification of the

---

[22] The only currently published version is §48 of the *Miscellaneous
Observations Concerning the Divine Decrees* (BT2, pp. 538–9), but this is a
heavily edited text.
[23] '... we are elected in Christ, as we are elected in his election' (p. 6 of
Schafer's transcript).
[24] For example: *Miscellanies* 993 (as yet unpublished); *Miscellanies* 1062,
published as the *Observations Concerning the Scripture Economy of the
Trinity* (in Helm (ed.), *Treatise*, pp. 77–94), which speaks of the 'mutual
free agreement, whereby the persons of the Trinity, of their own will, have
as it were formed themselves into a society, for carrying out the great
design ...' (p. 78); *History of Redemption* which insists 'The persons of the
Trinity were as it were confederated in a design and covenant of
redemption ...' (*YE9*, p. 118).
[25] As yet unpublished.

position reached in the entry considered in the previous paragraph, if not a modification), nor that we were elected alongside Christ. Instead, insists Edwards, we need to consider God's basic purposes and to understand the text in their light. God's 'special aim in all was to procure one created child, one spouse and body of his Son for the adequate displays of his unspeakable and transcendent goodness and grace'. So, although individuals are elected, they are elected as the Church ('as one body, one spouse, all united in one Head') to receive the benefits of election no other way than in Christ. Edwards presses the metaphor of the body to make his point: every atom of a particular body was chosen by God to be alive, but they are only alive in the body, animated by the soul, 'partaking of the vital influence of the Head and vitals of the body'.

So, God chose certain individuals to make up the elect body, the Church, which is vivified by its union with Christ, as His body and His spouse. As these individuals were to be human beings, God elected a human being to be the Head of the body and also the Head of creation (see Ephesians 1:10 which, as Edwards points out, is a part of the same discussion as the phrase 'chosen in Him'). This chosen human being is to 'have the most transcendent union with the eternal *Logos*, even so as to be one person'. So the election of Christ is first; the election of His spouse, or body, next, and the election of the members of that body only third. Jenson's conclusion seems inescapable: 'Edwards' doctrine of election anticipates at most points the justly praised "christological" doctrine of election developed by Karl Barth.'[26]

Finally, I should note that an apparent tension with my basic thesis is visible here: I have argued for the priority of God's act of self-glorification in Edwards' thought, and yet here the assertion is made that the first and basic decree is the

---

[26] *America's Theologian*, p. 106. This anticipation is arguably not such a departure from the tradition as Barth (perhaps) and some Barth scholars (certainly) have seen it: Heppe's synopsis of the Reformed Orthodox tradition, for instance, can claim, 'Of course the person of Christ is the foundation of election. To a certain extent he is the sole object of it ...' (*Reformed Dogmatics*, p. 168). See CD II/2, for Barth's doctrine of election.

election through crucifixion of Jesus Christ. This tension is, however, no more than apparent: I have already argued that in his mature thought Edwards sees self-glorification in terms of Christological (and pneumatological) participation; God's primal decision to glorify Himself is not in tension with the first decree that is Christ, rather they are the same decision viewed from two different angles, or described in two different ways. This may be seen explicitly in Edwards in *Miscellanies* 1062, published as the 'Observations Concerning the Scripture Oeconomy of the Trinity, and Covenant of Redemption'.[27] Here Edwards explores how the 'covenant of redemption' – the agreement between Father, Son and Holy Spirit that redemption should be executed this way rather than another[28] – relates to the 'natural order of subsistence' of the persons of the Trinity. God's desire to glorify and communicate Himself is basic, here as elsewhere, and this will inevitably be done in a manner appropriate to the internal Trinitarian relations. For Edwards, the economic Trinity is not so much identical with the immanent Trinity as coherent, or harmonious: it is a relationship of order and beauty, rather than identity (always remembering that beauty is a key category of ontology). The covenant of redemption is subsequent to this, God's inter-trinitarian decision to glorify Himself in this way, not another. Thus, the election of Christ to be the mediator of this redemption is subsequent, but it is inevitable (because beautiful in the light of the Trinitarian life of God) that Christ should be the one elected to be the mediator.[29] A similar argument may be constructed concerning the work of the Holy Spirit.

The object of election is Christ. The next stage of the

---

[27] Found in Helm (ed.), *Treatise*, pp. 77–98.

[28] This idea was a commonplace in covenant theology. See Heppe, *Reformed Dogmatics*, pp. 376–9 for the continental tradition and John von Rohr, *The Covenant of Grace in Puritan Thought* (AAR Studies in Religion no. 45) (Atlanta, GA: Scholars Press, 1986), p. 44 for the Puritan background.

[29] The point is made regularly in the *Miscellanies*, but to cite one example, from *Miscellanies* 772, Christ is fit to be the Mediator because He is 'the middle person between the Father & the Holy Ghost'. Edwards once (only, I think) makes the same point concerning the Spirit, in *Miscellanies* 1065.

argument, then, must be Christology. It has been one of the themes of this study that Edwards is best understood as within the Reformed tradition, albeit creatively within it, and I suggest that this is as true in Christology as elsewhere. The genius of Reformed Christology from the first has been its insistence on the genuine humanity of Jesus Christ. Calvin's disagreement with the Lutherans over the Eucharist, for instance, depends finally on his insistence that Christ's human body must be localised, because that is what it is to be human.[30] The theme is continued into the Reformed tradition. Turretin, for example, denies the Lutheran form of the doctrine of the communication of properties (*communicatio idiomatum*) in part because it would deny the true humanity of the (exalted) Saviour,[31] and echoes Calvin in insisting on the locatedness of the exalted Christ as appropriate to human being.[32]

This is not to argue that there is a distinctive formal Christology that may be called Reformed (as there is Lutheran, for example). Most Reformed theologians merely repeated the orthodox positions inherited from the medieval Catholic theologians. There was, however, I suggest, a distinct concern: the eucharistic controversy with the Lutherans, which continued throughout the late

[30] *Inst.* IV.17.30, where ubiquity is described as a 'monstrous notion'. This does not, however, confine theologians who follow Calvin to a Zwinglian view of the Eucharist, in which it is merely a memorial of Christ. Calvin claims a real feeding on Christ's body and blood in the Supper, made possible by our being joined to His heavenly presence by the Spirit (IV.17.31–34). In passing, it is interesting to note that an Edwardsean metaphysics can cut through this problem: God declares and knows the elements to be identical with the body and blood of Christ, and that knowledge defines the reality. An interesting account of Edwards' realistic understanding of the Eucharist may be found in William J. Danaher, 'By Sensible Signs Represented: Jonathan Edwards' Sermons on the Lord's Supper' *Pro Ecclesia* 7 (1998) pp. 261–87.

[31] *Inst. Elenc. Theol.* XIII.8, where the first, second, third and fifth reasons offered for rejecting the Lutheran position all turn on the suggestion that Christ would not be truly human if this were true (paragraphs 9, 10, 11 and 13).

[32] *Inst. Elenc. Theol.* XIII.18.9; see also I.10, where this matter is used as an example of the place of contradiction in constructing theological arguments.

sixteenth and the whole of the seventeenth century, turned, as far as the Reformed were concerned, on a Lutheran assertion that they regarded as incompatible with the true humanity of Christ. Thus in the controversy those points of traditional Christology which emphasised the real humanity of Christ were repeatedly stressed.

The peculiarly anglophone Reformed tradition of Christology that may be found in such writers as Richard Sibbes, John Owen and Edward Irving, then, may be regarded as a radicalisation of the basic Reformed position, in that it introduced doctrinal innovation with the intention of defending the same point, the genuine humanity of Jesus Christ. Owen insisted that the Logos is in union with the man Jesus not immediately, as traditional Christologies had taught, but mediately, through the Spirit.[33] Irving agreed with Owen, and further insisted that the humanity of Jesus was the same as that of those He came to redeem, which is to say fallen humanity.[34] Edwards agreed with Owen[35] and anticipated Irving. A long *Miscellanies* entry headed 'Incarnation of the Son of God and Union of the Two Natures of Christ'[36] ends with the assertion: 'In Jesus, who dwelt here upon earth, there was immediately only these two things: there was the

---

[33] John Owen (1616–83) was perhaps the greatest English Puritan theologian. He lived around the time of the Civil War, and was one of Cromwell's chaplains and vice chancellor of the University of Oxford under the Protectorate. The point in question can be found in his *Discourse Concerning the Holy Spirit*, Bk. II, chapters 3 and 4 (in *Works* vol. III, pp. 159–88); see also Alan Spence, 'Christ's Humanity and Ours: John Owen' in C. Schwöbel and C. E. Gunton (eds), *Persons Divine and Human* (Edinburgh: T&T Clark, 1991) pp. 74–97.

[34] Edward Irving (1792–1834) was a Church of Scotland minister. His distinctive Christological views developed whilst minister of the Caledonian Church in London, and led to his espousing an early form of pentecostal theology, and seeking the revival of miraculous spiritual gifts in the church. As a result of his heterodox views he was removed from the ministry, and went on to found the Catholic Apostolic Church, where his views could have free rein. For the point in question, see the 'Sermons on the Incarnation' in *Works* vol. V, pp. 9–446, and also Graham McFarlane, 'Strange News from Another Star: An Anthropological Insight from Edward Irving' in Schwöbel and Gunton (eds), *Persons*, pp. 98–119.

[35] Edwards had read Owen on the Spirit at least by the time he came to write *Miscellanies* 1047, since in that entry he quotes from the text.

[36] *Miscellanies* 487: *YE13*, pp. 528–32.

flesh, or the human nature; and there was the Spirit of holiness, or the eternal Spirit, by which he was united to the Logos.' This is Owenite Christology. A sermon on Luke 22:44 asserts: 'Christ, who is the Lord God omnipotent ... did not take the human nature on him in its first, most perfect and vigorous state, but in that feeble and forlorn state which it is in since the fall ...'[37] and *Miscellanies* 664 asserts that 'the [angels] saw him [Christ] in the human nature in its mean, defaced, broken, infirm, ruined state, in the form of sinful flesh ....'[38] These latter two quotations contain language that could have been found in one of Irving's pronouncements (although perhaps only one of the more temperate!).

Why insist on such positions? Fundamentally, to take with full seriousness the credal affirmation, 'He was made man.' This is Owen's central point: 'His divine nature was not unto him in the place of a soul, nor did immediately operate the things which he performed, as some of old vainly imagined.'[39] Thus Owen makes all the assertions that Apollinarian Christology is unable to: Christ grew in understanding, learnt new things, and acted in power only through the work of the Holy Spirit.[40] But there are soteriological imperatives at work also: 'that which He has not assumed He has not healed' insisted Gregory Nazianzen, against the extreme anti-human Christology of Apollinarius, and (whilst the question did not occur to the Fathers, to the best of my knowledge) the derivation from this of Christ's assumption of fallen human nature is uncomplicated. There is one further reason, characteristically Puritan in its concern with practical theology: if we desire to present Christ as the pattern or example of Christian life then we must recognise the true humanity of Christ. This emphasis can certainly be found in Owen, in that the whole structure of his *Discourse*, moving from the work of the Spirit in the life of Christ to the work of the Spirit in

---

[37] The sermon is printed in *BT2*, pp. 866–77; the quotation is from p. 866.
[38] *Miscellanies* 664 §8 (p. 10 of Schafer's transcript). This entry is not yet published in any form.
[39] Owen, *Works* vol. III, p. 169.
[40] Owen, *Works* vol. III, pp. 169–72.

believers, demonstrates this theme. Irving asserts a similar point, in arguing that, since Christ performed all His works of power through the Spirit, we should be able to do 'greater things than these' through the same Spirit.[41]

All three of these points may be found in Edwards – all are, after all, commonplaces of Reformed dogmatics. The denial of the *communicatio idiomatum*, the communication of the properties of the divine nature to the human nature of Jesus Christ, so that His flesh and blood could be ubiquitous; the assertion of the true humanity of Christ (classically in the *extra calvinisticum*, Calvin's assertion that the divine Son could not be limited to the Incarnate One, but continued to fill the universe, of which the positions outlined above are surely radicalised versions); and so the vision of a genuine possibility and expectation of sanctification; all form linked parts of Reformed polemic against the Lutherans.[42] The sermon on Luke 22:44, for example, which begins with the assertion that Christ's human nature was fallen and weak as ours is, ends with an exhortation to come before the Father in prayer as He did. This is a standard form of application for Edwards,[43] as for all Reformed preachers.[44]

---

[41] 'The Church with her Endowment of Holiness and Power' in *Works* vol. V, pp. 449–506. See especially pp. 459–67.

[42] This works better with the radical denial of the *communicatio idiomatum* taught by Owen and Edwards than with the more moderate form that was more often held by continental Reformed theologians. Owen and Edwards (along with various others, such as Sibbes or Irving) would insist that Christ took personal identity and nothing else from the divine Son, and so had no 'superhuman' abilities at all. Turretin, by contrast, argues for a real communication of properties from both natures to the person of Christ, whilst resisting what he takes to be the heart of the Lutheran view, that there is an abstract communication between the two natures. So Jesus Christ can be properly described as omnipotent, but the human nature of Jesus Christ cannot: *Inst. Elenc. Theol.* XIII.8.

[43] Examples abound, but consider the ordination sermon for Job Strong (28 June 1749), 'Christ the example of Ministers' (*BT2*, pp. 960–5), which contains, for example, the statement that Christ's 'example was set for us in our own nature, and so is especially fitted for our imitation' (p. 963). Of particular interest is a notebook (Beinecke Collection, Box 21, Folder 1259) entitled 'Christ's Example', which contains a list of Scriptures showing examples of moral virtue in Christ's life. The title makes the intended use clear.

[44] No doubt preachers from other traditions regularly make similar points,

The key Christological question concerns the description of the union of the two natures, divine and human, in the one person of Christ. Here, Edwards is able to cut through much that is complicating: the discussion in the last chapter showed that for Edwards created being is in being known and loved by God. An obvious corollary, and one Edwards draws in *Original Sin*,[45] concerns personal identity, which 'depends on God's sovereign constitution'.[46] That is, I am continuous with my earlier self because God knows me to be so, and for no other reason. The argument in *Original Sin* concerns imputation: the unity of the human race with Adam is established on the same ground as my personal identity with myself. If I can be held guilty of the sins I committed yesterday, then I can be held guilty of the sin of Adam in the same way.[47] When applied to the union of the two natures in Christ, this ontology reinforces other positions: 'God hath respect to this man and loveth him as his own Son; this man hath communion with the Logos, in the love which the Father hath to him as his only begotten Son. Now the love of God is the Holy Ghost.'[48] It is because God loves this man as His Son, that this man is His Son. The Trinitarian ontology that I described in the first half of the previous chapter and the Owenite (i.e. Trinitarian) Christology that is my present subject cohere in Edwards' thought in a remarkable way.[49]

---

but there is a coherence in the sort of Reformed dogmatics that Edwards held to which is lacking elsewhere. A preacher who held to the *communicatio idiomatum*, even in its moderate Reformed form, for example, surely could not exhort her hearers to do what Jesus did in the same uncomplicated manner, as the question would always arise: was this simply a human act, or was this a result of the working of properties the hearers could never hope to obtain?

[45] *YE3*, pp. 397–405.
[46] *YE3*, p. 399.
[47] This point will be more fully discussed in chapter 6 below. See pp. 229–32.
[48] *Miscellanies* 487 (*YE13*, p. 529).
[49] The same point may be found regularly in the *Miscellanies*. To cite only two examples, in entry 764b (as yet unpublished), the hypostatic union is said to be 'the consequence of God's communicating his Spirit without measure to [Christ's] human nature, so as to render it the same person with him that is God'; in entry 958 (also unpublished) Edwards asserts that 'All the endowments of both nature and grace which Christ had were given him of the Father for all are of the Spirit ...'. See also entries 614, 713, 737, 766 and 1043, amongst others.

However, Edwards will not allow the position to be that simple, at least in the *Miscellanies* entry under discussion. A second way in which the two natures are united is postulated: 'Tis not just any communion of understanding and will that makes the same person, but the communion of understanding is such that there is the same consciousness.'[50] Locke's influence is felt, and personal identity demands identity of consciousness,[51] so 'the man Christ Jesus was conscious of the glory and blessedness the Logos had in the knowledge and enjoyment of the Father before the world was, as remembering of it (John 17:5).'[52] Jenson gives a cautious welcome to this theme: 'neither the speculative vigour nor the exegetical difficulty ... can be missed ... it may well be that on *any* modern understanding of personhood Jesus' union with the Logos must be, as Edwards supposes, "doubtless ... some union of the faculties of his soul".'[53]

Let me put aside 'modern understandings of personhood', for a moment at least. 'Speculative vigour' is hardly unusual in Edwards; 'exegetical difficulty' is more so. Also unusual, and also not to be missed, is a theological incoherence. Edwards' argument here is an attempt to hold on to the genuine humanity of Christ ('Perhaps there is no other way of God's dwelling in a *creature* but by his Spirit' – my emphasis); and now we are presented with a baby who knows what it is to be God. Or with a dying man crying in agony 'My God, why have you forsaken me?' whilst knowing all the while that His perichoretic unity with the Father remains undamaged. These may be acceptable (or even necessary) deductions from an Alexandrian or Lutheran Christology (hence, one presumes, Jenson's welcome), but they stand in simple

---

[50] *Miscellanies* 487 (*YE13*, p. 529) Again, this point recurs in the *Miscellanies* – entry 738 (unpublished), for example.
[51] For this point in Locke, see *Essay* II.2,7.10.
[52] *Miscellanies* 487 (*YE13*, p. 529).
[53] *America's Theologian*, p. 121 (italics are original; the final quotation is from *Miscellanies* 487, and the ellipsis is Jenson's).

opposition to Reformed theology in its radical (Owenite) form.

I have had cause to insist before now that Edwards' *Miscellanies*, significant as they are, must not be taken as finished or polished statements of his theology. They are ideas, drafts, interesting points that he thought merited further consideration in the future. There is an incoherence here, based on two different conceptions of what constitutes personal identity. From his own metaphysics, Edwards was led to Owenite Christology; from Locke's arguments he was led to a Lutheran form. He apparently never resolved this. Even in *Original Sin*, continuity of consciousness is still necessary to identity, even if it is subordinated to, and guaranteed by, divine decision. Perhaps, as Jenson says, this must be true of '*any* modern understanding of personhood'.

Let me, however, change the emphasis: is the problem not that it is any *modern* understanding of personhood that this must be true of? In particular, a way around this may be found in the theological accounts of personhood that have been so important in recent years (whether 'postmodern' or 'a-modern'). Outside modernity, outside Descartes' incipient solipsism,[54] the assertion that relationality is definitive (or constitutive; the debates need not concern us at this point) of personhood allow a robust assertion that Edwards' own ontology is enough. I remain myself and not other because God relates to me as one. I do not need to know myself to be continuous for that to be true.[55] Outside modernity, that is to say, there is no need for the incoherence and the exegetical difficulty that Edwards introduces; the man Christ Jesus is one with the

---

[54] Beginning philosophy from the dictum, '*I* think, therefore *I* am', cannot but create a danger here.

[55] From the point of view of philosophy, one may question whether Locke's attempts to evade the question of amnesia are wholly successful. More pointedly, I as a pastor have encountered many Christian believers who do not know themselves (theologically or existentially) to be 'one with Christ'; yet I persist in my belief that God's knowledge of their being is decisive.

Logos because the Father knows Him to be His Son and loves Him as His Son.

The Process of Redemption: Atonement

This, then, is the Christ who is elect. In the eternal counsels of the Trinity, the Son chooses and is chosen to be one with this chosen man, to become incarnate in order to fulfil the purposes that Father, Son and Holy Spirit share. The next stage of the argument must be to ask how these purposes are fulfilled; to ask, that is, about the doctrine of atonement. It is something of a surprise here to find how little systematic treatment is offered by Edwards; the doctrine is everywhere assumed, certainly, but not often discussed at any length; and the two major discussions that are present in the corpus are interesting partly because they disagree. I will consider each briefly in turn, before offering some interpretative remarks.

The central section of the *History of the Work of Redemption*[56] deals with the time between Christ's incarnation and His resurrection (the ascension might have been a better choice, but let that pass). The proposition argued for is that 'from his incarnation to his resurrection, the purchase of redemption was made'.[57] This proposition immediately highlights the two major points of interest in the discussion: that atonement is the work of the years of the incarnation, not just the hours of the passion; and that the controlling metaphor is mercantile.

There are two aims to Christ's work of redemption: satisfaction, or the 'paying of a debt', and merit, or the 'purchase' of benefits.[58] These are both carried out throughout Christ's life, the one by the suffering and humiliation that He underwent, and the other by the obedience to the Father that He offered. Throughout these sermons, Edwards spells out in some detail how the

[56] *YE9*, pp. 294–343.
[57] *YE9*, p. 295.
[58] *YE9*, p. 304.

various events and experiences of Christ's life answer to these two ends, the purpose clearly being to insist that the details of the life of Christ are part of the gospel story, rather than just the fact of the death of Christ. It is striking in these passages just how prevalent the mercantile metaphors are, particularly in regard to the second purpose of Christ's work. Merit is almost always spoken of in terms of the 'purchase' of a benefit; satisfaction, by contrast, is often described in judicial metaphors, although the 'payment' of a 'debt' remains a recurring image.

This division of the benefits of Christ's work into satisfaction, the remission of the sins of believers, and merit, the imputation of righteousness to believers, is common in the tradition; often satisfaction is associated specifically with the death of Christ, which has the character of a sacrifice, cleansing the guilt built up by the people, and merit is associated with the positive righteousness of Christ's obedience during His life.[59] Edwards' particular choices of metaphors, however, are less usual; the tradition of theology that learnt more from the Church Fathers in the Latin-speaking Western provinces of the Roman Empire than those in the Greek-speaking Eastern provinces has tended to use mainly legal metaphors to describe the atonement.[60] Calvin, for example, mentions the remission of debts as a metaphor for the atonement only once in the *Institutes*, in discussing the clause of the Lord's Prayer that asks for forgiveness of debts, and even there he immediately interprets the phrase in judicial terms.[61] His example is typical.

It has been fashionable in recent times to decry legal metaphors for the atonement as inadequate or unworthy of God. This is an unfortunate if understandable

---

[59] See, for example, Calvin, *Inst.* III.11.2; Wollebius I.30.14–15; Turretin, *Inst. Elenc. Theol.*, XVI.4.

[60] Harnack's contention that this is due to the legal background of many of the Latin Fathers is accepted by more recent scholars such as Colin Gunton; see his *The Actuality of Atonement: A Study in Metaphor, Rationality and the Christian Tradition* (Edinburgh: T&T Clark, 1988) pp. 85–7 for the general point and a reference to Harnack.

[61] *Inst.* III.2,0.45: 'He calls sins "debts" because we owe penalty [*poenam debemus*] for them …'.

overreaction to an overuse of this one family of metaphors in the tradition, when the Biblical witness, which certainly includes such ideas, contains so many other pictures as well. Even amongst those most opposed to the language of the law court, however, it is unlikely that Edwards' alternative language of the market, of debt and repayment, will commend itself.

The second discussion that Edwards left, in the *Miscellanies*, entries 1352 and 1360,[62] invokes a different set of metaphors again. Here, Edwards is concerned to argue that it is 'reasonable and natural' for a 'patron' to intercede on behalf of a 'client' and that, as a result of this intercession, the patron's 'merit' with a third party may be transferred to (or shared by) the client. Edwards attempts to construct a calculus of such personal relationships, emphasising the union of patron and client that can be formed by the former considering the latter's interests his (or her) own, and the naturalness of the 'friend' regarding the client for the sake of an esteemed and loved patron.[63] As we are made one with Christ by His love for us, and by our spiritual union with Him, so it is not strange, but most natural for God to apply Christ's benefits to us; for, that is, atonement to happen. The metaphor now is one of personal relationships, and the emphasis is on the reasonableness of the proceedings.

This last point is important: the rationality, or beauty, of God's atoning action is central to Edwards. Gerstner, in his discussion of Edwards' understanding of the atonement, seems to have missed this, and so finds the texts riddled with evidences of a Grotian, 'moral government' theory

---

[62] As yet unpublished, but §3 of the *Miscellaneous Remarks on Satisfaction for Sin* offers an adequate text: parts 1–11 are entry 1352 and parts 12–19 are 1360. This text may be found in *BT2*, pp. 570–3. *Miscellanies* 1070 (also unpublished) shows Edwards moving towards this position, and contains (I think) the first reference to 'benefactors' as a metaphor for the atonement.

[63] As might be expected, precursors of this attempt can be found earlier in the corpus. *Miscellanies* 604, for example, asserts that 'It was a thing infinitely honourable to God that a person of infinite dignity was not ashamed to call him his God & to adore & obey him as such ...' (this entry has not yet been published). Although those for whom Christ acts are not mentioned here, there is the beginning of an attempt to understand what Christ has done, using the logic of interpersonal relationships.

with which he is distinctly uncomfortable. He has most
difficulty with *Miscellanies* 306:

> According to M 306, if God did not punish sin,
> 'nobody could charge God with any wrong.' How
> could an Anselmian like Edwards say that? ... pure
> governmentalism follows fast: 'As God's nature
> inclines him [to] order all things beautifully properly
> and decently, so it was necessary that sin should be
> punished ... There is this necessity, besides that which
> arises from the veracity of God.'[64]

Edwards is certainly here rejecting the assumption that
God has any need to act justly, rather than mercifully (an
'Anselmian' position, in Gerstner's terms, if not Anselm's),
but he is not embracing the idea that God chooses to
punish sin only because there was a need for God's law
to be seen to be upheld, having once been promulgated
('governmentalism').[65] Rather, Edwards is reverting to key
categories of beauty and decency to insist that, although
He is not required to act justly, it is appropriate to God's
nature so to act, and so He inevitably will.[66]

---

[64] Gerstner, *Rational Biblical Theology* vol. 2, pp. 435–6; the *Miscellanies*
text Gerstner is quoting can be found in *YE13*, p. 391.

[65] Edwards has no problems with a 'moral government' theory, and
indeed invokes such ideas more than once, but it is not the most
important metaphor for the atonement in his writings. However, there is
a minor thread in the notebooks concerning God's curse on Adam, 'Thou
shalt surely die': in a variety of *Miscellanies* entries around 1050–1100, this
threat is regarded as establishing the legal reason why Christ had to die,
which is indeed pure 'governmentalism'.

[66] The classic aesthetic argument concerning the atonement in the tradition,
of course, is Anselm's suggestion that the saints are redeemed to make up the
perfect number of inhabitants for heaven after the fall of the angels (*Cur Deus
Homo?* I.16–18). I am not aware of any evidence that Edwards had read
Anselm, or even of a survival of this idea in the Reformed tradition, but it is
interesting to discover that Edwards at one point makes the same argument:
the saints will 'fill up the room that was left vacant in heaven by their [viz. evil
angels'] fall ...' (*Miscellanies* 616, unpublished). In another context, this sort of
aesthetics is even offered as the reason for the resurrection of Christ: 'For if
God appointed his Son to redeem mankind from the calamities & miseries
that are come upon them by the fall, tis most meet that this redemption
should be compleat, and that all the evils of the fall should be abolished &
delivered from of which one is death': (*Miscellanies* 608, as yet unpublished).

Two points seem constant: Edwards wants to see the whole life of Jesus as redemptive, not just His death, and to insist on the rationality – or appropriateness – of the atonement. What is different, and markedly so, is the controlling metaphor used in the two discussions. It would be possible, at this point, to notice the chronological order, breathe a sigh of relief, and assert that Edwards put away crass economic language for the far richer pictures of personal relationship; after all, mercantile language sounds simply unworthy to be used to describe Christ's work to modern ears. I believe, however, that there is something to be learnt from giving attention to this disagreement, as I see an underlying continuity in the two accounts.

Edwards' concern in both pieces, I suggest, is to argue for the rationality of the atonement in personal terms. Perhaps the key point here is that it is not abstract 'Justice' or even 'Goodness' that must be satisfied, but that, for Edwards, what goes on in the life, death and resurrection of Christ must make sense as a relational event between Christ, His Father, and the elect. Just as the legal metaphors that Anselm used in his classic discussion of the atonement are radically depersonalised in the movement from feudal to modern society,[67] so Edwards' first, mercantile, metaphor can be seen as a picture of personal relationships in a context where money retains its old function of smoothing the interpersonal exchanges of goods, knowledge and skill that would have happened in any case. So 'purchase', 'debt' and similar terms do not function as abstract economic metaphors, but as ways of describing the interpersonal activities and obligations that would be familiar to the hearers of Edwards' sermon series. If, as seems likely given his friendship with John McLeod Campbell (who attacked Edwards' doctrine of the

---

[67] Anselm pictures God as a feudal overlord, who is required by his position to maintain the order of society, which means, amongst other things, to respond in the strongest possible way to anything which damages his own dignity. Thus sin becomes a matter of failing to relate appropriately to God and atonement the reordering of creation to honour God as it should. See my 'The Upholding of Beauty: A Reading of Anselm's *Cur Deus Homo*' *Scottish Journal of Theology* (forthcoming).

atonement in his own book on the subject), Edward Irving had Edwards partly in mind with his famous jibe about 'stock-exchange divinity', it may be that he was missing the very pertinent point that Edwards used trade language in a society that did not have a stock exchange!

So I suggest that the mercantile language is an earlier (and, I think, less satisfactory) version of the same project that Edwards is about in the *Miscellanies* texts – the attempt to show that a personal/relational rationality underlies the Christian doctrine of atonement.[68] This, surely, is also the import of the various uses of, and modifications to, traditional Reformed covenant language in Edwards:[69] his assertion that the 'grace' which Christ 'purchased' from the Father is the indwelling Spirit, rather than some list of 'benefits', is no more than an insistence that atonement is personal.[70]

This emphasis appears to have enabled Edwards to appropriate the best insights of the Reformed tradition when enquiring what benefits are gained by Christ's atoning work. Classically, a distinction had been drawn between justification and sanctification, and the problem faced by any theologian (or preacher) of salvation was to navigate between antinomianism and the doctrine of

---

[68] This is the attempt in these texts, at least. In Edwards' overall conception the argument is turned on its head, as has been implicit in earlier chapters and will become explicit before the end of this one. It is not so much that the atonement is a rational form of personal relationship; rather that particular forms of personal relationship are rational because they resonate or harmonise with the gospel story.

[69] Whether or not Edwards can properly be called a 'covenant theologian' (or 'federal Calvinist') seems to me a sterile question, depending more on the definition and delimitation of such terms than on any insight into his theology. For a glimpse of the debate, see pp. 13–17 of Paul Helm's 'Introduction' to the *Treatise*. *Miscellanies* 1091 is an attempt to find a mediating position between different varieties of covenant theology, and so might be the best source for a consideration of Edwards' doctrine of the covenants.

[70] It is true that Edwards' immediate reason for making this move in the *Treatise* is to demand 'equal glory' for the Spirit with the Father and the Son in the work of redemption – a point to which I will return later in this chapter and which should not be minimised – but the entire *Treatise* is devoted to the argument that saving grace is not some impersonal 'stuff' but the personal Spirit, and so the wider context admits and demands the interpretation which I am offering.

salvation by works. The former was an ever-present danger facing Puritan theology, which had surfaced in a famous controversy in New England a few years before.[71] Essentially, the Puritan insistence on the doctrines of unconditional election, total depravity and justification by faith alone could lead to an apparently logical deduction that, since I can do nothing to gain salvation, I should not try and, once saved, since my salvation is not dependent on good works, I need not strive to live well, and indeed perhaps should sin boldly so that my forgiveness will testify all the more to the overwhelming grace of God. The problem was hardly new; Paul foresaw it when writing to the Romans: 'Shall we then keep on sinning, so that there may be even more grace?' (Romans 6:1). The latter, salvation by works, was seen as the chief error of the Church of Rome, whereby God has so arranged things, albeit through the sacrifice of Christ, that we are able to save ourselves by our own actions.

Even with a clear-sighted appraisal of these twin errors, it was not always clear how to preach grace. A stress on the free justification of God guarded against the Roman error, but was in danger of sounding suspiciously antinomian. Equally, an insistence that all those who are truly saved will be sanctified by God, and so will be holy, avoids anti-nomianism, but links salvation and holy living rather too closely. Calvin's answer to this problem had been to insist that justification and sanctification were two results of one prior reality, union with Christ, a move that enables both free justification and genuine sanctification to be taught without confusion.[72] Whilst this insight was never wholly lost in the tradition, there is a sense in much post-Reformation soteriology that judicial declaration has replaced

---

[71] See William K. B. Stoever, 'A Faire and Easie Way to Heaven': Covenant Theology and Antinomianism in Early Massachusetts (Middletown, CT: Wesleyan University Press, 1978).

[72] So, for instance, Calvin's first statement concerning the work of the Spirit: 'He is called the "spirit of adoption" because he is the witness to us of the free benevolence of God with which God the Father has embraced us in his beloved only-begotten Son to become a Father to us ...': Inst. III.1.3.

personal union as the centre of the scheme, and the 'Golden Chain' of Romans 8:30 became a standard way of ordering such decrees. The most telling example of this, perhaps, is the relationship between justification and adoption: in Calvin, and in Edwards, these are parallel benefits;[73] in much of the tradition between, by contrast, adoption is a result of justification.[74]

Edwards' earlier discussions of the benefits that were won by Christ's atoning acts focused on the gift of the Spirit; the later focus is on incorporation into Christ.[75] This, once again, is not so much a change of mind as a refining of focus: it is incorporation into Christ that is the first and most proper work of the Spirit in the believer. Two systematic points stand out here: first, returning to the vision of Trinitarian overflow that I found to be basic to Edwards' concept of God's self-glorification, it is noteworthy that both the gift of the Spirit and incorporation into the Son are possible only because of this rich vision of the dynamism of God's life. Because God communicates Himself, we can speak of union with Him – speak, that is, of the Spirit indwelling us on the one hand and of our indwelling of Christ on the other. Second, the questions about the nature of personal identity discussed earlier in this chapter are of some help in understanding these points: understanding the (admittedly Biblical) language of 'incorporation' into Christ is not always easy, but in Edwards' scheme it is trivial: God regards the believer as one with Christ and so, ontologically, the believer is one with Christ. Under the metaphysical positions with which Edwards was working, it really is that simple.[76]

---

[73] Calvin, *Inst.* III.11.6: 'Whomever, therefore, God receives into grace, on them he at the same time bestows the spirit of adoption, by whose power he remakes them to his own image.' For the same point in Edwards, see, for example, *Miscellanies* 1093 (unpublished).

[74] See, for example, Wollebius (see Beardslee, *Reformed Dogmatics* pp. 157–76) or Turretin XV–XVII (see especially XVI.4–6, where Turretin explicitly states that adoption is a result of justification, rather than vice versa).

[75] This shift in focus can perhaps be best seen by reading the *Miscellanies* in chronological order.

[76] I am here assuming that Edwards' Lockean insistences on continuity of consciousness being necessary to personal identity were a mistake; they certainly complicate this point greatly.

Atonement is to be understood using a logic that is personal and relational. The results of atonement are in terms of personal union between the believer and the tri-personed God. Thus far in the exposition there is no hint that atonement is limited; this is, I think, significant. The logic of Edwards' theology in the areas of atonement, Christology and even predestination nowhere demands a limited salvation – the last because of the move that makes Christ the primary object of predestination. Edwards did, of course, hold to a doctrine of limited atonement – there was no other position admissible in New England Puritanism – but there is textual evidence that he was uncomfortable with the idea, which I shall highlight later. However, the effect of introducing a doctrine of limited atonement alongside the positions I have just outlined is striking: the gospel story becomes a relational narrative featuring Jesus, the Father, the Spirit and the elect. The rest of humanity (and, incidentally, the non-human creation) are excluded from this narrative, and so live their lives unconnected with the gospel. Here, then, the problem that I indicated in my consideration of Edwards' doctrine of predestination has consequences: if Christ is not connected to the reprobate as well as the elect, then the gospel has nothing to say about the reprobate. The most unacceptable results of this theology will become clear later; for now, I will turn to Edwards' arguments for the doctrines of grace.

Edwards' defence of the Calvinist scheme is built on an analysis of human fallenness and liberty, rather than a doctrine of predestination. Following the analysis of God's action in atonement, a discussion of these texts will form a necessary excursus before I explore the application of atonement in justification, faith, and sanctification. That is, conversion, at least in Edwards' scheme, is probably best understood by examining what it is a turning from before looking at what it is a turning to.[77]

---

[77] This might be seen as a weakness, but I suspect it is merely another example of Edwards' contextual theology. His understanding of conversion is decisively influenced by his experience of preaching, where this is the natural way round to work.

Two major texts are significant in this area: *Freedom of the Will* and *Original Sin*. The latter will be treated in some detail in Chapter 6; for now it will suffice to record that Edwards defends traditional positions concerning universal depravity and imputation, although the latter is defended in a novel way, as has already been indicated. The argument in *The Freedom of the Will*[78] is essentially that the freedom that human beings possess, when properly understood, is not inconsistent with our actions being predictable or even necessitated – not incompatible, fundamentally, with predestination. This is established by means of language analysis: 'the will' is simply 'that by which the mind chooses anything',[79] and so an 'act of will' is simply a choice. Given this, Edwards can assert that the will is determined by the strongest motive, in the view of the mind.[80] The image of a pair of traditional balance scales is not inappropriate here; I have a series of inducements to act one way or another, and (what I judge to be) the strongest set of inducements inevitably determines my choice. So, 'the will always is as the greatest apparent good is'.[81] 'Freedom', as commonly used, is simply the ability to do what we choose,[82] and so something may be described as free only if it possesses the ability to choose – if it possesses a will. So the will itself is not free, because it does not possess a will of its own; a person, by contrast, may properly be described as free, as one who does possess a will. This, briefly stated, is the position for which Edwards is arguing.

Edwards is aware, of course, that he will not carry the argument that easily, so in the second part of the work he turns to examining the opposing arguments. The basic position in this area is not so much that the 'liberty

---

[78] A fuller reading of *The Freedom of the Will*, together with some indications of the contemporary relevance of the book, can be found in my article 'Edwards on the Will', *International Journal of Systematic Theology* 1/3 (1999) pp. 266–85.
[79] *YE1*, p. 137.
[80] *YE1*, p. 141.
[81] *YE1*, p. 142.
[82] *YE1*, p. 163.

of indifference' claimed by his opponents is wrong as that it is nonsensical: '... to talk of liberty, or the contrary, as belonging to the very will itself is not to speak good sense ...'.[83] Asking whether the will is free or not is equivalent to asking if it is purple or not, and discussions based on this starting point are as likely to be useful! He asserts that the notion of 'free will' held by Arminians, Pelagians and others, who oppose the Calvinist view consists of three assertions: the self-determining power of the will; the indifference of the mind prior to the act of will; and the 'contingency' of the act of will, meaning that there is nothing that can be said to have 'caused' it.[84] The first of these assertions is simply incoherent, asserts Edwards; it can only mean that the person determines her own will, since the will is (as previously established) not an agent that can determine anything. But for a person to determine her own will, she must exercise choice, so every act of will is determined by a previous act of will. Edwards demonstrates the infinite regress by means of a *reductio ad absurdum*:[85] he posits a first act of will in the chain, and asks what caused that; by supposition, it is not a previous act of the will; yet if the will is self-determined, then it must be a previous act of the will; therefore, there must be an infinite chain of acts of will behind every decision, which Edwards dismisses as absurd. The assertion of the mind's indifference is again not so much wrong as incoherent: we are asked to suppose that, at the very moment of choosing one thing over another, our minds are indifferent as to which of the two we should choose. Finally, affirming the uncaused nature of choice (and, indeed, several attempts to evade his reasoning on the first two points which Edwards has explored along the way) establishes nothing. All that could be inferred if it were granted would be that from time to time the will randomly moves towards some thing or another with no motive, no morality, no rational

---

[83] *YE1*, p. 163.
[84] *YE1*, pp. 164–5.
[85] *YE1*, p. 172.

understanding possibly lying – by definition – behind the movement.[86]

At various points in the text, Edwards returns to his analysis of the notion of 'cause'. The most important issue here is the division into 'moral' and 'natural' cause. Moral causes are internal to the person choosing – a like or dislike; a moral imperative that is held in high esteem; a sense of some advantage to be gained by moving one way or the other. Natural causes are external – a gun held to my head or a locked prison door.[87] This distinction is vital for Edwards, and provides an epigrammatic way of stating his position: since the will merely weighs up conflicting motives, and comes down on the side of the strongest, and freedom is no more than the ability to do what I want, Edwards can insist that a free choice is one which is caused only by moral causes, a constrained choice is one caused, in part at least, by natural causes.

So much for the argument of *The Freedom of the Will*; what are we to make of it? In this book Edwards is working almost entirely philosophically, rather than theologically (although the boundaries were less clearly drawn in his day). The strongest evidence for this lies in the fact that the first reference to Jesus Christ occurs 175 pages into the text (of the Yale Edition). It is, then, perhaps unsurprising that the arguments appear less compelling in a different philosophical climate. Edwards' attempts at language analysis in the early sections, for example, must assume that only one language game operates, or at least that one is privileged, or there is no 'ordinary language' to analyse, and so the analysis of 'ordinary language' is not a possible or appropriate activity. After Wittgenstein and McIntyre, however, it seems difficult to make this assumption. What

---

[86] *YE1*, p. 179. Were they better versed in the history of philosophy, this point might give pause to those writers who regularly assail the public with arguments that the apparent randomness of certain quantum events makes room for 'genuine' human freedom in the scientific universe.

[87] Clearly there are grey areas in this definition, concerning the effect of mental illness and the like. The extent to which these correspond to important ethical questions concerning 'diminished responsibility' will demonstrate the usefulness of Edwards' analysis.

we call 'ordinary language' is a patchwork of elements of
different language games that have become common. Each
square of the quilt is itself a partial, and so probably
incoherent, subset of a wider game (one might think of the
elements of psychological or psychoanalytical language
that have passed into public usage, for example), and the
different squares certainly lack coherence with each other.
So, even if we could isolate something that we could
regard as 'the' common language of our society, Edwards'
position relies on the assumption that this language game
will produce meaningful and non-contradictory results
when subjected to rigorous philosophical analysis. Perhaps
Edwards did live in a society where the day-to-day
discourse was sufficiently unified and philosophically
robust to withstand such analysis, but simply to assume
that this is the case seems rather difficult today. Edwards'
mode of argument cannot be considered compelling in the
(post)modern world.

So must the *Freedom of the Will* be put to one side, a
brilliant piece of analysis relying on premises that are no
longer tenable? I think not. The mode of argument is open
to attack, but the work contains resources that suggest a
different way of arguing similar conclusions, one that is
theologically grounded. In Part III Sections 1 and 2[88]
Edwards is addressing the question of whether necessity is
incompatible with praise- or blameworthiness. He does this
by asserting that God is necessarily holy, and yet still praiseworthy (III.1), and that the holiness of Jesus Christ is again
both necessary and praiseworthy (III.2). In the first of these
sections, the argument is that God, of all beings, is worthy
of praise, and yet He is also necessarily holy – so necessity
cannot be a bar to moral worth. It would be equally cogent
to argue that God, of all beings, is *free*,[89] yet necessarily holy,
and so freedom is not incompatible with necessity.[90] If

---

[88] *YE1*, pp. 277–94.
[89] Although Edwards does suggest that some of his opponents are
denying this (pp. 277–8 and 203 n. 1). Later in the text (p. 364) he will
assert that 'God himself has the highest possible freedom.'
[90] Edwards comes near to making this argument in his discussion of the
necessity of the divine will: pp. 375–83.

God's freedom consists in the freedom to be who He is, then we cannot claim for ourselves any 'higher' freedom.[91]

In the second section, Edwards seeks to establish that it was indeed necessary for Christ to be holy, on the basis of the prophecies and promises of God given beforehand that He would be, and on the basis of His divine nature. Such arguments are clearly powerful from any position which, like Edwards', holds to a strong doctrine of the divine decrees. He next insists that Christ's actions are praiseworthy, and offers a similar argument to the one sketched above, which invites a similar reconstruction. This reconstruction becomes all the more forceful in the light of Barth's fundamental reorientation of anthropology. Barth argued, in essence, that to assert that we know what it means to be human and then to apply what we know to Christ because He is human is wrong; we should rather assert that we know what it is to be human only because Christ is human, and we can see humanity in Him.[92] If we follow this reversal, and define humanity by looking at Christ, then the few pages of exegesis in this section of Edwards' book offer a theological basis for the whole. Christ was, as Edwards argued, necessarily holy; His holiness was praiseworthy; to be praiseworthy it must have been freely entered into; thus in Christ we see a freedom that is compatible with necessity. Edwards finds an example here, but it is possible to find a definition: we know what it means to be human only as we look to Christ, so *this* freedom, subject to necessity as it is, is definitive of true human freedom.

I therefore suggest that, by invoking theological arguments like these, Edwards' arguments may be given foundations that are perhaps more lasting than those which he offers from the philosophical methods of his day. As a parenthesis, one final criticism suggests itself: if the

[91] In Edwards' terms this necessity for God to be holy is of course a moral necessity – inevitable because beautiful, in the light of God's triune self.
[92] Geoffrey Bromiley states the point well: 'Both noetically and ontically, anthropology rests on christology': *Introduction to the Theology of Karl Barth* (Edinburgh: T&T Clark, 1979) p. 123. Barth's own words offer a terser statement: 'this man is man': *CD* III/2, p. 43).

argument suffers from being philosophical, then it is surely no surprise that the conclusion does so too. Edwards' definition of freedom is based on the meaning of the word in common speech, not what it means in the New Testament. There, *eleutheros* and its cognates are soteriological words; freedom is a category of Christian being, not a category of 'natural' human being. It is the freedom to serve God as a child of God – to borrow another insight from Barth, to live as children of God is our only possible way of living; any other existence must be in some sense inauthentic, unreal and impossible.[93]

This position may appear to be radically different from that of Edwards, but actually differs on only one point: the nature of the moral agent. Edwards defines a moral agent as a 'being that is capable of those actions that have a moral quality, and which can properly be denominated good or evil in a moral sense'.[94] In this, a certain autonomy is assumed, but theologically (as Edwards well knew) the nature of humanity is fundamentally contingent: we are created by and for God, determined to serve God and to live as children of God. This, surely, must be relevant to a discussion of human freedom. If we paraphrase Edwards' position as 'the only freedom we can consider is the freedom to be who you are', the point becomes clear: we are, at least in part, that for which we are determined; as such to live in any other way than as a child of God is to be something less than free. A felicitous expression of this occurs in an unexpected source, when the (now sanctified) soul of Gerontius says '... I feel in me ... a sense of freedom, as I were at length myself, and ne'er had been before'.[95]

It may be argued that only the elect are determined to live as children of God, but this raises again the problem that I am concerned to expose in this chapter: if human ontology is (even in part) teleologically defined, and if this

---

[93]   See especially *CD* II/2, pp. 349–54.
[94]   *YE1*, p. 165.
[95]   In the first speech of the soul in Part Two of the abridged version of the *Dream of Gerontius* that Elgar used for his libretto.

is not true of all humanity, then the reprobate are ontologically other than the elect and so not truly human. Now,
Edwards' ontology as I have sketched it in the previous
two chapters clearly has a teleological component – the end
of all being is the End when God is glorified through the
ekstasis of Son and Spirit to His creatures – so this is a
genuine problem. I will return to this theme, but first the
exposition of Edwards' account of the doctrines of grace
needs completion.

On the basis of his analysis of the nature of freedom,
Edwards feels able to deal with the five points of
traditional Calvinism in little more than one paragraph
each. His argument in each case is similar: the doctrines are
generally accepted to be the most natural way of understanding Scripture, but it has been held that they are
logically difficult, usually because of a commitment to an
understanding of freedom of the sort Edwards has been
concerned to debunk, so in each case he may insist on the
doctrine by showing how the objections to it rely on that
particular account of freedom. Thus, the major objection to
the doctrine of total depravity is that it is inconsistent with
free will, but Edwards has shown this to be a meaningless
term, and there is no inconsistency between total depravity
and freedom as he has defined it, so that the doctrine may
stand, at least until further objections are raised. When we
turn to irresistible grace, so long as this is understood to
create a moral, rather than a natural, necessity of acting, it
is also consistent with human freedom as defined by
Edwards and so again may remain.[96] The same arguments
may be made in relation to unconditional election and the
final perseverance of the saints.

Finally comes limited atonement, and Edwards'
comments are worth quoting at length, as they indicate

[96] The same point is made in a different way in *Miscellanies* 665 (unpublished), where Edwards argues that irresistible grace does not imply that
the will cannot resist, since grace acts on the will, and so the will just will
not oppose the workings of grace. The argument in the *Freedom of the Will*
adds only that this is not an infringement of the convert's freedom,
properly understood.

that uneasiness with the doctrine that I commented on earlier:

> From these things it will inevitably follow, that however Christ in some sense may be said to *die for all*, and to redeem all visible Christians, yea, the whole world by his death; yet there must be something *particular* in the design of his death, with respect to such as he intended should actually be saved thereby ... God pursues a proper design of the salvation of the elect in giving Christ to die, and prosecutes such a design with respect to no other, most strictly speaking; for 'tis impossible, that God should prosecute any other design than only such as he has: he certainly don't, in the highest propriety and strictness of speech, pursue a design that he has not ... for 'tis as impossible, in strictness of speech, that God should ...[97]

Not only the insistence on a genuinely universal ('the whole world'!) sense to the work of redemption, but also the constant qualifiers concerning strictness of speech, indicate that Edwards, whilst certainly wanting to hold to the theological point, is unhappy with the mode of expression. In *Miscellanies* 424[98] Edwards is working at the same point, and suggesting that there is genuinely a universal component to the atonement, that by it all people should 'have an opportunity of being saved'. The doctrine of limited atonement is both important and difficult for Edwards, because he was (rightly!) so impressed with the magnitude of the sacrifice of Christ. This must be to accomplish something definite, rather than merely establishing a possibility, and a doctrine of limited atonement offers this certainty. On the other hand, the same vision of the magnitude of Christ's death leads him to struggle with the idea that anything could remain untouched by it. This unease is surely related to the ontological questions I have been raising in this chapter: if, as I have argued Edwards

[97] *YE1*, p. 435.
[98] *YE13*, p. 478.

held, the whole of the being of creation is defined by the gospel story, then the being of the reprobate must be so defined, or they become some special class separated from not just true humanity – the elect – but God's creation as well. Edwards was too sharp a thinker to miss this line, and so felt the need to speak of some universal component of the atonement.[99]

The Process of Redemption: Conversion

The doctrine of atonement is an exploration of the new possibility for human living provided by the work of Christ. The most important question, however, at least for a preacher and a pastor such as Edwards was for much of his life, is how this new possibility may be realised in a particular human life. How, on the basis of all of the above, can a particular (elect) person come to enjoy the benefits that are available to (elect) human beings through the work of Jesus Christ? Edwards' most complete answer came in a key sermon text. 'Justification by Faith Alone'[100] is in its published form an expansion of one of a series of anti-Arminian sermons that were instrumental in sparking off the first revival that Edwards witnessed at Northampton.

Edwards' sermons broadly follow a standard Puritan pattern,[101] in which an exposition of the text would lead to a statement of the 'doctrine' of the sermon, a proposition drawn from the text which the preacher sought to convince his hearers of. This would be followed by several points of discussion of the doctrine, explaining its meaning, defending it against possible criticisms, and relating it to other parts of Scripture. Finally would come

[99] One of the notebooks containing source material for *Freedom of the Will* and *Original Sin* demonstrates the same point: 'Universal Redemption: in some sense Redemption is universal of all mankind all mankind now have an opportunity to [respond? the word is unclear] otherwise than they would have had if Christ had not died a door of mercy is in some sort now open for them.' (Beinecke Collection, Box 15, Folder 1205, p. 10).
[100] *BT1*, pp. 622–54.
[101] For details of the pattern and the modifications Edwards made to it see Kimnach's 'General Introduction' to *YE10*, particularly pp. 27–41.

several points of application, or 'improvement', under which the doctrine would be used to urge particular actions on particular classes of people. The text for this sermon is Romans 4:5: 'But to him that worketh not, but believeth on him who justifieth the ungodly, his faith is counted for righteousness.' The doctrine asserts, 'We are justified only by faith in Christ, and not by any manner of virtue or goodness of our own.' Christ, Edwards states, has 'purchased' (again!) justification – that is, both a remission of guilt and an imputation of righteousness. Given this, 'there may be certain qualifications found in some persons which . . . is the thing that in the sight of God renders it a meet and condecent thing, that they should have an interest in this purchased benefit'. There is no sense of desert here – no human person deserves to be justified by God, or can do anything which would merit this, that was the burden of *Original Sin*, and a fixed position in Edwards' thought.[102] However, it is a datum confirmed by Scripture, tradition and pastoral experience for Edwards that some people receive God's gift and others do not, and so there must be some reason for this division. Clearly, the reason is faith, but Edwards' construction of how faith is a 'condition' is very careful. Justification is based on God choosing to treat Christ and each believer as a single moral agent – there is an effective moral union.[103] We are justified not *because* we are united with Christ but *by* being united with Christ: in union Christ's merits are ours, and so there is no need for a subsequent decision of the Father to justify those He has chosen to unite with His Son. Faith is the instrumental cause, on our part, of this union.

The danger here, and one that Edwards recognises, is that this can make faith merely another 'work' – another way for human beings to save themselves, rather than

---

[102] The reason regularly given by Edwards for this position is that to assert otherwise would detract from God's glory – a further example of the centrality of my theme to his thinking.

[103] The discussion of the patron–client relationship in *Miscellanies* 1352 and 1360 is no more than an attempt to uncover the logic of this divine choice.

relying wholly on the grace of God.[104] Edwards responds to this in a number of ways. Firstly, the grounds on which God makes faith the decisive condition are not moral, but aesthetic – it is not that those with faith deserve to be saved (united with Christ), but that it is beautiful in God's eyes that they should be. Secondly, faith is the act of union, not a prior act to which union/justification are attached as a reward: '... faith is the very act of uniting or closing *on our part*. As when a man offers himself to a woman in marriage, he does not give himself to her as a *reward* of her receiving him ...'.[105] Thirdly, Edwards' belief in predestination requires that faith itself is an unmerited gift of God – a requirement that merely moves the problem a stage backward.

'There is', asserts Edwards, in the 'doctrine' of another published sermon,[106] 'such a thing as a divine light, immediately imparted to the soul by God, of a different nature from any that is obtained by natural means.' Matthew 16:17 was the text, and the words 'flesh and blood did not reveal this to you, but my Father in heaven' were the focus. All knowledge is from God, according to Edwards, but in imparting most knowledge he makes use of 'flesh and blood' as a 'mediate' or 'second' cause. This knowledge, by contrast, was imparted immediately, with no 'intermediate natural causes'. The knowledge is 'a true sense of the divine excellency of the things revealed in the word of God, and a conviction of the truth and reality of them thence arising'. Faith is a reflex act in response to this

---

[104] The question of why or how faith is made the condition for justification is probably the single most frequent subject of *Miscellanies* entries. Edwards' mature answers do not go very far beyond this sermon text, but it becomes ever clearer that he sees union with Christ as the fundamental soteriological category, and faith as an appropriate, or beautiful, way for us to be united with the Saviour. See, for example, *Miscellanies* 1042 (unpublished): '... there is a particular beauty in his [God's] so ordering it that those sinners that heartily consent to & with their whole souls comply with Christ as a Mediatour should be looked upon & they only as in him or belonging to him'.

[105] 'Justification...' II.4.3 (*BT1*, p. 640) See also on this point the 'Appendix' to the 'Observations Concerning the Helm (ed), Trinity' in *Treatise*, pp. 95–8.

[106] 'A Divine and Supernatural Light' *BT2*, pp. 12–17.

knowledge: one who sees the beauty of the gospel story cannot but be seized by it and so respond in faith.

So, the prior gift of God is this 'light'. Edwards' construction of this is characteristically careful. The light is emphatically not any new notional knowledge; it is an appreciation of the beauty and moral majesty of the notional knowledge of the gospel that is already present. Edwards' common illustration is of experiencing a taste – I might have been told of a liquid that tastes of seaweed and peat smoke, and might even believe that this could be a pleasant experience, in the sense of giving intellectual consent to such a proposition, but only when I taste the whiskies of Islay will I really understand what was meant, and be seized by the desire to discover more.[107] This is the 'sense of the heart' to which Edwards regularly refers.

This introduces an important topic that may be called the psychology of conversion, which I will return to in the next chapter, and examine with the help of Edwards' revival treatises, but the main point in this sermon is the one I noted earlier, concerning the role of the Spirit as the benefit given to the elect in salvation. The 'light' is 'divine' and so the person of the Holy Spirit, acting 'in the mind of the saint as an indwelling vital principle'. The Spirit brings 'knowledge' in the sense that, renewed by the Spirit, a person is able to see the beauty of the gospel story that they already knew. The image is perhaps a light coming on in a dark room – I might have established that something was there by shadows and touch, but that it was a sculpture by Michelangelo had escaped me. More than this, however: the coming of the Spirit does not just give me light to see the beauty of the gospel story, but it gives me the conceptual framework to appreciate this beauty as well. Further still, salvation is an ontic change in which a new basis ('indwelling vital principle') is given to the life of the person converted.

So, a person is converted because the Spirit illuminates

---

[107] Edwards' own illustration was of the sweetness of honey, but honey is perhaps a more prosaic foodstuff today than when Edwards spoke of it, and so his analogy communicates less well than it did.

their mind, or is given to them by the Father. We are back in the realm of the divine decrees, and so no further Why? questions may be asked. In the beautiful melody that unfolds from God's first thought of the death of His Son, it is appropriate that x should hear and respond, that y should hear and be hardened, and that z should never hear. But the question recurs: how can the hardening of y and the loss of z be beautiful in this system? If the tonic note of the melody is really the cross of Christ, then in what sense is it appropriate or harmonious for a person to be lost? This, surely, is a discordant note, dissonant with not just the life of the Church but the universe around. It is all the more dissonant because, as I have tried to show, the theme (to continue the musical metaphor) that is the life and loss of the reprobate has no relationship to this tonic note, no connection to the cross of Christ. Beauty, as I discussed in the previous chapter, is defined by relationship – so this cannot be beautiful. Worse than that however: beauty is also a category of ontology, so the question is not finally how the hardening of y and the loss of z can be beautiful, but how such things can be. God simply should not think like this.

Conclusion and Prospect

In the previous chapter I argued that, for Edwards, the being and history of creation were defined by the gospel story; this chapter, has been an attempt to tell that story, which is irreducibly theological. The narrative is a Trinitarian one: '... the persons of the Trinity, of their own will, have as it were formed themselves into a society, for carrying on the great design of glorifying the deity and communicating its fulness....'[108] The language here invites words like 'daring' or 'unguarded'. As ever, it is important to remember that this is not material prepared for publication, and so perhaps not so carefully phrased as it might

---

[108] *Miscellanies* 1062, published as 'Observations Concerning the Scripture Oeconomy of the Trinity ...' in Helm (ed.), *Treatise*, pp. 77–94: p. 78.

have been if reworked. The image, however, is a powerful one – the narrative into which the world is to be read is a story of dynamic inter-Trinitarian relationship. Hence the point I made in passing earlier:[109] it is not that the atonement is rational in personal terms – rather, the atonement, being the centre of the personal inter-Trinitarian relationships that make up the narrative that defines the being and rationality of the world, is definitive of all personal rationality. The point is similar to the one the writer of Ephesians makes in connection with marriage – the wife-husband relationship may be used as an image of the Christ-Church relationship, but the logic of what is going on demands that the direction of the analogy is properly understood: marriage makes sense only because there is a rationality derived from Christ's love for the Church.[110]

The atonement is the central event of this narrative; the phrase I have repeatedly quoted concerning the crucifixion as the first and foundational decree of God makes this point, as does the supralapsarian form of Edwards' theology. Creation, history, and all other divine actions (which is to say all else that is) can be regarded as the necessary backdrop for God to glorify Himself through the death of His Son, and the outpouring of His Spirit. This was, simply, His first and best thought, to which all else is subsequent.

There is much is to be celebrated in Edwards' account: the basic vision of his Christology cuts through much that is complicating, and at every point Edwards can be seen to be striving to be more pneumatological and hence Trinitarian than the tradition he inherited. I have suggested, however, that there is one major systematic problem here, perhaps illustrated by a phrase I have already quoted: Jenson's assertion that 'Edwards' doctrine of election anticipates at most points the justly praised "christological" doctrine of election developed by Karl Barth,'[111] is undoubtedly correct, but it leaves open the

---

[109] Note 68 on p. 147 above.
[110] Eph. 5:21–33.
[111] Jenson, *America's Theologian*, p. 106.

question of reprobation. If, as I argued in the previous chapter, created being was for Edwards mediated Christologically and pneumatologically; and if, as I have argued in this one, that the same is true of election and the salvation that is dependent upon it; then it is not just that the determination of the reprobate is other than that of the elect, but that their being is – they are, and there is no other way of saying it – less human (or at least 'differently human') than the elect.

When John Calvin treated the doctrine of election in his *Institutes*, he laid down one vital boundary condition: there can be nothing in the elect that makes them any different from the non-elect prior to their coming to faith and salvation.[112] Faith and conversion would necessarily radically change those who came through it, and the doctrine of the Spirit's indwelling demands that this change is more than merely a change of belief or behaviour, but prior to the moment of conversion there could be nothing that separated those who infallibly would come to believe because they were predestined to, and those who would not, because of their prior determination. If this were not the case, if there was, as Calvin terms it, a 'seed of election' present, then we would have to posit two different sorts of sinful human being. The logic of Edwards' arguments, I suggest, does precisely this, and in such a way that we see not just a seed, but the largest of the trees of the field.

It is instructive to consider how this problem arises, because it is a direct result of the advances I described in the previous chapter. In developing a Trinitarian theology of creation, Edwards exposed the flaws in a Reformed tradition that had always seen the reprobate as Christless and Spiritless. It is noticeable in Calvin's account of predestination that, whereas the name of Christ is linked in a number of ways with the elect,[113] the rejected live out their determination with no reference to

---

[112] *Inst.* III.24.10–11.
[113] This is helpfully considered by J. K. S. Reid, 'The Office of Christ in Predestination', *Scottish Journal of Theology* 1 (1948), pp. 5–19 and 166–83.

Christ.[114] As Reformed orthodoxy developed, this feature became fixed: Beza's *Tabula praedestinationis,* and Perkins's *Golden Chaine* (which is based closely upon it) firmly in their diagrammatic form place Christ with the elect on one side and leave the reprobate totally unconnected to Christ on the other.[115] The most striking illustration of this tendency is perhaps from a modern commentator: Richard A. Muller's *Christ and the Decree,* conceived as a defence against the charge that Reformed orthodoxy separated Christ and the doctrine of predestination, regularly demonstrates how Christ was connected with *election.* The shadow side of the decree proceeds with no influence from the Son and no work of the Spirit.[116]

If one can be human without reference to Christ – if, that is, for example, human being is defined in relationship to Adam, not to Jesus – then this tradition may stand. The Creator, it is true, is properly named as Father, Son and Spirit, but with an infralapsarian understanding, it is

---

[114] This can be seen very strikingly in *Inst.* III.2.4, where sections 1–11 describe the fulfilment of the determination of the elect and refer regularly and in many ways to Christ, and sections 12–17 describe God's dealings with the reprobate. These latter pages contain a number of references to Scripture introduced with words like 'Christ Himself said,' and one temporal reference ('before Christ's advent'), but Christ is mentioned only once in any theological sense, when the reprobate are described as 'strangers to Christ's body'. Given that Calvin introduces election as a means of offering assurance to believers, the problem in his doctrine may be simply that he is not interested in reprobation. This defence certainly could not be made for much of the following tradition.

[115] Theodore Beza, 'Totius Christianismi ...' in *Tractationum Theologicarum* (Secunda Æditio) Eustathii Vignon, Anchora, 1576, pp. 170–205. The table is on p. 170 (Notice particularly the first two sets of parallel boxes: first, 'To elect in Christ' is opposite 'To reject and throw into eternal punishment on account of their own voluntary guilt'; then 'The free love of God because, although corrupted in themselves, in Christ they are freely destined elected and saved' is opposite 'The just hatred of God, because they are corrupted in themselves, as a result of the sin passed on through Adam'). William Perkins, 'A Golden Chaine ...' in *Works* vol. 1 (Cambridge: 1612), pp. 9–114.

[116] R. A. Muller, *Christ and the Decree: Christology and Predestination in Reformed Theology from Calvin to Perkins* (Grand Rapids, MI: Baker Book House, 1988²). See, for example, p. 95 for the point concerning Beza, p. 171 for Perkins (and the startling point that Adam fulfils a role for the reprobate equivalent to Christ's for the elect), and pp. 171–3 for a series of assertions that this move characterises the whole period.

possible to speak about the *Logos asarkos* (the unincarnate Word) and suggest that the Incarnation was an afterthought. But I have suggested in the previous chapter that Edwards shows up the weaknesses in this tradition. God is known only in the gospel story, and so creaturely being, and hence human being, can be known only in the gospel. If this is the case, then to speak of a Christless, Spiritless existence for the reprobate is to deny them any humanity.

5
The Community of God's Glory

There are two fundamental destinies for humanity. In asserting this, Edwards is merely teaching standard Christian doctrine, which has always envisaged an eschatological judgement and separation ('When He comes in glory with His angels, the King ... will put the sheep on His right and the goats on His left ...' – Matthew 24). The linkage of the outcome of this decisive judgement with questions of faith, church membership and sacramental participation is also commonplace, however much the debates may rage over the precise weight and ordering of these three linked areas. The question that was raised in the previous chapter is not about different destinies but about different existences. There is one human race, from which particular people will reach one destiny or the other; it can never be legitimate theologically to suggest that there are two humanities.

To address this question, the next two chapters will explore these two destinies. This chapter will be devoted to the first of the two ways of life that Edwards sees as human possibilities, life in Christ and so in the Church.[1] That Jonathan Edwards was a theologian and philosopher of immense stature must not be allowed to obscure another fact: all his adult life, save for a year or two as a young man and the final months, he was employed not in an academic role but as a preacher and pastor. It should be no surprise, then, to find that the controversies which first caused him to write for publication concerned the nature and life of the Church. In analysing the revivals, Edwards was offering rules and advice for ministry, not academic treatises on psychology; the appropriate comparisons are with Puritan manuals of practical divinity, not with William James on the *Varieties of*

---

[1] I have been following the now reasonably common practice of using 'Church' to refer to the universal church and 'church' to refer to a local congregation throughout. Given the importance of this distinction in this chapter, however, it is as well to make it explicit.

Religious Experience.[2] Again, the disagreement that led to his removal from the Northampton pulpit was over qualifications for communion, not a nice point of Calvinist doctrine. Here I intend to get behind the immediate topics of controversy to demonstrate that the underlying vision of what it is to be the Church that drives Edwards owes much to his understanding of God's basic act of self-glorification.

Entering the Community: The Psychology of Conversion

Historically, the first controversy that Edwards engaged in was over what we might call religious psychology. The series of revival treatises – *The Narrative of Surprising Conversions* (1736), *The Distinguishing Marks of the Spirit of God* (1741), *Some Thoughts Concerning the Revival* (1742),[3] and *The Religious Affections* (1746)[4] – is an increasingly careful set of statements of fundamentally the same approach to the question of how a supposedly spiritual experience may be adequately identified as such, and so how a person's claims to have been converted may be tested. To these may be added some of the published sermons, particularly the *Five Discourses* prefixed to the American edition of *The Narrative of Surprising Conversions* in 1738,[5] and some autobiographical and biographical writings: the *Personal Narrative*,[6] although not apparently intended for publication, is an attempt to work through the same questions in relation to his own experience of grace; and the *Life and Diary of David Brainerd* may, I think, be read as an attempt to continue the

---

[2] This is explicit in most of the revival treatises; see especially *YE4*, pp. 260–88 (the section on application from the *Distinguishing Marks*); 370–83 (the duties of various sorts of people in a time of revival from *Some Thoughts*); and 496–530 (what ought to be done to promote the revival, from *Some Thoughts*).

[3] All found in *YE4*.

[4] *YE2*.

[5] *BT1*, pp. 620–89.

[6] *YE16*, pp. 790–804.

same argument by offering an example.[7] As this list will indicate, many of Edwards' published writings treated this area, including the most popular ones, and so it is no surprise that this area of his thought has excited much interest, leading occasionally to his being regarded as merely a religious psychologist. I hope that my reconstruction of Edwards' theology thus far will have demonstrated that this is due more to historical accident than to any particular focus of his thought in this area; these questions were pressing, and so he dealt with them and people read what he had to say. The fact remains, however, that he devoted himself to puzzling out these problems also, and some discussion of his answers is necessary here in order to offer a relatively complete account of his theology.

Calvin's account of the divine decrees had bequeathed a problem to Reformed theology. The doctrine of the perseverance of the saints, taught by Calvin,[8] is one of the five points of traditional Calvinism, and asserts that no one who has truly been converted can ever be lost from the Church. At one point in his discussion Calvin raises the possibility of people possessing 'temporary faith', of those who appear to be converted but actually are not.[9] This idea coheres well with experience, as it is not uncommon that somebody who has shown every sign of being a faithful church member should for some reason drift away from the faith and finally become indistinguishable from someone who has never claimed to believe. If the doctrine of perseverance is to be held on to, then some theory to account for the progress of such people must be advanced.

However, if a theory of temporary faith has once been admitted in a predestinarian scheme, a question is raised that affects every believer: how do I know that my faith is real and so saving, and not merely the sham faith of

---

[7] YE7. Norman Pettit, the editor, says: 'The major works that Edwards published between 1736 and 1746 were efforts to describe the revivals and to define the religious life. His *Life of Brainerd* should be grouped with these' (p. 5).

[8] *Inst.* III.24.6–11.

[9] *Inst.* III.2.11–12; see also III.24.7.

someone who is not elect and so has no hope? This pressing pastoral issue led to a strong interest in religious psychology amongst the Puritans, as ways of discovering the truth or falsity of the experience of religiously serious and worried people were necessary. The standard answer given was to observe a series of steps through which God would lead all converts, and to measure a person's conversion experience against this standard. To cite merely one example, God would always, it was asserted, use the law to lead to the gospel, and so a convert must be able to testify to a growing conviction of his or her own sinfulness before finding salvation in Christ.

Edwards' *Diary*[10] famously records his doubts over his own conversion, centring on a worry that, as he had not gone through the steps of the process of conversion mapped out by the tradition, and in particular lacked a strong sense of the work of preparation, the humbling before the law that was thought necessary, there must be some want or deficiency in his experience. This question might be considered to lie behind much of his writing in defence of the revival, where the central question is 'how can a genuine work of the Spirit be identified?' and the answers given always include an insistence on its being 'not by a particular order of experience'.

This concern over identifying true and false religious experience may seem foreign to Christians today, but two factors combined to make it extremely relevant to Edwards and his contemporaries. The first is theological: a Reformed and Puritan tradition of seeking to give assurance through a syllogism that included evidence of one's own conversion was bound to result in questions about what evidence was valid. The second reason – and perhaps the more powerful one – is sociological. Edwards had a sense of the prevalence of 'natural religion' – the attitude of unconverted people who were seeking selfish religious gratification, particularly, perhaps, some sort of freedom from the fear of hell. Today, the person who is in search of such selfish religious pleasure in New England will

[10] *YE16*, pp. 759–89.

probably find it in whichever version of new religious practice is currently and locally fashionable. In Edwards' day such a person would have appeared diligent in Christian practice. Thus he faced the need to address a question that is unlikely to trouble pastors greatly in our own time.

The series of treatises that Edwards produced in defence of the religious experiences of those who were affected by the revivals began with a simple account of events in the first, localised, awakening of 1734–5. *A Faithful Narrative* originated as a letter to a friend, but was gradually worked up into a more polished description of Edwards' first experience of ministering during a revival.[11] Such local revivals were not novel in New England; Stoddard had seen five such during his ministry,[12] and Edwards himself had been moved (although not to conversion, in his own estimation) by a similar event which had occurred in his father's church.[13] The Great Awakening, by contrast, was something new: a work of the Spirit so geographically widespread, and so temporally sustained was indeed remarkable – and, according to some, dangerous. Thus there was a need for analysis and defence of revivalistic preaching, and of the reality of revival experience.

In the *Faithful Narrative* Edwards offers his first attempt at what we might call doing theology through biography (an idea revived and, with nice irony, applied to Sarah and Jonathan Edwards, by James McClendon[14]). Edwards wrote up the experiences of two people that illustrate the piety that he is recommending. The same procedure inspires his own *Personal Narrative*, his use of the experience of his wife, Sarah, in *Some Thoughts*[15] and his edition of *Brainerd's Diary*. Thus, alongside the more carefully logical and psychological

---

[11] See C. C. Goen's 'Introduction' to *YE4*, pp. 32–46, for the (somewhat convoluted!) history; *YE4*, pp. 99–109 for the original letter, and pp. 144–211 for a definitive text of the final published version.
[12] Edwards claims continuity with this heritage in the *Faithful Narrative*: *YE4*, p. 190.
[13] See the *Personal Narrative* in *YE16*, p. 790.
[14] *Ethics*, pp. 110–31.
[15] *YE4*, pp. 331–41.

arguments of the later revival treatises, Edwards offered a series of portraits of what he thought spiritual experience looked like, what have been called 'case studies to authenticate the revival',[16] implying rather than arguing for a particular way of discerning truth from falsehood in this area.

The Distinguishing Marks represents Edwards' first attempt to provide theological analysis and defence of his position.[17] This text is a sermon on the need to 'try the spirits' as referred to in 1 John 4:1. In it Edwards introduced an idea that was to remain central throughout his involvement in the controversy: that of a 'negative sign'. There were positive signs, signs that would demonstrate by their presence that the Spirit was genuinely at work in this or that situation. But what Edwards regarded as negative signs were to become more controversially important, if of less lasting theological significance. These were epiphenomena; happenings which proved nothing either way regarding the presence or absence of a true work of the Spirit. Yes, some might cry out in fear as they listened to a sermon on hell, and later feel an overwhelming sense of relief at the mention of Jesus' name, but such proved nothing. A true work of the Spirit may well be accompanied by heightened emotion, and so cryings out could not be dismissed as hysteria that precluded the Spirit's presence. Such emotions could equally well be merely the natural responses of an unconverted sinner who falsely believes that he has hope, however.

As the controversy over the revivals went on, Edwards found himself fighting on two fronts. Not only did he need to oppose those who, led by Chauncy, condemned the revivals out of hand, but he also had need to oppose those whose enthusiastical tendencies were giving revival a bad name and leading to the work being damaged, in Edwards' eyes (James Davenport is most famous of these).[18] One can

---

[16]   Pettit's phrase from *YE7*, p. 7, echoing Goen in *YE4*, pp. 69–70.
[17]   For the occasion, see Goen in *YE4*, pp. 52–6; for the text, pp. 226–88.
[18]   For a summary of the history, see again Goen in *YE4*, pp. 51–2. For a fuller account, Joseph Tracey's *The Great Awakening* (Edinburgh: Banner of Truth, 1976) dates from the nineteenth century but is probably still as good a source of historical data as any. See pp. 230–55 for Davenport, and also my comments in the next chapter, p. 212.

imagine a woman crying out whilst listening to a sermon, with Davenport saying, 'She's saved', Chauncy saying, 'She's mad', and Edwards saying, 'This proves nothing' with some degree of exasperation!

If these things prove nothing, what does? Edwards' analysis is complex, particularly so in its mature form in the *Religious Affections*.[19] 'True religion', according to the 'doctrine' of that work (which, despite its length, retains the classic Puritan sermon form), 'in great part, consists in holy affections',[20] that is, in willing, and especially in loving; affections are immediately defined as 'the more vigorous and sensible exercises of the inclination and will of the soul'.[21] The proof of this from the Scriptures is a simple matter: the fear of the Lord, love, and actions which spring from fixed intentions are constantly held up by the Biblical writers as central to piety.[22] This being proved, however, Edwards proceeds to offer his most extensive and comprehensive list of negative signs. The existence of affections, even strong affections, is no proof that they are truly gracious; neither are their ordering, their multiplicity, their source or any surprising effects, such as bodily responses or facility in religious conversation.[23] Even a life well lived, a zeal for worship and prayer, and a confidence in (assurance of?) salvation is no proof that the Spirit has been at work.[24] Edwards still makes the old point, that these things to excess are no proof against the presence and activity of the Holy Spirit, but the emphasis seems to have moved. The question now is whether anyone may really know where the Spirit has been at work.

This work was published in 1746; it was some years since Edwards had seen people leaping out of their seats and throwing themselves to the floor whilst listening to a sermon, but those whom he had once hoped were genuinely touched and changed by the Spirit were now the

---

[19] *YE2*.
[20] *YE2*, p. 95.
[21] *YE2*, p. 96.
[22] *YE2*, pp. 99–119.
[23] *YE2*, pp. 125–63.
[24] *YE2*, pp. 163–90.

ones who stood against him as he sought to require holiness of living amongst the church members.[25] Reading in chronological order through the various works written in defence of revival, one can, I think, sense a declining confidence in his own ability to recognise the work of the Holy Spirit in a particular person's life.

Even in the *Affections*, however, Edwards continues to assert that such discernment is necessary, and so offers twelve positive signs by which holy affections may be identified, describing their source, their nature and their results.[26] This is prefaced by an admission that there is no chance of certainty in judging the lives of others, and that hypocrisy may well blind us to the extent that we are unable to judge our own case.[27] Truly gracious affections come from the indwelling Spirit of God and the change of nature that accompanies that indwelling, consist of an appreciation of the beauty of God, and of 'divine things', and a disinterested love for God, and result in a humble, Christ-like, beautiful spirit that shows itself in Christian living.

The details of the individual signs have been much studied, and only the briefest repetition of that material is necessary here.[28] The first, third and fourth signs describe the source of truly gracious affections. Their origin is in spiritual, supernatural and divine operations on the heart, as the Holy Spirit dwells in the saints and becomes their new 'vital principle', 'communicating himself' to them 'in his own proper nature'.[29] As a result, those who are so blessed see and respond to the world in a new way. They are able to grasp the surpassing beauty of the moral perfection of God, and of what He has done in the gospel

---

[25] The 'bad book affair' (see chapter 1, p. 5) had occurred in 1744; David Hall, tracing the history of Edwards' deteriorating relationship with his congregation, cites this as the beginning of much that was to go wrong, and links this with examples of falling away offered in the *Religious Affections*. See *YE12*, p. 58.

[26] *YE2*, pp. 191–461.

[27] *YE2*, pp. 193–7.

[28] John E. Smith's 'Introduction' to *YE2* is a good summary, and a useful pointer towards the wider literature.

[29] First sign, *YE2*, pp. 197–239. The quotations are both from p. 201.

story, and it is this that leads to the affective response that is the mark of true holiness.[30] Equally, they are able to understand who God is and the nature of what He has done in a new way, and this too is necessary for truly gracious affections to arise.[31]

The first important point of this chapter may now be made, although it was at least implicit already in Chapter 2. There, I discussed Edwards' account of how God glorifies Himself by communicating truth to His intelligent creatures through the gift of His Son and communicating delight or love to His intelligent creatures through the gift of His Spirit.[32] He is glorified by His creatures knowing and delighting in His perfections. Now, in the *Religious Affections* we are told that the sources of truly gracious affections are the true knowledge of, and delight in, God that are given by the Spirit. The *Affections* is the earlier work, and so the connection is not as obvious as it might have been, but a clear systematic congruity is visible, leading to the conclusion that the Church is precisely a way in which God glorifies Himself. God's election, as it is made actual in conversion, faith and membership of the Church, is an act of self-glorification.[33]

When we turn to the nature and results of the affections, as indicated by Edwards, then we should expect to find further congruities with the process of God's self-glorification that he described. The second, fifth, sixth, seventh and tenth signs describe the nature of truly gracious affections. Firstly, those who have such affections see that divine things are beautiful in themselves, rather than just seeing personal advantage in them.[34] A hypocrite who believes in the general truth of the Christian scheme may

---

[30] Third sign, *YE2*, pp. 253–66.
[31] Fourth sign, *YE2*, pp. 266–91.
[32] Chapter 2, pp. 54–8.
[33] Sairsingh has argued a similar point in an unpublished Harvard Ph.D. dissertation, 'Jonathan Edwards and the Idea of Divine Glory: His Foundational Trinitarianism and its Ecclesial Import' (1986). I find this ecclesial reading of the *Two Dissertations* illuminating, although I have some questions, which I will raise in my discussion below. See pp. 188-90.
[34] Second sign, *YE2*, pp. 240–53.

be zealous in religion for a time, but such zeal is merely a selfish attempt to gain personal advantage, rather than a heartfelt response to the overwhelming perfection of God. This is not to say, as Edwards has sometimes been accused of saying, that a true Christian should be willing to be damned for the sake of God's glory, something Edwards never suggested, but it is to say that a true response to God is not merely selfish. To share in God's delight in His own perfections is a part of what it means to glorify Him, and so that is what truly gracious affections will lead to.

Secondly, and similarly, it is of the nature of gracious affections to include a conviction of the reality of those things that are seen to be beautiful. That is, there is, according to Edwards, a 'natural' prejudice against divine things; a person who lacks the appropriate affective response will find it difficult to believe that such things could be, that God could be as He is in the gospel narrative.[35] In a sense, this is to say little more than the commonplace observation that we are all predisposed to believe those things that we would like to be true. It links, however, with an important piece of analysis in Edwards, usually described by the term 'the sense of the heart', which I will describe shortly.

Thirdly, truly holy affections bring with them both 'evangelical humiliation' and a change of nature.[36] The first is a standard term in Puritan discussions of conversion. It is only natural for all people who hear the demands made by God to be humbled, but there are different sorts of humiliation, which superficially appear similar. There is a purely natural humiliation, which has no beneficial results and soon passes, resulting at most in an intention to live better, which is of course beyond the power of natural human beings. By contrast, there is a genuinely evangelical humiliation, which is a work of the Holy Spirit, and leads in time to a conviction of the hopelessness of our condition, and so finally a looking to Christ for pardon and help. The

---

[35] Fifth sign, YE2, pp. 291–311.
[36] The sixth sign deals with evangelical humiliation (YE2, pp. 311–40); the seventh with the change of nature (pp. 340–4).

change of nature is again standard: conversion leads inevitably to sanctification, and so the person who is converted will be different.

What is interesting about these two points, however, is what Edwards is doing with these standard terms: he relativises them and relates them to a more basic reality, the gracious affections. This is where the scope of Edwards' opening assertion, that 'true religion, in great part, consists in holy affections',[37] becomes clear: he is insisting that all the realities of the common Puritan descriptions of conversion can be reduced to the effects of the affections.

Finally, in considering the nature of gracious affections, Edwards suggests that they exist in 'beautiful symmetry and proportion'.[38] On one level the point is merely obvious, and indeed Edwards does not devote very much time to its development. To display unbalanced zeal in one area of Christian belief or practice, and to ignore other areas, is an indication that, at best, something is badly wrong with the way we express our religion. What is more suggestive, however, is the language Edwards employs to discuss this point: 'symmetry', 'proportion' and 'beauty' are the terms that were used to describe both God's perfections, and the reason behind the ordering of His creation. Conversion is a work of God, and as such is congruous with the whole created order of the universe. In the light of the cross of Christ, God's first and best thought, it is beautiful that those created after the pattern of Christ[39] should react in this particular set of ways, and, because God is glorified by the communication of His self-knowledge and His delight in Himself, the beauty of their response should be primarily analysed in terms of balanced and appropriate affections.

The remaining positive signs by which truly gracious affections may be recognised, the eighth, ninth, eleventh

---

[37] YE2, p. 95.
[38] Tenth sign, YE2, pp. 365–76. The quotation is from p. 365.
[39] I am not aware of any place where Edwards discusses humanity's creation in the image of God in the light of the New Testament passages that describe Christ as the 'image of the invisible God' (e.g. Col. 1:15), but the point would be entirely congruous with the sweep of his theology.

and twelfth signs, describe the result of their presence. Gracious affections 'beget and promote such a spirit of love, meekness, quietness, forgiveness and mercy, as appeared in Christ'.[40] Equally, they 'soften the heart', and so produce a 'tenderness of spirit'.[41] The point is unexceptional: true Christianity, which is here being defined ('in great part') by the affections, changes people. Therefore, and once more unsurprisingly, they produce a hunger for their own increase[42] – the more God is loved, the more desire there will be to love Him more, and so with the hatred of sin, and other religious affections – and they find their final fulfilment in Christian practice[43] – the result of an overwhelming hatred of sin will be the avoidance of the same, and similarly with other affections.

A link has often been made between the *Affections* and a key concept in Edwards' psychology of conversion, the 'sense of the heart'. This term has been regularly discussed in the secondary literature,[44] as it is perhaps the most important idea that Edwards developed in response to Locke. In essence, it is knowledge that is emotionally affecting, or an act of will that coincides with held notions, when a person's whole self, both mind and will, is caught up in the experience of conversion. If, as I have argued, a congruity may be traced between the account of God being glorified through the (intelligent) creation in the *End of Creation* and the response of those converted and so added to the Church in the *Religious Affections*, then this theme is potentially very interesting: in the *End of Creation*, the creatures' knowledge of God was a Christological category, and their delight in God was a pneumatological one. An attempt to connect the intellectual and volitional

---

[40] Eighth sign, *YE2*, pp. 344–57; the quotation is from p. 345.
[41] Ninth sign, *YE2*, pp. 357–64; the quotations are both from p. 357.
[42] Eleventh sign, *YE2*, pp. 376–83.
[43] Twelfth sign, *YE2*, pp. 383–461.
[44] A selection: Terrence Erdt, *Art*, makes repeated reference to the topic (unsurprisingly, given the subtitle), as does H. P. Simonson, *Heart*. Briefer discussions may be found in Anri Morimoto, *Jonathan Edwards and the Catholic Vision of Salvation* (University Park, PA: Pennsylvania State University Press, 1995), pp. 22–3; Cherry, *Reappraisal*, pp. 19–20; and Jenson, *America's Theologian*, pp. 70–1.

aspects of conversion, then, could be regarded as a form of Trinitarian theology.

Puritanism prior to Edwards had worked with a 'faculty psychology' that appears to owe much to the logic of Peter Ramus.[45] The human psyche was divided into a mind, having the ability to think, and a will, having the ability to desire. The work of the mind is to distinguish truth from falsehood; the work of the will to distinguish good from bad. In discussions of conversion, a controversy may be traced[46] between those who thought that truth was primary and so conversion was first a work of the mind, and those who thought that commitment was primary, and so conversion was first a work of the will. Edwards repeatedly finds ways of cutting through this controversy: the 'sense of the heart' language; the description of true religion in terms of affections, which on the one hand arise from an awareness of both the excellency of divine things and the right understanding of the same, and on the other hand bring with them both the ability to see the beauty of the gospel story, and a conviction of its truth; even the discussion of the work of the Spirit in the sermon 'A Divine Light ...', which uses the image of a known truth being delighted in for the first time to describe conversion.[47] On the basis of the theological connections described here, and the terminological arguments which I sketched in an earlier chapter,[48] I suggest that at least a part of the reason for these various attempts to avoid this controversy over conversion is that either of the previously available answers would, with Edwards' account of God's action in the world in glorifying Himself, have offended against basic positions in Trinitarian dogma.

This is perhaps an illustration of a more general point concerning the secondary literature on Edwards' accounts of conversion and the religious affections: the interest that

---

[45] For Ramus, see chapter 1, pp. 13–14.
[46] For an illuminating discussion of this point, together with references to primary texts and a discussion of the importance of Locke in helping Edwards cut through the problem, see Cherry, *Reappraisal*, pp. 12–17.
[47] See my comments in the previous chapter, pp. 161–3.
[48] Chapter 2, pp. 54–8.

has been focused on the psychological aspects of Edwards' account of Christian conversion has sometimes obscured the more directly theological aspects. Edwards was certainly concerned to offer an adequately Trinitarian account of how men and women came to be included in the Church, and so to be a part of the glorifying of God that is the purpose of the whole of creation. The one point in his discussions of soteriology where Edwards admits to being innovative concerns the way in which salvation is applied: 'If we suppose no more than used to be supposed about the Holy Ghost, the honour of the Holy Ghost in the work of redemption is not equal in any sense to the Father and the Son's; nor is there an equal part of the glory of this work belonging to Him.'[49] The old theology that had held that the Spirit merely applied the gifts of salvation that the Son had 'purchased' from the Father would not do; rather, the Spirit must Himself be seen as what is purchased. The Spirit 'acts in the mind of a saint as an indwelling vital principle ... [He] exerts and communicates himself there in his own proper nature .... The Holy Spirit operates in the minds of the godly, by uniting himself to them and living in them, exerting his own nature in the exercise of their faculties.'[50]

At this point Edwards has succeeded in describing the conversion of the saints in terms of the Trinitarian relationships. An (unpublished) *Miscellanies* entry makes this point in remarkably vigorous language:

> It was not fit that he [the mediator] should be either God the Father nor a fallen man because he was to be Mediatour between the Father & fallen man. Upon the same account tis not fit that he should be either the Father or the Spirit for he is to be Mediatour between the Father & the Spirit. In being Mediatour between the Father & the saints he is Mediatour between the Father & the Spirit. The saints as saints act only by

---

[49] Helm (ed.), *Treatise,* pp. 68–9; see 'An Essay on the Trinity' in the same volume, pp. 123–4, for the same point in another place.
[50] 'A Divine and Supernatural Light' I.1 (*BT2*, p. 13).

the Spirit .... There is a need of a mediatour between
God and the Spirit as the Spirit is a principle of action
in a fallen creature . . .'[51]

This indwelling of the Spirit naturally leads to sanctification. Here, Edwards remains with the mainstream
Reformed tradition, insisting that sanctification is to be
expected, but regarding it as a long-term and partial
reality. If Christian practice is the chief positive sign
through which genuinely gracious affections can be identified,[52] still '[t]rue saints may be guilty of some kinds and
degrees of backsliding, may be foiled by particular tempta-
tions, and fall into sin, yea, great sins.'[53] But, Edwards
insists, a perseverance and growth in holy living will be the
mark of all true saints, until the end of their lives.

However, that Edwards had little that was original to
say on the subject of sanctification does not mean that he
was uninterested in it. Gerstner estimates that this is the
single most common theme in the sermons manuscripts
that Edwards left,[54] and it is clear that he regarded the
holiness of the saints as central to Christian living. This
should not be surprising: if the Church is a primary
recipient of God's communication of His glory to His
creation, and a part of that communication is a participation in God's own love for Himself, which is to say the
gift of the Spirit, then life in the Church should be marked
by a love for God, which is to say holiness. Thus sanctification, understood precisely as the work of the Holy Spirit
and interpreted as the outworking of a love for God, is a
concept that may be derived straightforwardly from basic
positions.

I have been arguing that God's self-glorification is a key
concept for Edwards, and that it should be understood in
Trinitarian terms. In glorifying Himself in the work of
redemption, there must be equal glory for Father, Son and

---

[51] *Miscellanies* 614 (unpublished).
[52] Which it would seem to be, if only because Edwards devotes to this
last sign one third of the space used to discuss the twelve positive signs.
[53] YE2, p. 390.
[54] *Rational Biblical Theology* III, p. 224.

Spirit, insists Edwards, and his account of conversion and its outworking is bent towards giving appropriate weight, and hence glory, to the work of the Spirit. God mediates salvation by His Son and Spirit, and so draws us into relationship with Himself. The language of the *Two Dissertations* is appropriate here – through His Son and Spirit the Father knows and loves us, and so salvation consists in our pneumatic response, in Christ, to the Father's *ekstasis* – our entry into ever-deeper relationship until 'the creature must be looked upon as united to God in an infinite strictness'.[55]

Ecclesiology: The Shape of the Community

The *Religious Affections* was the last direct contribution that Edwards made to the debate over the revivals;[56] before he turned to writing the major dogmatic treatises of his last years, he engaged in one further, and directly ecclesio-logical, controversy. This argument was very personal, in that it finally led to him being dismissed from his ministry in Northampton; it concerned the qualifications necessary to be admitted to communion. There is a prima facie incoherence between the position Edwards adopted over this issue and the account he had given of the *Religious Affections*; I hope to show that both these positions depend on the vision of the Church as the primary locus for God's act of self-glorification.

In the communion controversy, Edwards sought to reverse the position of his predecessor and grandfather, Solomon Stoddard,[57] and insist that only those who were able to give the church a satisfactory account of their Christian experience should be admitted to communion. At first sight this seems an odd point of view for Edwards to adopt: the *Religious Affections* had at least given the

[55] *YE8*, p. 534.
[56] His edition of *Brainerd's Diary* came after the *Affections*, in 1749, and has at least some relevance to the controversy over the revivals, however.
[57] On Stoddard and Stoddardeanism, see chapter 1, pp. 4–5.

impression that there was no way for a person to be certain of his or her own state before God, and had certainly suggested that there was no possibility of certainty in judging others;[58] if this is the case, then to insist, as he did just three years later, that the church have an opportunity to seek to judge a person's spiritual state before admitting them to communion is at least incongruous. This is even more the case if David Hall's reconstruction of the history of Edwards' change of mind over Stoddardeanism is accepted,[59] according to which Edwards had changed his mind before writing the *Affections*, but did not feel ready to tell the church for some years.[60]

This change of heart was not an absolute commitment to a particular ecclesiology either. After he had been dismissed from Northampton, Edwards engaged in some discussion with his regular correspondents in Scotland about the possibilities of taking up ministry there. In the course of this, he indicated that he would have no trouble subscribing to the Westminster Confession, which teaches a Presbyterian polity.[61] As things turned out, Edwards remained within the (Congregationalist) New England system. Certainly he was committed to the gathered church ideal (i.e. that a local church should be composed as far as is possible only of Christians), but he seems to have regarded other, still-current, debates concerning the ordering of the church as matters of some indifference, inasmuch as he expressed a long-standing preference for the Presbyterian scheme but did not feel the need to remove himself from a Congregationalist context, or to bring his unease over the issue to the attention of the church, as he finally did over communion.

Perhaps the first point to make concerning this issue is

[58] YE2, pp. 193–7.
[59] See Hall's 'Editor's Introduction' to YE12, and particularly pp. 51–62.
[60] Edwards himself suggests that he had come to the opinions expressed in *An Humble Enquiry* by the time he wrote the *Affections* in his preface to the former: YE12, p. 171.
[61] 'For the better government, and further edification of the Church, there ought to be such assemblies as are commonly called synods or councils' (Ch. 31.1). For Edwards' comments on this, see his letter of 5 July 1750 to John Erskine (YE16, pp. 347–56).

that Edwards, unsurprisingly given the quality of his mind, never lapsed into incoherence: in insisting on a public testimony before accepting a person to communion, he was always careful to distinguish between the quality of testimony that should satisfy the church and the reality that lay behind the testimony. This is the case throughout his writings on the communion controversy, both the *Humble Enquiry* and the later *Misrepresentations Corrected*.[62] At one point in the controversy with his church, Edwards offered four model professions, presumably to illustrate what he had in mind. These are extant amongst Edwards' papers, and each begins 'I hope ...', or else with some similar statement expressing lack of certainty.[63]

There is, then, no absolute incoherence. There is, however, incongruity. The force of this should not be missed: if it were simply a case of Edwards thinking through an issue and reaching a point which happened to contradict an area of his previous practice, we might let it pass. Such examples are commonplace in the intellectual biography of any creative thinker. Instead, however, we see Edwards developing his thoughts on two different issues concurrently, and reaching positions which are surprisingly difficult to reconcile. This is surely a question that should be pressed.

Faced with deteriorating relationships with his congregation over the question of admission to communion, Edwards wrote his *Humble Inquiry* very quickly early in 1749, with the intention of asking his people to read the

---

[62] Both texts may be found in YE12: *An Humble Enquiry*, on pp. 165–348 and *Misrepresentations Corrected,* on pp. 349–503. The particular point may be found almost *passim*, but see especially pp. 174–81 and pp. 355–7. The volume contains also Edwards' *Narrative* of the controversy; this was a private account, not prepared for the press, and so although of great historical interest will be referred to here only when the more careful statements are in need of supplementation.

[63] These may be found amongst the Edwards' manuscripts in the Beinecke Collection, Box 21, Folder 1245. Three begin 'I hope ...' and the last and longest begins, 'I do now appear before God and his people to solemnly & publickly to [sic] profess, as far as I know my own Heart ...'. Two of the shorter professions were included in *Misrepresentations Corrected* (YE12, p. 361), where Edwards cites them to make precisely this point.

text and to allow him to expound it from the pulpit before making any precipitous judgements, although in fact he was never given occasion to do this. He begins by defining the terms of the controversy:[64] it relates to adults in ordinary membership of the church, not on the one hand children, and not on the other ministers or officers; the question is not whether a person must be converted, but whether a 'credible *profession* and *visibility*' of conversion should be required;[65] the standard of proof required is not absolute, but sufficient to convince the church; finally, there is no suggestion of, or attempt to found, a pure church, and so these procedures are not designed to apply to a congregation collectively.

Edwards then turns to offering eleven reasons which lead him to assert that such a probable confession is necessary before a person is admitted to the benefits of full church membership, primarily attendance at communion.[66] This is followed by the usual (in Edwards' works) lengthy series of refutations in advance ('prebuttals', in modern political parlance) of almost every conceivable objection, and several objections which, one suspects, would never have been conceived of, had Edwards not raised them in order to knock them down.[67] What is at stake here is a particular understanding of the nature of the visibility of the Church.

Edwards follows the standard practice of distinguishing sharply between the invisible Church, composed of all who are truly converted, and the visible Church, consisting of those who are in membership of local churches (and their baptised children). In New England, only the separatists ever believed in the possibility of collapsing this distinction and so sought to create pure churches. The debate between Edwards and the supporters of Stoddardeanism concerned the precise nature of this distinction. Edwards suggests that the logic of his opponents separates Christianity into

---

[64] Part I; *YE12*, pp. 174–81.
[65] The quotation is from p. 176; the emphasis is original.
[66] Part II; *YE12*, pp. 182–262.
[67] Part III; *YE12*, pp. 263–325; Edwards here enumerates twenty objections, and offers multiple responses to many of them.

an outward part – intellectual assent to doctrinal propositions and non-scandalous living – and an inward part –
true belief and true holiness. Further, the practice of only
requiring the former and refusing to enquire into the latter
suggests that there is no particular connection between
them, or at least that the interior reality of faith can exist
only where the exterior practice also exists, but that such
exterior practice does not depend in any way on the
interior reality.

It is this logic that Edwards refuses to accept. Again, this
may seem difficult in the light of all the complications
introduced in his analysis of the *Religious Affections*, but all
the qualifications made in that work do not begin to
suggest that the event of conversion, the gift of the Spirit,
and the gracious affections thus engendered, make no
difference to a person's life, only that sometimes the
difference made will not be so obvious as to provide incontrovertible evidence of its underlying realities. In
particular, unconverted people are not able to live holy
lives, as an overwhelming love for God is both a necessary,
and a sufficient, condition for the growth of holiness.

So, for Edwards, true interior holiness will necessarily
be visible – not so visible as to be unmistakable, but visible
nonetheless. On this basis, it should and will be possible to
observe the existence of a gracious nature in a person's life
with a sufficient degree of confidence to warrant turning
some people who do not exhibit the appropriate evidence
away from church membership and the sacrament. That
this is possible is only half the question, however; and the
remainder is more theologically interesting: why should
acting on this possibility be desirable?

I have already made brief reference to Sairsingh's
interpretation of the *Two Dissertations* as ecclesiological
works;[68] this understanding will form a convenient starting
point for the discussion. The claim made is thus: 'In the
beauty of spiritual community the glory of God becomes
visible'.[69] Sairsingh develops this claim by arguing from

---

[68] N. 33 on p. 177 above.
[69] Sairsingh, 'Foundational Trinitarianism', p. 3.

the *End of Creation* that the primary recipients of God's communication of God's self-knowledge in His Son and self-delight in His Spirit are the saints. This suggests that the Church is 'an image or representation of God's Triune existence ...'[70]

Given this understanding of the first *Dissertation*, Sairsingh reads *True Virtue* as a specifically ecclesiological work, describing what the Church should be, if it is intended to thus reflect God's own life, and so to show forth His glory.[71] The language of 'consent to being' in *True Virtue* is here understood as a re-visioning of Puritan covenantal concepts of the Church,[72] and Edwards' 'separatism' is described as 'the ecclesial expression of the nature of true virtue'.[73] The saints are those who, because they love being-in-general, find harmony with one another.

As I have already intimated,[74] I am not wholly convinced by this account. It is, I think, broadly acceptable in its positive claims, but misses the point to some extent in the exclusiveness of those claims. Thus the Church is certainly a recipient of God's self-communication and so a place where His glory is imaged forth, but (as should be clear from earlier chapters) it is by no means the only recipient, or the only way the creation images forth God's glory. Equally, and consequently, *True Virtue* does not describe a merely ecclesial ethic, but a vision of the harmony of the whole world.

As a result, Edwards' theology must be seen as far less sectarian than Sairsingh's understanding permits. Indeed, the point is made by one of the quotations just cited, which described Edwards' understanding of the Church as 'separatism'. Edwards was abundantly clear in a number of his writings that he was not espousing separatism; he did not believe in the possibility of a 'pure church', and disowned those whose attempts to create such a body led

[70] Sairsingh, 'Foundational Trinitarianism', pp. 207–8.
[71] Sairsingh, 'Foundational Trinitarianism', pp. 214–52.
[72] Sairsingh, 'Foundational Trinitarianism', p. 223.
[73] Sairsingh, 'Foundational Trinitarianism', p. 290.
[74] N. 33 on p. 177 above.

to their denouncing ministers as unconverted, and encouraging 'true Christians' to separate from the town churches.[75] He believed in a gathered church, but not a separated one; the world also reveals God's glory, and so was to be celebrated, represented and converted, not disowned.

That said, the strength of Sairsingh's exposition is the recognition that the Church is the paradigmatic example of God's act of self-glorification through the giving of His Son and Spirit. As a result, the Church should be a place, indeed the primary place, where God is known through Christ and worshipped in the Spirit. Thus, despite the very real problems that are involved in restricting church membership to those who are judged to be truly converted, and so to know God and to be filled with the Spirit, the attempt must be made for the Church to be what God has intended it to be, a manifestation of His glory. If the Stoddardean policy is followed, if people who have only a notional knowledge of religious things are admitted indiscriminately to full membership of the church, as signified by the communion service, then the result will be a church body where God is less perfectly known and less perfectly loved than would otherwise be the case.

The point must be made even more strongly, however: with Edwards' understanding of God's self-giving through the Son and Spirit, he cannot admit that the notional knowledge of the things of God that these half-way saints possess, or the natural commitment to live according to the law of the gospel that they offer, have anything to do with true piety. True knowledge of God is a participation in Christ; these people do not participate in Christ, so whatever knowledge they have, it is not true knowledge of God. Equally, true holiness is a participation in the gift of the Spirit, and so whatever morality these people can offer has nothing to do with true virtue. Precisely the categories that lie behind the slippery and complex nature of the positive tests in the *Religious Affections* demand that,

---

[75] See especially *YE12*, pp. 170–1, where Edwards expresses a very strong desire not to be thought to be teaching such ideas.

however difficult it may be, those tests be applied, or the Church will fail to be what it should be.

I suggest then that understanding the being of the Church as a part of God's act of self-glorification as it is described in the *End of Creation* illuminates Edwards' various comments about ecclesiology and the apparent problems that they present when taken as a whole. Whilst there is a tension between the need to test the reality of a person's Christian commitment, and the difficulty of doing so, for the Church to fulfil the role it must fulfil in the wider sweep of Edwards' theology, this tension must be maintained, since both sides of it are important consequences of the same basic positions.

Love and Hatred in the Community

The various places in which Edwards discusses the Church offer a further datum: relationships within the Church, fundamentally love-relationships, were absolutely crucial for Edwards. Gerstner, in his survey of both published works and unpublished sermons, makes this point with nearly twenty examples from the texts, and the assertion, 'Edwards never seemed to tire of this subject.'[76] Amongst the published writings, the *Humble Attempt to Promote Explicit Agreement and Visible Union of God's People in Extraordinary Prayer* makes the point most powerfully, even in its long title, cited here.[77]

This text is Edwards' attempt to give public support to a proposal that had originated amongst evangelical ministers in Scotland for widespread meetings for united prayer amongst evangelicals, which would promote unity particularly by being held on the same days in every location. The proposal was circulated in a 'Memorial', and several hundred copies were sent to the American colonies. It is again in sermonic form, and begins with a brief intro-duction to the text that Edwards selected, Zechariah

---

[76] Gerstner, *Rational Biblical Theology*, III, p. 380; the examples may be found on pp. 378–84.

8:20–22, which speaks of people from 'many cities' encouraging each other to seek the Lord.[78] Edwards then states the use he will make of this text, in asserting the 'duty' of Christians in America to respond to the 'Memorial' sent from Scotland, which had proposed a united 'concert' of prayer. He offers a brief history of this call to prayer,[79] and then inserts a verbatim copy of the 'Memorial'.[80] Most of the remainder is then taken up with a series of reasons to support this movement[81] and a longer section answering anticipated objections.[82]

Edwards' interpretation of the text is already relevant to my purposes here: it speaks of the future age of the Church's triumph, which will be brought about by 'great multitudes in different towns and countries taking up a *joint resolution,* and coming into an express and visible *agreement,* that they will, by united and extraordinary *prayer,* seek to God ...'[83]; this, we are told, is 'a very suitable thing, and well-pleasing to God'.[84] It is beautiful in God's eyes, not just that churches should be united, but that the Church should be united, and visibly so, a point that is stressed more than once in these few pages.

The various reasons proposed by Edwards in the second part of the work are also interesting in this respect. There is, first, to be a future time of great glory of the Church. This is clear, as many Scripture prophecies represent the Church in a much better state than has ever been the case throughout recorded history, so this time must lie in the future. It is, thinks Edwards, a precursor to the coming millennial reign of Christ and the saints, after which Christ will return to bring resurrection and judgement.[85] This coming world-wide revival 'is an event unspeakably happy and glorious ... wherein God and his Son Jesus

[77] *YE5*, pp. 307–436.
[78] *YE5*, pp. 312–20.
[79] *YE5*, pp. 321–4.
[80] *YE5*, pp. 324–8.
[81] Part II; *YE5*, pp. 329–67.
[82] Part III; *YE5*, pp. 368–431.
[83] *YE5*, p. 314; emphasis original.
[84] *YE5*, p. 320.
[85] *YE5*, pp. 329–37.

Christ will be most eminently glorified on earth . . .' .[86] This will, second, be a time of great increase in knowledge of divine things, and of great unity in the whole Church, which will '[shine] with a reflection of the glory of Jehovah risen upon it'.[87] Taking the third and fourth points together, we read also that this is the time when the Holy Spirit, who is the sum of all that Christ won for His Church by His sufferings, will be given most fully, and so the time for which Christ mainly suffered.[88]

Continuing the theme, Edwards points out that this will be the day of redemption for the whole of creation, not just for the Church, quoting from Romans 8: 'the whole creation is . . . groaning and travailing in pain to bring forth the felicity and glory of it.'[89] Again, the Scriptures encourage us constantly to be praying for the coming of this time,[90] and according to Edwards there were many providential signs in the mid-1740s to encourage belief that this was a particularly hopeful moment to seek to see this day come.[91] Finally, he offers two points concerning the appropriateness of such togetherness in religious duties. The first is a panegyric to human unity in general and so to visible world-wide unity in the Church in particular. '[T]is the glory of the church of Christ, that she, in all her members however dispersed, is thus *one*, one holy society, one city, one family.'[92] the second is an account of the promised success of united prayer in Scripture.

I have tried to indicate something of the quality of the language in this section by the brief quotations. There is a repeated use of the language of glory, and a repeated stress on not just on unity, but on its visibility. Edwards' great

---

[86] *YE5*, pp. 337–41; the quotation is from p. 337.
[87] *YE5*, p. 339.
[88] *YE5*, pp. 341–4.
[89] *YE5*, pp. 344–7; the quotation is from p. 344.
[90] *YE5*, pp. 347–57.
[91] *YE5*, pp. 357–64. In part this is a jeremiad – was the nation ever in such a low state, and so much in need of revival, as now? Edwards also believes he can see particular signs of God's mercy, however, in surprising victories in the ceaseless war against Antichrist, which is to say the Roman Catholic nations of Europe.
[92] *YE5*, pp. 364–6. The quotation is from p. 365, and the emphasis is original.

vision of these concerts of prayer is that the Church will be
united and be seen to be united, and that is what God will
use in part to answer the prayers of the Church, as others
see this glorious unity and are drawn to God as a result.

This coheres fairly naturally with the point discussed in
the previous section: if it is amongst the chief characteristics of God's Church to be united, to be one, then there is
a necessity for a unity of feeling and purpose in the
Church, which is to say a necessity for a Church of like-
minded members. Given the radical difference that,
according to Edwards, conversion makes to both
knowledge and desires there is thus a need to seek to keep
the Church pure, however difficult this will inevitably
prove in practice.

In both the communion controversy writings and the
Humble Attempt, Edwards expresses a repeated concern for
the visibility of the Church. Further, in the latter work, at
least, this language of visibility is closely linked with
language of glory. This connection deserves some investigation in the context of the arguments that I have been
advancing. I suggest that the understanding of the Church
as the community of God's glory may explain this point as
well: in the Church the beauty of God, which is the
presence of the Holy Spirit, should be seen, and so there is
a need for harmony and consent amongst the members of
the Church. If the Church, that is, is to reflect God's own
beautiful nature back to Him, then it must be beautiful.
Thus, unity, in the rich sense of communal consent, is
essential to the very being of the Church. Equally, if God
is to be glorified by this unity, it must be seen, and so the
Church's necessary unity must be visible unity.

Thus far the point is relatively trivial: the systematic
connections are not difficult to trace, nor are they
suggestive of any major shifts in understanding. There is,
however, a problem in all of this, concerning the
relationship between the beautiful community that is
the Church and the beautiful order of the creation as a
whole. A brief return to Edwards' basic definitions of the
nature of beauty and consent will illuminate this problem:
in both *True Virtue* and the *Notes on the Mind*, Edwards

suggests that it is a part of consent to being to dissent from that which does not itself consent to being. In slightly more familiar language, it is appropriate and virtuous for one who loves God to hate that which hates God. In the *Notes on the Mind* this is taught very simply: greatness of existence is both excellency in itself (as mere existence is pleasing and so excellent) and 'the capacity for excellence'; however, if such capacity is perverted, as when a great being dissents from being in general, then the perversion is the more odious the greater the capacity, and 'his greatness ... does nothing towards bettering his dissent from being in general, because there is no proportion between finite being, however great, and infinite being.'[93]

The discussion in *True Virtue* is slightly more nuanced, but tends in the same direction. There, it will be recalled,[94] love of being is taken as the essence of true virtue, and this is analysed into benevolence and complacence. The former has as its primary ground the love of being for the sake merely of being, and as its secondary ground the love of virtuous being, since all love will be the greater if the beloved displays the same temper as the lover. The latter, love of complacence, has this as its primary ground, since it is the love of that which is lovely.[95] Under this analysis, being which does not consent to being in general, which is to say a creature that does not love God, is to be loved for its mere existence, but hated for its hatred towards God.

In these analyses of the nature of beauty, then, Edwards envisages situations in which the beautiful, and thus the virtuous, thing to do is to dissent from, or hate, another being. It is true that in *True Virtue* this is balanced by a calculus that suggests reasons to respond to a being who hates God with both love and hate, but little is made of this complexity. Now, the creation is fallen, and so cursed and in whole or in part (the human part, at least) in rebellion against God. This suggests that the appropriate and virtuous response to large sections of the human creation,

---

[93] YE6, pp. 362–6.
[94] See chapter 2, pp. 59–61 above.
[95] YE8, pp. 545–9.

at least, will be simple hatred on the part of the Church. As I will show in the next chapter, Edwards does in fact follow this logic through in a number of sermon texts, where he portrays the saints rejoicing in the punishment and unimaginable sufferings of the damned.[96]

However, this line of argument would seem to lead to precisely the sort of sectarian understanding of the Church that I have just indicated that Edwards refused, and was correct to refuse on the basis of his own logic. That is, if Edwards' account of God's self-glorification is not just confined to the Church, but embraces the whole of created history as well, the beautiful history of consensual relationships that images forth God's glory cannot be confined to the Church but must also embrace the whole of creation; and yet here there is a line of argument present in Edwards that insists that the Church must respond to a large part of the creation[97] with simple hatred. Once again, a possible incoherence is in view. The problem here arises from the ambiguous goodness of the created order: in the case of the human (and, presumably, angelic) parts of creation at least, there are those who are in rebellion against God; consequently, notwithstanding their status as creatures of God and participants (albeit unwilling ones) in the history of God's self-glorification, these are regarded as separated from the community that glorifies God, and so are to be shunned, dissented from and hated.

This is a problem only because in his discussions of creation and its history, Edwards links the doctrine of creation to the gospel story. By so doing, he includes every creature and every event within the beautiful community that is the recipient of God's gifts and so the display of God's glory – the being of the world is defined by the cross

---

[96]   See pp. 213–15 below.
[97]   Particularly in this context, Edwards' insistence in the *End of Creation* that the intelligent creation is the most significant part of the whole (see chapter 2, pp. 50–1), and his 'idealism', to use the standard, if inaccurate, shorthand (see chapter 3, pp. 86–90), make the problem much sharper than it might have been otherwise. It is not that the grand sweep of the universe is in harmony, and a few insignificant creatures cause a slight disruption to that; rather, the greater portion of the most important part of the creation is in rebellion against God.

of Christ.[98] Precisely because of this, the Church is not a second example of God's act of self-glorification, which would entail a decisive separation between the realms of creation and redemption. This was the old error which I have suggested Edwards managed to avoid. Instead, according to Edwards, the Church is one particular and important part of the single history of redemption and creation by which God brings about His single purpose: all else that exists reveals God's glory to the Church, which glorifies God in knowing and delighting in what He has revealed.

Given all this, we can make sense of everything that Edwards had to say only if we are able to understand the dissent that the Church is asked to display to certain people and events as itself a part of the wider web of beautiful consent. This seems difficult, however, and demands further investigation – how can it be? There are not, according to Edwards, two cities or two histories constantly at war with each other in the world; there is one history, the history of God's act of self-glorification, which includes within itself a basic hatred and yet is the primary example of the shining forth of God's beauty. To describe the problem in these terms, however, is merely to restate the question that was left open at the end of the previous chapter: in the light of the cross of Christ, how can the hardening and final loss of certain human beings be beautiful?

---

[98] See my comments on this towards the end of chapter 3; pp. 120–3.

6
God's Self-Glorification in the Damnation of Sinners

A question is pressing: how can Edwards, given the account of God's purposes in creation, which is to say all that He does, have a doctrine of reprobation? Put another way, what possible reason can there be for God to send people to hell? Such is the burden of this chapter. That God is glorified in His gracious salvific action, as the previous chapters have been devoted to arguing, is hardly a controversial point. The same, however, emphatically may not be said of the converse, at least in the present theological climate: the idea that God may glorify Himself in the rejection and punishment of impenitent men and women, that, if it must happen, this can be anything other than a cause of the most grievous divine sorrow, is rejected as a particularly gruesome and old-fashioned Calvinistic excess of which we are most grateful to be rid.[1]

Perhaps – the point may certainly be found in Calvin.[2] Jonathan Edwards, although other things as well, was nothing if not an old-fashioned Calvinist, however. He believed that the Reformed and Puritan construction of theology that he had inherited was, in all important respects, adequate. The recent revival of interest in Edwards has sought to play down the note of 'hellfire' in his preaching (particularly), arguing that American literature anthologists perpetrated a major crime against his memory in ensuring that he was known only through 'Sinners in the Hands of an Angry God'.[3] This is, of course,

---

[1] This emphasis can be found even in a broadly sympathetic treatment such as John Colwell's 1992 Drew Lecture, which I had the privilege of hearing (published as John E. Colwell, 'The Glory of God's Justice and the Glory of God's Grace: Contemporary Reflections on the Doctrine of Hell in the Teaching of Jonathan Edwards', *Evangelical Quarterly* 67/4 (1995), pp. 291–308).

[2] *Inst.* III.24.14.

[3] See, for example, Cherry, *Reappraisal,* p. 58; Jenson, *America's Theologian,* p. 101. Many other examples are readily available.

true: there is far more to Edwards' thought than is hinted at in this sermon, even if it does offer a particularly potent example of his rhetoric. But if not a crime, it would certainly be a distortion of his memory if this note were eradicated from it. At best, we would lose an important reminder that, whatever else he was, Edwards was a preacher in the Puritan tradition; at worst we might lose an important, if unpleasant, clue to interpreting his theology. One assumes that medical professionals do not enjoy all the examinations they are asked to perform; that there would be less medical knowledge available to us if they shrank from such tasks, however, is obvious. In this chapter I shall attempt a general survey of Edwards' doctrine of hell before showing how this relates to the wider theme of this book.

A comparison of the reaction to Edwards' writing on hell with the reaction to, say, Dante's *Inferno* makes an important initial point: there is significantly less comfort with ideas concerning hell in Edwards than with very similar ideas in Dante. This, presumably, can only be because of an implicit assumption that Edwards, being more 'modern', is culpable for invoking such ideas in a way that Dante is not. A medieval author is permitted to be 'obsessed' with the pains of hell;[4] a philosopher conversant with Locke, living on the cusp of the great Enlightenment social experiment that was the founding of the American state, is not. The fashion in early American Studies for comparisons of Edwards with Benjamin Franklin[5] is an indication of this: if Franklin can be such a thoroughly modern 'Yankee', why is Edwards, in the same age, stuck with trying to rewrite the old 'Puritan' script?

As there is an increasingly apparent discomfort with, or at least questioning of, the values and intellectual positions of the Enlightenment, we may assume that at least the

---

[4] The charge of 'obsession' is as unfair to Dante as it is to Edwards, of course, but the relative current popularity of the *Inferno* compared to the other two parts of the *Comedy* makes the comparison an apt one, particularly as the *Purgatorio* and the *Paradiso* are regarded as 'difficult' because their content is more philosophical than that of the more popular work.

[5] See my discussion of this point in chapter 1.

assumption of culpability on Edwards' part that has been commonly made will quietly pass away. Indeed, one of the (many) merits of Robert Jenson's appreciation of Edwards is the recognition that his particular recasting of the first colonial American social experiment, the Puritan 'city on a hill', has much to say to a culture that preferred to listen to Franklin's new vision and is still living with the consequences of that. [6] The point that prompted these reflections, however, is still to be answered: how can Edwards, living in an age which is at least beginning to be Enlightened, speak as he does about the doctrine of hell?

Before levelling accusations that Edwards was obsessed with hellfire or similar, it seems only reasonable to investigate the extent to which he differed from the community and tradition of which he was a part. His pictures, although shocking, would not be out of place in the high Puritanism of the mid-seventeenth-century American colonies, but they would be in the young, forward-looking, and Enlightened nation of 1800. We may usefully ask where the break came: if we press the motif noted above, whilst removing notions of blame, the question becomes is Edwards anachronistic, or Franklin prophetic? Or do they perhaps between them show the tensions of a nation 'between the times', providing an all-American mythology for our own 'postmodern' culture? I will begin this chapter by, seeking, albeit very briefly, to identify Edwards' context on this point.

Visions of Hell in the Early Eighteenth Century

Edwards' heritage, at least, was Puritan. More than that: until such figures as Franklin found an alternative mythology[7] in

---

[6] Jenson, *America's Theologian*; Jenson's initial statement of his purpose makes the point: 'Edwards knew what to make of the great eighteenth-century Enlightenment, and America and its church are the nation and the church the Enlightenment made': p. 3.

[7] Using 'mythology' in the sense of 'foundational story', not with any assumptions about truth value attached. My own convictions about the Enlightenment paradigm will no doubt be clear to the reader, but this point, at least, stands whether or not they are accepted.

Enlightenment philosophy, the only heritage available to colonial America was Puritan. It is there, then, that I will begin my sketch. My intention is to trace both the substance and the presentation of belief in hell in the Puritan period, and how this developed in the decades afterwards, in order to provide a background to Edwards' own theology and rhetoric.[8]

Carl Trueman has offered a useful, if brief, survey of Puritan thinking on heaven and hell.[9] He begins by commenting on the brevity of the presentation of heaven and hell in the *Westminster Confession*, itself significant: there was presumably sufficient doctrinal agreement in the mid-seventeenth century for there to be no need to define truth and combat error in the documents of the Assembly.[10] In analysing this doctrinal consensus, Trueman first explores the significant borrowings Puritan writers made from the medieval heritage, and identifies two particular points: the adoption of Aristotelian categories and logic;[11] and wholesale borrowings from scholastic theology – this latter including, for example, the *poena sensus–poena damni* distinction.[12]

---

[8]   The concern with presentation ('rhetoric') alongside substance in the earlier parts of this chapter is based on the assumption that, with such an emotive subject as eternal human suffering, the language chosen to present a given idea can be just as important – and damaging – as the idea itself.

[9]   Carl R. Trueman, 'Heaven and Hell: 12 In Puritan Theology', *Epworth Review* 22/3 (Sep.1995), pp. 75–85.

[10]   The only references are in 32:1, which teaches '... the souls of the wicked are cast into hell, where they remain in torment and utter darkness, reserved to [the last judgement]'; 32:3, which states that, at the final judgement, 'the bodies of the unjust shall, by the power of Christ, be raised to dishonour ...'; and 33:2, which asserts that part of the reason for the judgement is the display of '[the glory of] his justice in the damnation of the reprobate who are wicked and disobedient,' and goes on to insist that 'the wicked ... shall be cast into eternal torments, and be punished with everlasting destruction from the presence of the Lord, and from the glory of his power.' Notable here is the total lack of controversy in comparison with much of the *Confession*: no opposing positions are named and rejected.

[11]   'It is tempting to describe *The Saint's Everlasting Rest* as the greatest application of Aristotelian physics to the service of Christian piety in the history of the church': Trueman, 'Heaven', p. 76.

[12]   Trueman, 'Heaven', p. 77. The *poena sensus* ('punishment of sense') refers to the torments actively inflicted on those in hell; the *poena damni* ('punishment of the damned') refers to the loss of the joys of heaven, and particularly of the sight of God.

There is, according to Trueman, an asymmetry in the doctrine of the last things in Puritanism. Heaven is coloured by a Christological focus; hell is, in essence, absence from God. Because of this, to speak of heaven is to be about theology proper in a way that to speak of hell is not. The language of physical suffering was recognised as inadequate of hell by the Puritans, but was still used with some freedom.[13] Puritan writers assert both that heaven is visible from hell, and the pains of the damned are thereby increased, and that hell is visible from heaven, with a corresponding increase of the joys of the saved.[14] Finally, with Edwards quoted as an example, Trueman speaks of 'a basic Puritan pastoral preoccupation with indifference towards hell ... '[15]

In order to amplify this basic picture slightly, and particularly to demonstrate some features of the rhetoric to which Edwards was heir, I shall examine two Puritan writings on hell briefly. I have deliberately chosen authors who have the reputation of being among the more gentle breed of Puritan, in order to make more forcefully the point that such rhetoric was commonplace. The writings are Richard Baxter's *The Saints' Everlasting Rest*[16] and John Bunyan's *The Resurrection of the Dead*.[17]

Baxter's *Saints' Rest* should need no recommendation; occupying amongst Puritan devotional literature a pre-eminence similar to that of its author's *Reformed Pastor* and *Christian Directory* in the field of pastoral theology, it is one of the gems of the religious writing of the period. It may be a matter of some surprise, then, to find within this work a series of chapters describing in some detail the sufferings of those who are found at the last not to be saints. More so,

[13] Trueman, 'Heaven', p. 80; some examples of my own will be found below.
[14] Trueman, 'Heaven', p. 79–80.
[15] Trueman, 'Heaven', p. 81.
[16] Baxter's *Works* are published in 23 vols., with a *Life* and appreciation by William Orme; the *Saints' Rest* may be found in vol. 22 of Richard Baxter, *Works* (London: James Duncan, 1830).
[17] *The Resurrection of the Dead* is included in a recent scholarly edition of Bunyan's *Miscellaneous Works*: John Bunyan, *Christian Behaviour; The Holy City; The Resurrection of the Dead: Miscellaneous Works* vol. 3 (ed. J. Sears McGee) (Oxford: Clarendon Press, 1987).

perhaps, when it is realised that these chapters occupy a position of significance: the first of the 'uses' found for the doctrine of rest is 'Showing the unconceivable [*sic*] misery of the ungodly in their loss of this Rest'.[18] Baxter here follows a common Puritan practice of including an 'alarm to the unconverted'[19] in his text; my intention is to focus attention on the contents of that 'alarm'.

Baxter is, very simply, seeking to scare his readers into heaven: 'I am a messenger of the saddest tidings to thee, that ever yet thy ears did hear .... This sentence I am commanded to pass on thee, from the word: take it as thou wilt, and escape it if thou canst.'[20] To this end, he offers three sections, demonstrating the greatness of the loss of heaven, those things that aggravate this loss, and the positive torments that are added to that loss.[21] The damned lose God, their own possibility of a glorified existence, all the benefits of God, and the company of the saints and angels.[22] This loss is aggravated by the increased ability to understand their condition which they will then know; by the strengthening of their consciences; by the increased ability to feel; and by the clarity of their memories – particularly of the opportunities to escape the torment they spurned.[23] Then follows a list of the pleasant things of this world, which will be lost, just as surely as the delights of heaven,[24] before finally Baxter turns to the positive torments that the damned experience. The greatness of these is demonstrated by the fact that God is the Author of them, by the seriousness with which He takes the work of glorifying His justice, by the 'delight' He will take in punishing the wicked, by the identity of their tormentors, viz. Satan and themselves, by the way these torments will

[18] Baxter, *Works*, 22, p. 361; this use is discussed in the Third Part, ch. 1–4.
[19] The phrase is the title of a book by John Alleine; the concept will be recognised by anyone familiar with Puritan literature.
[20] Baxter, *Works*, 22, pp. 361–2.
[21] In passing, it is notable here that the *poena sensus–poena damni* distinction underlies Baxter's thought, without explicit invocation.
[22] Baxter, *Works*, 22, pp. 365–71.
[23] Baxter, *Works*, 22, pp. 371–95.
[24] Baxter, *Works*, 22, pp. 395–415.

affect every part of soul and body continuously, by the lack of any hope of an end, and by their eternity.[25]

This summary will have given some flavour of these sections, but to truly convey a taste of the rhetoric I must quote at some length:

> Is it not a terrible thing to a wretched soul, when it shall lie roaring perpetually in the flames of hell, and the God of mercy himself shall laugh at them; when they shall cry out for mercy, yea, for one drop of water, and God shall mock them instead of relieving them; when none in heaven or earth can help them but God, and he shall rejoice over them in their calamity?[26]

> How God will stand over them with the rod in his hand, (not the rod of fatherly chastisement, but that iron rod wherewith he bruises the rebellious,) and lay it on for all their neglects of Christ and his grace. Oh, that men would foresee this, and not put themselves under the hammer of revenging fury ...[27]

> So also, when the time comes that he will purposefully manifest his justice, it shall appear to be indeed the justice of God. The everlasting flames of hell will not be thought too hot for the rebellious; and when they have there burnt through millions of ages, he will not repent him of the evil which is befallen them. Oh! wo [sic] to the soul that is thus set up for a butt, for the wrath of the Almighty to shoot at; and for a bush, that must burn in the flames of his jealousy and never be consumed.[28]

These sections occupy a significant proportion of the text,[29] and these examples could be multiplied, but the point should now be made: Trueman could as well have picked Baxter as Edwards as an example of his 'basic pastoral

---

[25] Baxter, *Works*, 22, pp. 415–25.
[26] Baxter, *Works*, 22, p. 419.
[27] Baxter, *Works*, 22, p. 418.
[28] Baxter, *Works*, 22, pp. 417–18.
[29] 72 pages out of 514 in the edition used.

preoccupation' with a neglect of the seriousness of the threat of damnation. More briefly, let me add a third name to this list, which should serve to establish that such imagery was common currency amongst Puritan divines.

John Bunyan is perhaps the greatest of the Puritan authors, judged on purely literary terms; *Pilgrim's Progress* is in the very first rank of English literature both in terms of popularity and influence and, whilst none of his other work approaches this, such texts as *Grace Abounding* are still read, and deservedly so. For the present purpose, I will turn to a very brief treatise, making no comment on its theological merit or otherwise, in order to demonstrate that Bunyan, too, shared in the common Puritan rhetoric of damnation. In this work[30] Bunyan discusses at great length in narrative form the final judgement, with various 'books' being opened, and heaven and hell visible to all humanity before the bar. With considerable literary skill, he paints the desperation of those under judgement to be let into paradise and even across the centuries the writing is capable of conjuring feelings of urgency and suspense. My concern, however, is with the description of hell that Bunyan builds. The simplest way to communicate the flavour is to resort to quotation:

> ... they will most famously behold the pit, the bottomless pit, the fire, the Brimstone, and the flaming beds that Justice hath prepared for them of old .... Fire is that which of all things is the most insufferable, and insupportable. Wherefore, by fire, is shewed the grievous state of the ungodly, after Judgement. Who can eat fire, drink fire, and ly down in the midst of flames of fire? yet this must the wicked do. Again, not onely fire, but everlasting fire .... [31]

> The Holy shall be in everlasting Light: But the Sinner in everlasting Darkness. Without light, I say, yet in Fire ever burning, yet not consumed, always afraid of

---

[30] Bunyan, *Works* III, pp. 197–292.
[31] Bunyan, *Works* III, p. 286–7.

death and hell, vehemently desiring to be annihilated to nothing. Continually fearing to stay long in Hell, and yet certainly sure they shall never come out of it. Ever desiring the Saints happiness [sic], and yet alwayes envying their felicity. They would have it, because it is easie and Comfortable; yet cannot abide to think of it, because they have lost it for ever. Ever loaden with the delight of sin: and yet that is the greatest torture, alwayes desiring to put it out of their Mind, and yet assuredly know [sic] they must for ever abide the guilt and torment thereof.[32]

These passages are not pleasant; their authors never intended them to be pleasant and, in an age less used to such descriptions, they border on the horrific.[33] They have been included for a reason, however: there is a widespread assumption that Edwards is in some sense culpable for the doctrine of hell he espouses, and preaches. In assessing the validity of that charge, the tradition of rhetoric that he inherited must be taken with full seriousness.

Two monographs offer helpful discussions of the movements that occurred between the writing of such passages and Edwards' prime: Walker's *The Decline of Hell* and Almond's *Heaven and Hell in Enlightenment England*.[34] Both survey the period around 1700, as mainstream Puritan and other, stranger, conceptions from the Commonwealth radicals gave way to an increasingly universalistic picture. Following these authors, and Camporesi in *The Fear of Hell*,[35] I will identify several

[32] Bunyan, *Works* III, p. 290.
[33] Although one might cogently argue that for modern society to object to such descriptive language in print or pulpit whilst supporting the right of film directors to produce some of the sicker fantasies that have emanated from Hollywood in recent years is hypocrisy on a quite breathtaking scale.
[34] D. P. Walker, *The Decline of Hell: Seventeenth-Century Discussions of Eternal Torment*, (London: Routledge and Kegan Paul, 1964); Philip C. Almond, *Heaven and Hell in Enlightenment England* (Cambridge: Cambridge University Press, 1994).
[35] Piero Camporesi, *The Fear of Hell: Images of Damnation and Salvation in Early Modern Europe* (tr. Lucinda Byatt) (Cambridge: Polity Press, 1990).

common features of the background to Edward's own thought on this subject:

Firstly, Walker and Almond both make a link between the doctrine of hell and changing notions of punishment: 'For Baxter, as for his contemporaries, the purpose of punishment of those convicted of crime was retributive, and the conscious infliction of physical suffering in a public context was central.'[36] This point is worthy of some attention: whilst retributive punishment, as described in the quotation, was regarded as ethically acceptable, there was little to oppose the inherited notion of hell. The concept of 'desert' was widely held, and this legitimated eternal punishment (once some argument concerning the infinite guilt of sin was constructed, and such arguments were commonplace[37]). Equally, whilst the visibility of punishment was considered important, the 'vision across the chasm', so repugnant to twentieth-century sensibilities, was almost demanded for God's action to be just – and with this concept in place, the fact of the eternal bliss of the saints could demand the eternity of the torments of hell – God's justice would not be perfect, and hence their enjoyment of God not perfect, if they could not see justice being done on the impenitent.

As ideas of punishment became more focused on restoration and deterrence, so ideas of hell inherited from the Middle Ages became less in tune with the temper of the times. Thus, the idea of vision across the chasm from both sides gradually disappeared after 1700. Significantly, however, this was not the result of sustained criticism; the concept vanished quietly because, apparently, it was simply no longer part of the way people thought. There was now no need for punishment to be seen for it to be effective (obviously deterrence must be seen, but it must be seen in this life: the saints need no convincing to remain holy[38]).

---

[36] Almond, *Heaven*, p. 84.

[37] See pp. 219–20 below for a discussion of the standard argument as Edwards constructs it.

[38] Walker actually notes (*Hell*, p. 101) one writer who uses the need for the saints to be eternally deterred from sinning as an argument for the eternity and visibility of hell, but this was hardly a common position.

Almond offers a further datum: the hordes of demons and their ruler Satan, which formed part of the standard description of hell prior to 1700, rapidly disappeared in the new century. Either God was seen as directly punishing those in hell, or universalism was embraced.

The connection between understandings of hell and legal theories of justice is a natural one in a Western tradition which has usually understood the atonement in forensic terms.[39] If this is followed, then once retributive theories of justice have been discounted, there can be little support for the doctrine of hell, in its traditional form of eternal conscious torment with no hope of an end. Such an understanding does not 'restore' the 'harm' done to God by sin; traditional doctrines of impassibility make any such language meaningless, and so restorative theories of justice offer little help.[40] If such ideas of justice are to be used, then some scheme such as that of Anselm, which proposes a need for a debt to be paid in order for propriety to be satisfied must be invoked, and it is difficult to see how this differs, except in the language used, from straightforward retribution.[41] As already noted in passing, for hell to have any deterrent effect it must be visible in this life, not the next, and so any such effect ceases to be relevant at the eschaton. Whilst it may be argued that the pains of hell must continue into eternity for the deterrent threat to be honest, such sophistry hardly seems reason enough for God to do such a terrible thing, if His character is anything close to what has been commonly assumed in the Christian tradition. Reformative theories of justice, of course, lead

[39] On the connection between atonement theories and the ethics of judgement see Timothy G. Gorringe, *God's Just Vengeance: Crime, Violence and the Rhetoric of Salvation* (Cambridge: Cambridge University Press, 1996) and Walter Moberly, *The Ethics of Punishment* (London: Faber & 1968).
[40] The widespread desire amongst recent theologians to recast (or remove) the doctrine of impassibility hardly alters this point: whilst some wish to speak of God suffering as a result of our sin – it is easy to see how this could be used as an argument in favour of traditional doctrines of hell – there would seem to be little desire to make this a reason (excuse?) to reintroduce such doctrines.
[41] Anselm, *Cur Deus Homo* I.12–23.

one to the final universalisms of Origen and Hick,[42] not to any support for the traditional doctrine of hell. In my examination of Edwards' doctrine, I will return to this question of the relationship between doctrines of hell and understandings of justice.

Secondly, the 'static' nature of hell is highlighted, by these authors: there is a complete 'moral freezing' at death, such that there can be no further guilt incurred, but also no hope of repentance. This view can be found in Aquinas.[43] Walker[44] links this to the deterrent value of the idea of hell,[45] a theme which he regards as important.[46] Such a moral freezing removes an obvious defence of the existence of hell – that the impenitent continue to sin, and so remain in punishment.[47]

Thirdly, Walker traces the systematic connection between the doctrine of hell and other doctrines, particularly the atonement.[48] If Christ, as truly God, suffered and died for our redemption, then, within a retributive scheme, sin must be infinitely culpable: the moral calculus here is a reversal of Anselm's in *Cur Deus Homo*: he argued that, since sin must be infinite, only God could atone;[49] now the argument is that since God has atoned, sin must be infinite.[50] Walker makes the point that this made it very easy for Socinians and Arians to reject the orthodox doctrine of hell, although others may wish to place more stress on a common cause for the

---

[42] John Hick, *Evil and the God of Love* (London: Macmillan, 1985²): Hick's understanding is not necessarily universalist, in that he preserves a place for indeterminate human freedom – see n. 144 on p. 236 below.
[43] *Summa*, IIa IIae q. 13 art. 4.
[44] *Hell*, p. 23.
[45] That hell has a deterrent value is undisputed throughout the period; the object of the discussion of justice above was to indicate that if hell has no more than a deterrent value, it becomes difficult to defend its existence.
[46] Various authors are quoted to the effect that, if the doctrine of hell is questioned, crime will necessarily increase – see pp. 1–4, and *passim*.
[47] According to Walker (*Hell*, pp. 24–5) Leibniz, amongst others, actually offered this defence.
[48] *Hell*, pp. 26–9.
[49] *Cur Deus Homo*, II.6.
[50] One thinks of Barth's argument that we understand what sin means only by seeing Jesus accepting its consequences on the cross.

rejection of various orthodox doctrines than on a theological consequent like this. Walker offers a fourth section, concerned with what I have called the 'vision across the chasm'. In discussing this under the question of retributive justice, I hope I have indicated theological linkages which may not be wholly evident in Walker's account.

In summary, then, the Puritan tradition which Edwards inherited stood in broad continuity with the medieval tradition both in doctrine and rhetoric concerning hell. I have highlighted the connection with theories of justice that led to common views of hell changing during the early decades of Edwards' life, and the 'vision across the chasm', the decline of which demonstrates this shift well. In addition, I have followed Walker in noting other aspects of the received doctrine which were being challenged in Edwards' day.

Edwards' Doctrine and Rhetoric of Hell

With this background in place, it is now possible to examine Edwards' own understanding, and presentation, of hell. When Edwards' sermons on the subject are read alongside the descriptions quoted earlier, what is striking is actually his reticence in graphic description of hell.[51] His preaching ministry was carried out less than a century after the origin of these illustrations, and so one is forced to conclude that, in his rhetoric, Edwards was no more than in step with his times. He certainly can – and regularly does – use language to shock and grab the attention of his congregation, but usually it is not the pains of hell itself he stresses, but their immanence, their

---

[51] The crude anthropomorphism of God's infliction of torments seen in Baxter, for instance, could not be paralleled within Edwards' corpus. Equally, the reader of Edwards' *Miscellanies* cannot fail to be struck by the sense that his abiding interest is in the joys of heaven, not the pains of hell, and he is far more graphic in describing the former, even with much less scriptural material on which to build.

unavoidability, their eternity, and the sovereignty of God.[52]

It is worthy of note, even if only in passing, that in choosing to preach in such ways Edwards was not out on a limb; his own criticisms of revivalist excesses suggests that many were so affected by their experiences of the revival that they preached in ways even Edwards found wholly unacceptable. James Davenport is the name almost always mentioned in this connection, although it is unclear whether he was the most culpable, or just the most notorious, culprit. Reading the history, I am left with an uncomfortable feeling that he is blamed most because he detailed his own failures in a retraction. One could hope that Christian theologians rehearsing this history would have been more conscious of the impropriety of heaping guilt upon a person precisely because they have repented.[53] It is also relevant to this point to note that Edwards' practice here differed little from that of Wesley or Whitefield.[54]

---

[52] It has been regularly remarked, but serves as an ideal example here, that the images of 'Sinners in the Hands of an Angry God' terrify by stressing instability – whether the spider is kept from or engulfed by the flames depends only on the good pleasure of an angry Deity – not by stressing the pains of hell. This makes the doctrine of God an even sharper question of course, and one I shall return to. For further examples of the point, see my analysis of the various published 'hellfire' sermons below.

[53] For brief accounts of the history of this part of the controversy over the revivals, see *YE2*, pp. 2–8; *YE4*, pp. 51–2; 60–61; for Edwards' explicit statements that he feels some have been emphasising the terrors of hell too much, see *YE4*, pp. 246–8. For Davenport's retraction, see *Confessions and Retractions* in Alan Heimart and Perry Miller (eds), *The Great Awakening: Documents Illustrating the Crisis and its Consequences*, (Indianapolis: Bobbs-Merill, 1967) pp. 257–62. The editors describe Davenport as 'a convenient target': p. 257.

[54] This point may be demonstrated by reference to James Downey's study, *The Eighteenth Century Pulpit: A Study of the Sermons of Butler, Berkeley, Secker, Sterne, Whitefield, and Wesley* (Oxford: Oxford University Press, 1969). Downey says of Whitefield's predilection for such preaching: 'It is little wonder that, projecting such graphic descriptions of hell, he sent many away from his services distraught with fear. But Whitefield made no apology for this. He believed that it was "better to have some soul-trouble here, than to be sent to hell by Jesus Christ hereafter".' (p. 162). According to Wesley, Downey suggests, '[c]ongregations must never be allowed to forget the ineluctable fate of the impenitent' (p. 192). Downey quotes at length from both preachers, and a glance at the relevant passages will offer considerable support for the point.

Turning to doctrine, rather than presentation, if we search Edwards for visions of demons and Satan, we again find that he was in step with his times. His vision of hell is between God and the damned, perhaps all the more shocking for today's Christian reader because of that,[55] but there is little or no room for great armies of demons with twisted faces tormenting the damned, as there had been in the Puritans of the previous centuries. Certainly Edwards believed in the devil and the fallen angels; his (Reformed) orthodoxy was, here as elsewhere, impeccable;[56] it is simply that he was not especially interested in them, and saw little use for pictures painted involving them.[57]

It is when we turn to what I have termed the 'vision across the chasm', to the saints rejoicing over the sight of sinners being punished and sinners suffering more from seeing saints in glory, that Edwards' doctrine appears, famously, out of step. An entire sermon, 'The End of the Wicked Contemplated by the Righteous',[58] is devoted to defending this point, and it regularly appears in other texts.[59] This sermon, on Revelation 18:20, begins by asserting: 'When the saints in glory shall see the wrath of God executed on ungodly men, it will be no occasion of grief to them, but of rejoicing.'[60] Scripture, according to Edwards, plainly teaches that heaven and hell are each visible from the other. Further, when the righteous see the sufferings of hell, 'They will not be sorry for the damned, it will cause no uneasiness or dissatisfaction to them; but on the contrary, when they have this sight, it will excite them to joyful praises.'[61]

---

[55] If only in that such immediacy may imply some uncomfortable things about God.

[56] For references, see the *Miscellanies* entries listed in Edwards' table: *YE13*, p. 130 (under devils) and p. 145 (under Satan).

[57] A brief passage such as the one in the sermon entitled 'The End of the Wicked Contemplated by the Righteous' (*BT2*, pp. 207–12), referring to the lack of any pity in the devils that torment the damned, (see IV.1.3, p. 211) only proves the point: it is simply not characteristic of Edwards' preaching.

[58] *BT2*, pp. 207–12.

[59] See, for instance, 'Wicked Men Useful in their Destruction Only' (*BT2*, p. 127).

[60] Section 1.

[61] Section 1 Prop. 2.

This is so out of tune with our own times that it is in danger of exciting simple revulsion. As I indicated in the introduction to this chapter, this should not be allowed to prevent us tracing Edwards' logic on this point. It is a part of his theology, and one I intend to show to be important in understanding his vision of glory, and the flaws therein.

Edwards offers several arguments for his contention that the saints will praise God at the sight of the damned. Firstly, and negatively, it is not because of any ill disposition in the saints. They have no love and no pity for the damned, because they love only what God loves and God does not love the damned. Secondly and positively, God glorifies Himself – His justice, power and majesty – in the punishment of sinners, and the saints will rejoice in any display of His glory, so they will rejoice at the sight of the sufferings of hell. Thirdly, in seeing what they have been saved from, the saints have a greater sense of their own happiness and a greater sense of God's love and grace; both gratitude for salvation, and this further glorification of God as the depths of His love are seen, excite them to worship. Edwards is aware of the objection that any modern reader would raise, although not perhaps of the emotional force with which it would be raised, and he answers the point that this appears to be a less than perfect action on the part of the saints in several ways. An examination of these shows that they essentially reduce to his fourth argument: that the exercise of a virtuous disposition is different in different circumstances. So the saints are called to love sinners now because they do not know whether a particular person may be amongst the elect and hence later converted; then they will know, and so may respond with simple hatred for those whom God hates.[62] Again, in the suffering of the reprobate the saints see God's glory, and they are more aware of His love for them, and so it is appropriate for them to rejoice at the sight, but this is not the case with human suffering seen in this life, which

[62] This would seem to presuppose a limited atonement, at least with Edwards' Calvinist presuppositions; for Edwards' views on this issue see pp. 157–9 in chapter 4 above.

appropriately generates pity and compassion in a virtuous person. The difference, according to Edwards, is in the nature of the suffering, not in the virtue of the person who sees it.[63]

So, my examination thus far suggests that Edwards was broadly in tune with his times, if fairly traditional, in both his rhetoric of damnation and in most areas of his doctrine. The single glaring exception is the 'vision across the chasm' and the use he makes of that. As with his commitment to Calvinist expressions, Edwards can be seen here to be firmly holding to a doctrine that is rapidly being discarded all around, presumably because it forms an important plank in his theological scheme. My purpose in the next part of the chapter, then, will be to use this anomaly as a way in to explore the doctrinal concerns that lie behind Edwards' understanding of damnation. This will take up the next two sections, the first being an examination of the writings (mainly sermons) that treat directly of hell, and the second an examination of an area of theology which will form an important part of the background to this question in Edwards' own thought.

The Use of Hell in Promoting God's Glory

The key texts for an examination of Edwards' doctrine of hell come from the published sermons: 'The End of the Wicked Contemplated by the Righteous',[64] 'The Wicked

---

[63] The strongest argument that Edwards advances in favour of these ideas is actually found in the *Miscellanies*. In entry 1356, Edwards constructs a series of arguments against the idea that hell is reformative, rather than punitive, in the course of which he asserts: 'There is nothing in the accounts of the day of judgement [in Scripture] that looks as tho the saints had any love or pity for the wicked, on ac[count] of the terrible long-continued torments which they must suffer. Nor indeed will the accounts that are given admit of supposing any such thing. We have an account of their judging them & being with Christ in condemning them, concurring in the sentence ... but no account of their praying for them, nor of their exhorting them to consider and repent...' (p. 12 of Schafer's transcript). These observations are significant, and must be taken seriously by any theology that is committed to the authority of Scripture.
[64] BT2, pp. 207–12.

Useful in their Destruction Only',[65] 'Wrath upon the Wicked to the Uttermost',[66] 'The Justice of God in the Damnation of Sinners',[67] and, famously, 'Sinners in the Hands of an Angry God'.[68]

This is an unpleasant selection of titles, but notice what it means: there is almost nothing in Edwards' major published works which touches on the doctrine of hell – a brief comment in the section of *True Virtue* concerning conscience;[69] a few pages towards the end of *History of Redemption*;[70] but, overall, very little. The comparison with Baxter's *Saints' Rest*, to which I have already referred, is instructive: nearly a sixth part of that work is devoted to discussing hell. This cannot be put down to subject matter: *Original Sin, True Virtue*, and any or all of the Revival Treatises could have included an 'alarm to the unconverted' without raising any surprise amongst those used to Puritan literature. A relatively small collection of sermons[71] and a number of *Miscellanies* entries[72] are the entirety of Edwards' output in this area and, whilst their contents should not be minimised, nor should they be over-emphasised simply because of their sensational nature.

I will treat these sermons in a theological, rather than chronological, order, beginning with 'Wrath upon the Wicked'. The doctrine of this sermon states: 'When those that continue in sin shall have filled up the measure of their sin, then wrath will come upon them to the uttermost.' –

---

[65] *BT2*, pp. 125–9 (dated July 1744).

[66] *BT2*, pp. 122–5 (dated May 1735).

[67] *BT1*, pp. 668–79 (the fourth of the 'Five Discourses' which Edwards published as his anti-Arminian series which, he claims, were a catalyst for the first revival he saw at Northampton, in 1734).

[68] *BT2*, pp. 7–12 (preached at Enfield on 8 July 1741, and at Northampton a few months earlier).

[69] *YE8*, pp. 597–9.

[70] *YE9*, pp. 505–6, 512.

[71] In addition to those listed, only one of the sermons thus far published is devoted to hell: 'The Torments of Hell are Exceeding Great' in *YE14*, pp. 301–31.

[72] Edwards' Table, which is exhaustive, lists 70 of the 1400+ entries as having some reference to hell, or about 5% – almost exactly the same number as refer to heaven. See *YE13*, pp. 134–6. There is little in these entries that is not present in the sermons that I am considering.

the points stressed being that there is a limit permitted to the sin of any wicked person, and that when that limit is filled, God's wrath will fall without any restraint. The use of this is to encourage those still unconverted to seek salvation. Wrath will come without restraint, without mercy, without limit and without end, because 'sin is an infinite evil'.[73] This sermon is a simple threat; there is little other than standard Puritan ideas contained therein, although the rhetoric focuses on the immediate action of God in punishing those in hell, an emphasis entirely in accord with Edwards' regular stress on God's immediacy. This focus is emphasised when the most famous of Edwards' imprecatory sermons is considered; as already noted,[74] the stress in 'Sinners ...' is not so much on the pains of hell as on their immediacy and the instability of the unconverted sinner – again and again, the image is of the hand of God, the God the listeners are told they have provoked to anger and hatred, being the only thing that keeps them out of the fire. This is unsurprising when the doctrine of the sermon is considered: 'There is nothing that keeps wicked men at any one moment out of hell, but the mere pleasure of God.' Immediacy and instability are the hall marks.

Wilson Kimnach, in his long and significant intro-duction to the various volumes of Edwards' sermons in the Yale Edition, has traced the genre of this sermon to 'hands' sermons, preached to criminals condemned to execution and often later published.[75] The rhetorical trick Edwards used is to take the language of these sermons, delivered to those on the point of certain death, and to apply it to his listeners in Enfield to stress the instability of their position. Edwards' vision of immediacy reached a terrifying climax here: everything is stripped away, God and the sinner are the only two beings in view, and God is characterised as being primarily powerful and angry.

These two sermons point to the first aspect of

[73] BT2, p. 123.
[74] N. 52 on p. 212 above.
[75] YE10, pp. 167–79.

Edwards' understanding of hell that I want to draw out: the note of immediacy. Edwards' vision of the immediacy of God's relations with men and women has been mentioned before in this study, but this is the point where he might have been expected to finally draw back from it. After all, according to Trueman, a basic description of hell in the Puritan tradition was the *poena damni*, the absence of God. For Edwards, this is not the case: hell is the presence of God, but of God in His anger and wrath. What hell is not, however, and the texts will be searched in vain for any counter-evidence, is the presence of the Trinitiarian God. God's close relationship with His creation, is Trinitarian – most obviously in the divine self-giving to the world, which is the sending of Son and Spirit. In redemption, it is the closeness of the saints' relationship to Christ, and the presence of the indwelling Spirit which demonstrate the closeness of God. Here, in hell, it appears that a different God is present. I will return to this theme.

Bracketing this Trinitarian question, we may observe that Edwards' position (insisting that hell is the presence, rather than the absence, of God) has a certain strength theologically, in that he takes with full seriousness the contingent nature of human creatureliness. There is always a certain suspicion that what is at work in accounts which stress the absence of God is a borrowed Greek view of the necessary immortality of the soul, and so a concept of hell as the soul living out its life apart from God.[76] Edwards' conviction that continued existence of any sort must be solely by the active will of God is surely truer to the Biblical texts, but raises an acute problem: why, if this is the case, are the damned resurrected at all?

It may be that the truth of this position can be established by exegesis, at least for anyone with a 'high' view of

---

[76] Perhaps Odysseus' experiences in the Underworld come to mind, as he praises the shade of Achilles for the high regard in which he is held in the realm of the dead. Achilles' response is to insist that to be a slave but alive would be better than his current state. *Odyssey* Book 11.

Scripture[77] – and certainly this would be the case for Edwards. This is not, however, the challenge: when Edwards adopts the realist understanding of virtue of which *True Virtue* is an exposition, and particularly when he does so in full knowledge of Locke's attempt to make justice and similar concepts self-defining, the pressing question must be how Edwards can consider such a position theologically possible. When Bruce Davidson wrote an article entitled 'Reasonable Damnation: How Jonathan Edwards Argued for the Rationality of Hell' he was raising the right question.[78]

I will address this question by examining the remainder of the sermons listed at the beginning of this section,[79] starting with 'The Justice of God in the Damnation of Sinners'. This sermon, preached on Romans 3:19, 'That every mouth may be stopped', is a defence of the doctrine of hell on precisely this point: how can it be just? Edwards answers on the basis of two data: human sinfulness and God's sovereignty. On the first, he adopts a traditional defence, in arguing for the infinite guilt of sin. This can be appropriately dealt with only by either suffering of infinite worth, as in the self-offering of Christ on the cross, or suffering of infinite duration, as in the eternal punishment of the wicked. Edwards' construction of the argument is typically careful, and must have been shattering to hear preached. Punishment, he asserts, must be proportional to the crime punished; this is simple (retributive) justice. The heinousness of a crime is, in turn, proportional to the strength of the obligation offended against. Obligations to

---

[77] '. . . if a specific sense be attached to words, never-ending misery is enunciated in the Bible. On the presumption that one doctrine is taught, it is the eternity of hell torments.' The claim is vastly overstated, but makes the point. It is taken from W. G. T. Shedd, *The Doctrine of Endless Punishment* (Edinburgh: Banner of Truth, 1986) p. 118.

[78] Although I find the answers he gives lacking in penetration. The article is: Bruce W. Davidson, 'Reasonable Damnation: How Jonathan Edwards Argued for the Rationality of Hell' *Journal of the Evangelical Theology Society* 38/1 (March 1995) pp. 47–56.

[79] An early attempt at a defence can be seen in 'All God's Methods are Most Reasonable' (*YE14*, pp. 165–97), particularly Sections I, II and V. The arguments in the sermons that I analyse in the main text cover the points made here more carefully, so I will not include an analysis of this sermon.

love, honour or obey are proportionate to the degree of loveliness, 'honourableness' or authority in the person in question – this is the definition of these words. But God is infinitely lovely, etc., and so, tracing the chain back, any offence against God is deserving of infinite punishment. Therefore, 'the *eternity* of the punishment of ungodly men renders it infinite: and renders it no more than infinite' – so punishment is proportionate, and hence just.

There is a more careful construction of this in *Miscellanies* 713,[80] where Edwards (presumably independently) reaches the same conclusion as Aquinas[81] in arguing that all sins are infinite in one respect but not in another. Edwards invokes the image of cylinders of infinite length, which may still differ greatly in diameter and yet all be infinite. In the same way, considered as offence against God, all sin is infinitely culpable, but considered in other ways sins may be much greater or less than each other.[82] Aquinas follows this by insisting that punishment is infinite in its duration but finite (and varying) in its intensity – not a point Edwards makes as far as I am aware, but one from which he is only one step away.

Considering the question from the standpoint of God's majesty, Edwards is concerned to make three points: that God is under no obligation to prevent us from sinning; that it is just for God to impose the federal scheme; and that God may choose to redeem or not as He pleases, when fallen humanity is in view. The first of these is defended on the grounds that it would be unreasonable to insist that God makes us in such a way that it is impossible for us to sin, and so we cannot blame Him when we do. Further,

[80]   As yet unpublished, but cited in this connection in *YE3*, p. 41 n. 1.
[81]   *Summa*, Supp. q. 99 art. 1 *responsio*.
[82]   Edwards' precise words – 'it may be doubled & trebled yea & made a thousand fold more by the increase of other dimensions' (*Miscellanies* 713) – lack mathematical rigour, in that the volume of a cylinder of infinite length and *any* finite diameter is the same. One could seek increases by invoking Cantor's theory of transfinite numbers (unknown in Edwards' day, of course), whereby the volume of a cylinder of infinite diameter would be a larger infinity than the first (an aleph-1 set as opposed to an aleph-null set), but Edwards' point is made by his illustration, whatever the mathematical niceties!

God may permit sin justly, even if He knows it is certain we will fall into sin, or if He so orders the creation that it is inevitable that we should fall into sin.[83] The second of Edwards' contentions is that there is no reason why God should choose to treat us as individuals, rather than as a federal whole under Adam,[84] as the latter is no more inherently dangerous to us than the former. Once again, there is apparently a certain doublethink present here, as this can be the case only if Adam's sin is not foreknown and foreordained. Lastly, he argues that with fallen humanity in view, God may justly choose whom to redeem and whom not to, since all are guilty.

These points, taken together, are unsatisfactory. Each on its own may indeed work. It is, however, integral to Edwards' theological scheme that such decisions do not come on their own. It is not that God creates *homo labilis* (human beings with the potential to fall) and is then 'surprised' and forced to take a new decision when we fall; it is not even that God creates *homo labilis* in full knowledge that we will fall; as I have tried to show, Edwards' understanding of creation is such that history is all immediately present to the mind of God – with this understanding of the relationship between eternity and time, Edwards is asking us to believe that God creates not just *homo lapsus* (fallen humanity) but the *massa damnata* (the collection of the damned). The arguments he deploys will not defend against the charge of injustice levelled here.[85] Once again, this difficulty is related to Edwards' predestinarianism, and I will return to it in the next section.

The two remaining sermons address a slightly different question: the usefulness of hell. This will not stand as a

---

[83] In this final step, the defence of his predestinarian scheme, Edwards may appear vulnerable. I will return to this question in the next section.

[84] The federal scheme, unsurprisingly given its cultural *milieu*, does not mention Eve in this connection. It is not clear to me that the inclusion of Eve would alter the system in any significant way, however.

[85] To be fair to Edwards at this point, we cannot expect the theological rigour of his later treatises within the confines of a sermon. My purpose here is not to dismiss the arguments of the sermon, but to indicate that they are inadequate to answer the general question, however valid in context.

defence on its own, of course: hell may not finally be accepted because it is useful, although unjust. It is, however, a second strand to Edwards' attempts to justify the existence of hell, and a further guide to his understanding of hell. I will begin with his sermon on Ezekiel 15:2–4, 'The Wicked Useful in their Destruction Only'.

With a certain horrific logic, Edwards presses the image in the text of Scripture of a barren tree being useful only for fuel to assert that those who do not 'bring forth fruit to God' are useful only when burning in hell. The 'end of their being' is to glorify God; if this cannot be obtained by living for Him, then in eternal death they can bring glory to God: God's majesty is glorified in that the greatness of it is seen by the awfulness of offending against it; God's justice is glorified in that He does not shrink from delivering the damned to what they deserve; and God's love and mercy are glorified in that the saints are given a sense – and a sight – of what they have been freed from by the mere grace of God.

Edwards focuses on God's glorifying of Himself in the punishment of the reprobate, which is made an occasion for worship and thanksgiving when seen by the saints. So, in the final sermon that I will consider, 'The End of the Wicked . . .', which I have already discussed at some length, Edwards asserts that, while God glorifies Himself in everything He does, He does so principally in the eternal fate of His intelligent creatures – whether to life or death.[86] In the eternal death of the wicked, He glorifies His own justice, His power and majesty, and His grace and love, in the ways described above. The use of hell is that God is glorified through it, by the display of His perfections. Assuming it is just for God to send people to hell, this point must be considered valid.[87] Once again, however, the same question recurs: in his basic account of God's self-glorification, in creation and in redemption, God's glory is

---

[86] As Edwards maintained in *End of Creation*. See my analysis in chapter 2, pp. 50–1.

[87] Although I will raise some objections to it at the end of the chapter, pp. 233–4.

defined by Trinitarian concepts and the gospel narrative. These are only conspicuous by their absence in the writings on hell.

Again, leaving a full consideration of this point until the end of the chapter, on Edwards' own terms the question remaining is one of justice, and the sharpness of it, as I have indicated, depends on his predestinarianism.[88] In order to explore this question more fully, then, I shall need in the next section to devote space to the last of Edwards' major works to be considered in this book, and to explore Edwards' doctrine of reprobation.

Edwards' Calvinism in *Original Sin*

If the doctrine of hell Edwards adopts is to be treated with full seriousness, both doing justice to the uses he makes of it and highlighting possible weaknesses within it, it must be viewed in connection with his predestinarianism. Certainly, if an 'Arminian' understanding of freedom and salvation is once admitted, it is easier to defend eternal, conscious torment – indeed, the defences already explored could be considered sufficient from such a starting point. Edwards, however, does not start from here. I looked at the first part of his projected defence of his variety of Calvinism in *The Freedom of the Will* in the previous chapter; I will now introduce the theme in this chapter with a reading of the second, *Original Sin*.[89]

Edwards finished this work in 1757, intending it, as he tells us, not just as a reply to Turnbill and Taylor, the interlocutors named in the preface, but as a *'general defense* of

---

[88] *Miscellanies* 779, for instance, contains a long defence of the appropriateness of God's punishing of sin, which works on its own terms, but (again) ignores the way in which the arguments must be adjusted if it is held that God ordained the sin in the first place.

[89] *YE3*; key secondary texts relating to this work include Clyde A. Holbrook's Editor's Introduction (*YE3*, pp. 1–101); C. Samuel Storms, *Tragedy in Eden: Original Sin in the Theology of Jonathan Edwards* (London: University Press of America, 1985); and pp. 141–53 of Jenson, *America's Theologian*. In addition, Haroutunian, *Piety* will be found to reflect this controversy on almost every page, although it is only rarely in the foreground.

that great important doctrine'.[90] In John Taylor of Norwich, Edwards seems to have found an opponent worthy of his foil; unlike the various works addressed in *Freedom of the Will*, Taylor's *The Scripture Doctrine of Original Sin, Proposed to Free and Candid Examination* was written by a scholar of no mean ability, who was skilled both in Biblical languages and contemporary philosophy and theology.[91] The book itself had apparently rapidly gained a reputation of being unanswerable, despite attempts by, among others, Isaac Watts.[92] The nature of what Edwards called 'Arminianism' in New England has already been noted, and a moment's thought will show how amenable such a mood would be to an apparently reasonable and learned attack on one of the most offensive of the 'old Calvinist' doctrines.[93] This said, however, Edwards' response is a piece of constructive theology: he gives an account of the doctrine as he understands it, pausing from time to time to address particular points of controversy. Edwards' positive arguments are usually more interesting than the controversial sections, and if the latter were lacking, the book would still form a coherent whole.

Original Sin is divided into four parts, with the first three designed to demonstrate the truth of the doctrine and the last designed to answer objections raised against it. The first two parts, roughly equal in length, discuss evidence for original sin in 'facts and events' and Scripture, respectively; the third, much shorter, part offers a theological argument based on the doctrine of redemption. The work as a whole suffers in comparison with its companion volume, *The Freedom of the Will* – but then, most books

---

[90] *YE3*, p. 102; italics original.

[91] For a brief biography of Taylor, see *YE3*, pp. 68–70. His *Scripture Doctrine* was published in either 1738 or 1740 – see *YE3*, p. 2 n. 5.

[92] See *YE3*, p. 3, where both this reputation and the various responses are discussed.

[93] Jenson states: 'The rising bourgeoisie found the notion of original sin the single greatest religious offence to its ideology and aspirations' (*America's Theologian*, p. 144) This may be overstated – certainly the doctrine of predestination would be a close challenger – but the basic point, that this linked nexus of predestinarian doctrines was inimical to the rising American mood, holds.

would. One might describe *Original Sin* as competent rather than brilliant; its one original contribution, the doctrine of imputation put forward, has been considered as misconceived by most commentators.[94] Other than this point, the book is little more than a solid restatement, mainly built on Biblical exegesis, of the mainstream Christian position. Edwards displays his usual clarity, and his usual cumbersomeness, in his restatement, and does a solid job of defending against the particular attack he was facing.

Edwards' preparation of the ground is characteristically careful: in theological use 'original sin' refers only to human depravity, whereas in lay use it refers to the (linked) doctrines of depravity and imputation;[95] depravity means a particular disposition of the heart, which may be discerned by observing what is common to the same event in a wide variety of circumstances.[96] In the particular case in question, we must be careful to look at the reaction of humanity apart from the effect of divine grace.[97] Equally, we must not make arguments about the relative preponderance of good and bad: depravity implies that we are always liable to sin, not that we are liable to sin always.[98] Again, arguing that we are good naturally, but just corrupted by this world is irrelevant: this world is our proper place; if we are corrupt in our proper place then we are corrupt.[99] On the basis of these foundations, Edwards seeks to demonstrate the universality of human sin. The texts cited are the usual ones, as are most of the arguments; two of the latter, however, are worthy of further comment.

The first is a cluster of arguments in the second chapter, which is entitled 'Universal Mortality Proves Original Sin.'[100] Edwards is here addressing the regularly-made

---

[94] Any survey of the literature will demonstrate this – including, most conveniently, Holbrook's in his 'Introduction'. See *YE3*, pp. 97–101. My own estimation will follow the minority line – see later.

[95] *YE3*, p. 107.

[96] *YE3*, pp. 107–9.

[97] *YE3*, p. 109.

[98] *YE3*, pp. 120–7.

[99] *YE3*, pp. 125–7.

[100] *YE3*, p. 206.

point that death is a great benefit to humanity, given by God for many good purposes.[101] For Edwards, death is 'a calamity above all others terrible'.[102] Behind this argument is the Panglossian nature of the Enlightenment thought of which Taylor is such an able representative. Whatever is, is good; death is; so death must be good. Taylor had tried hard to defend this position, arguing that death teaches and trains us, and so is to be welcomed as a good gift of God.[103] Edwards responds with almost angry derision – death is a tragedy; Christ meets death as an enemy;[104] it is the ultimate sign that there is something fundamentally wrong with the world.

Secondly, Edwards constructs arguments for the ubiquity of sin from the dullness of religion in the world.[105] Once again, this highlights a fundamental divergence between Edwards and the coming Enlightenment. The moral calculus of *True Virtue*, which insists that an action's value can be judged only in relation to God, and that heroic deeds in another context are finally sinful, is beyond Taylor.[106] Edwards' point is one that I have had cause to mention before now: that which appears good and harmonious viewed against part of reality may yet be seen to be disharmonious with the whole, and hence wrong. A theme, however attractive in itself, will grate if it occurs in a piece of music in a different key.

When Edwards feels he has established the doctrine, by arguments and citations, he turns in Part IV[107] to discuss various objections that are raised. Much of the genuinely

---

[101] Perhaps Holbrook's statement of the position will make the point best: 'It is God's love, his fatherly concern for his children's welfare, his grace, that has brought about death.' *YE3*, p. 32.

[102] *YE3*, p. 206.

[103] John Taylor, *The Scripture Doctrine of Original Sin Proposed to Free & Candid Examination* (London: J. Wilson, 1740). On this point see the appendix to the first part of the work, pp. 65–70, where Taylor argues that death could be just only if God had '*kind* and *beneficent* Ends' in view (p. 65; all emphases original), and so offers a series of reasons for regarding death as a benefit.

[104] *YE3*, p. 212.

[105] *YE3*, pp. 147–57.

[106] Taylor, Supplement, pp. 62–77 (part IV).

[107] *YE3*, p. 373–433.

interesting material in the book is here. Two areas stand out: the suggestion that this doctrine makes God the author of sin (which speaks directly to the questions about the justice of hell which prompted this examination), and the doctrine of imputation advanced. I will consider these in reverse order.

The doctrine of imputation has provided difficulties throughout the history of the Augustinian tradition of theology. The fact of imputation – that we are guilty by virtue of Adam's sin and holy by virtue of Christ's obedience – is easily derived from a fairly natural reading of Paul's argument in the early chapters of Romans; problems arise when attempts are made to account for this fact theologically. Augustine's own version was developed, like so much of his theology, in the midst of controversy – the Pelagian disputes, in this case. The student of Edwards learns to appreciate the particular difficulties that doing theology controversially brings, and it is a measure of Augustine's greatness that he was able to produce creative and powerful work in the heat of argument so regularly. On the doctrine of imputation, however, he is almost universally regarded as having made a false move.

Augustine argued, simply, that the essence of sin is concupiscence – inordinate desire. Sin is inherited, from Adam and Eve down, because concupiscence is always a part of reproduction as sexual intercourse cannot take place without desire. On an abstract level, this is very neat: it makes sense of troublesome passages concerning sinning in Adam, and the status of the virgin birth is immediately established as the reason for Christ's sinlessness. It is the practical and pastoral consequences concerning the denigration of God's good gifts of sexuality and hence embodiment which are disastrous; theologically, this ties up with a commonly perceived failure in Augustine's theological scheme to celebrate the goodness of creation.[108]

There is no need here to explore further attempts to

---

[108] For Augustine's position, see the various anti-Pelagian writings (conveniently collected in the *Nicene and Post-Nicene Fathers* First Series vol. 8), but especially 'On Marriage and Concupiscence' (pp. 260–308).

formulate the doctrine.[109] Within the Reformed tradition, Edwards would have found a confused legacy, which sought to move away from Augustine's position without really knowing what, other than the bare fact of imputation, to put in its place.[110] Given this, it is hardly surprising that Edwards should make an original contribution when he comes to this point.

Edwards advances his theory of imputation in the third chapter of Part IV of *Original Sin*,[111] devoted to dealing with the charge that imputation is unjust. Characteristically, the treatment begins with a careful statement of what imputation is. God's covenant with Adam was such that in every step of His dealings with him He treated his posterity as one with him.[112] The essence of Adam's first sin was in his disposition, not in his act, which was merely the outward manifestation of the inward disposition: 'His sin consisted in wickedness of heart, fully sufficient *for*, and entirely amounting *to*, all that appeared in the act he committed.'[113] Part of the punishment for this sin was God-forsakeness, resulting in depravity of nature as a fixed principle in Adam, and in all who follow.[114]

Taylor had insisted that it was unreasonable and unjust to consider Adam and his posterity, manifestly different individuals, as one.[115] Once again, a standard

---

[109] A long, although not necessarily unbiased, discussion will be found in F. R. Tennant's Hulsean Lectures, published as *The Origin and Propagation of Sin*, (Cambridge: Cambridge University Press, 1902) pp. 1–112. See also Norman Powell Williams' Bampton Lectures: *The Ideas of the Fall and Original Sin: A Historical and Critical Study* (London: Longmans, Green & Co., 1929).

[110] Heppe's regular desire to impose order and unanimity on the tradition only makes his witness to confusion on this point more powerful: see pp. 341–8.

[111] *YE3*, pp. 389–412.

[112] *YE3*, p. 389.

[113] *YE3*, p. 390.

[114] *YE3*, p. 390–1.

[115] 'Guilt always denotes the having committed a wicked Action, by which a Person becomes obnoxious to Punishment, it is evident our Sinfulness cannot, in the Nature of Things, consist in the guilt of *Adam's* first Sin; because we could not possibly commit that Action in any sense, so we could not, upon account thereof, become obnoxious to punishment.' Taylor, *Doctrine*, p. 99. Again: 'We do understand, and by our Faculties must necessarily judge, according to all Rules of Equity, it [imputation] is *unjust*.' (p. 150). (emphasis original in both quotations).

Enlightenment note is being sounded here: the desire to define my freedom *against* the community, rather than *for* and *by* the community – in this case, the community of the whole human race.[116] The precise objections are twofold: that this damages those of us who are descended from Adam, and also that it is simply fictional, and so improper, for God to act thus. Edwards simply dismisses the first objection – it was much fairer to humanity to do things this way round, as Adam had far more reason, and so was far more likely, to obey than any who follow. Enlightened pleas of self-sufficiency are met with the contempt they deserve: '... no man's vain opinion of himself, as more fit to be trusted than others, alters the true nature and tendency of things, as they demonstrably are in themselves.'[117]

It is in dealing with the second objection, that this oneness between Adam and his descendants is fictional, that Edwards advances novel views. These depend on an analysis of what is meant by identity: 'the seeming force of the objection arises from ignorance or inconsideration of the degree, in which created identity or oneness with past existence in general, depends on the sovereign constitution and law of the Supreme Author and Disposer of the universe.'[118] Only God has 'absolutely independent identity';[119] all other identity is dependent on God's pleasure. A tree, for example, is 'so exceeding diverse, many thousand times bigger, and of a very different form, and perhaps not one atom the very same' as the shoot from which it grew, but God has 'in a constant succession communicated to it many of the same qualities, and most important properties, as if it were one'.[120] Locke saw personal identity as identity of

---

[116] On this point, see Jenson, *America's Theologian*, pp. 154-68; Colin E. Gunton, 'God, Grace and Freedom' in Gunton (ed.), *God and Freedom: Essays in Historical and Systematic Theology* (Edinburgh: T&T Clark, 1995) pp. 119–33, and my own article, 'Edwards on the Will', *International Journal of Systematic Theology* I (1999) pp. 266–85.
[117] *YE3*, p. 396.
[118] *YE3*, p. 397.
[119] *YE3*, p. 400.
[120] *YE3*, pp. 397–8.

consciousness;[121] Edwards wants to say that it is more than this, but he accepts that this is essential, and insists that it 'depends wholly on a divine establishment.'[122]

Edwards offers a proof for this, at first sight surprising, contention: the existence of a body in a given moment is not necessary, so it must be dependent on some cause. That cause is usually thought to be its existence in the previous moment, but this cannot be the case. Firstly, many previous existences are entirely passive – a stone, for example, cannot be considered as exerting itself to cause its continuation. Secondly, the previous existence is, by supposition, no longer existing at the moment of present existence, and nothing can cause an effect in a place, or a time, where it is not present. The past moment is gone, and can have no more effect on the present than a moment of existence twenty years ago. So momentary existence must be the immediate action of God.[123]

These arguments do not work, of course. Ingenious as the second line is, Edwards had allowed as far back as *Of Atoms* that the condition of being adjacent was sufficient for cause to apply spatially;[124] if the temporal analogy may not be made, he needs to demonstrate why. The first argument is simply question-begging: he wishes to argue that something cannot be the cause of its own continuation, on the basis of an assertion that it cannot be the cause of its own continuation. Apparently, Edwards recognises these problems, since his next move is to allow 'that the established course of nature is sufficient to continue existence, where existence is once given'.[125] This prompts him to expose his underlying argument: on the basis of his understanding of the nature of created reality, 'the established course of nature' is nothing other than God's agency. So we have a statement of a standard theme in reference to

---

[121] *Essay Concerning Human Understanding* 2.27.11.
[122] *YE3*, p. 398; see my earlier comments on Edwards' construction of personal identity in relation to Christology: chapter 4 pp. 139–42.
[123] *YE3*, pp. 400–1.
[124] See p. 83 in chapter 3 above.
[125] *YE3*, p. 401.

creation: 'God's *preserving* created things in being is perfectly equivalent to a *continued creation*, or to his creating those things out of nothing at *each moment*.'[126]

I have already discussed the validity of this understanding of creation,[127] but with it, Edwards' doctrine of imputation follows naturally. If all created identity is arbitrary divine constitution, then to object that God cannot establish such-and-such an identity because to do so would be arbitrary is to pursue a signally fruitless line. Jenson sees much of the breakdown of communal identity in the Enlightened nation of the United States as due to precisely this flaw: identity can be imposed only by arbitrary divine decision; to attempt to live without recourse to the divine, the grand Enlightenment experiment, is inevitably to attempt to live without identity, even, in the last analysis of Sartre, identity with myself.[128]

Turning to Edwards' response to the accusation that his doctrine makes God the author of sin, the reply is far less satisfactory. He makes a distinction between the idea of sin as something added to human nature, and the witholding of certain divine influences without which human nature will inevitably fall into sin.[129] As already noted, part of the punishment for Adam's transgression is God-forsakenness, so all who follow Adam are solely under the influence of natural and inferior principles, and so become wholly corrupt, as Adam did.[130] Thus a distinction between God creating sin and permitting sin is introduced, but the force of Edwards' argument depends on a further invocation of his understanding of providence as continuing creation, and a simple *tu quoque*

---

[126] *YE3*, p. 401.
[127] See pp. 92–4 in chapter 3 above.
[128] Jenson, *America's Theologian*, pp. 150–1.
[129] *YE3*, pp. 380–1.
[130] *YE3*, p. 383. Once again, Edwards is reminiscent of Aquinas in his understanding of depravity. This is all the more striking since Calvin, at the start of the Reformed tradition, had offered a different, and arguably better, understanding, of every human faculty being ruined, rather than a divine faculty being taken away and the rest left untouched. See *Inst.* II.1.8-11; *Summa* Ia IIae q. 85.

argument:[131] if Edwards' position makes God the author of sin because human beings are created in sin, then so do his opponents' positions, because human beings are permitted to continue in sin.[132] This is Edwards' first response to the same issue when he turns to it in *Freedom of the Will*:[133] once again, the *tu quoque* argument is to the fore.

In order to be as fair as possible to Edwards at this point, we must recognise that he assumes that there is no position which does not make God the 'author of sin' in some sense – God created all things, and so, finally, all things come from Him.[134] Edwards' point in his *tu quoque* is that this is no more the case for a 'Calvinist' than for an 'Arminian'. This given, his point must be accepted, although we might have wished he had displayed more concern about the issue.

So much for *Original Sin*. My question for this chapter concerned the justice of hell: can it ever be just for God to create human beings for no purpose other than to glorify Himself by damning them, as, according to Edwards, He does? The responses I have found in Edwards reduce to a bracketing of the problem of theodicy. He *argues* that his opponents have as much trouble with this issue as he does; on the basis of this, he *asserts* that there is no theological scheme which can offer a better answer, and so takes refuge in the classical, 'Who are you, O man, to answer back to God?'. This, however, will not do. In the federal theology, with a broadly nominalist understanding of God's goodness, this approach was available; even for

---

[131] 'tu quoque' = 'you also'; this refers to an argument which attempts to establish that the opponent also believes the very thing that he or she is castigating the speaker for. It may be observed very regularly in political discourse. To have any serious logical force, however, the argument must establish that there is no possible position which does not assume the disputed point, otherwise the most that can be proved is that 'we're both wrong'.

[132] *YE3*, pp. 386–8.

[133] *YE1*, pp. 397–9.

[134] '... it is impossible in the nature of things to be otherwise....' (*YE3*, pp. 399–400). This point depends, of course, on the supposition that Edwards' contention that views of the will as self-determining are incoherent is accepted.

Calvin, who seems to be more realist in his thinking, an invocation of the doctrine of accommodation made this line possible (if not useful[135]); for Edwards, however, with an understanding of virtue that is not just realist but Lockean, so that what is just must be self-evidently so (at least to the saints) such an approach simply could not be acceptable.[136] Edwards must have believed, on his own premises, that the transparent justice of his position was demonstrable, even if he did not have a demonstration. A comfortable refuge in mystery was simply not an option.

Concluding Reflections

For Edwards hell, like every other area of the great drama of God's actions in creation and redemption, was bent towards the increase of God's glory. To show that it would achieve this purpose, he must demonstrate that it was entirely in accord with divine justice. My contention thus far has been that, finally, he failed to do that. This final section is an attempt to explore other discussions concerning the nature and use of hell in order both to see how Edwards' thought may be appropriated, and to discover possible lines for recasting Edwards' doctrine in a stronger form.

Firstly, I wish to return to the incoherence that I have suggested is present in Edwards' position: even bracketing the question of theodicy, his arguments concerning the usefulness of hell prompt a question. If we accept that

---

[135] To the extent that Calvin's attempts to give assurance to believers through the doctrine of election founder on the hidden decree, as Barth, amongst others, suggest (*CD* II/2, pp. 334–9), this move is the problem.

[136] This point is perhaps best demonstrated by comparisons with what has gone before: 'beauty' is self-defining, according to *True Virtue*; the 'new simple idea' of God given in salvation 'naturally shines' – justice, then, must also be visibly just, at least to the regenerate mind. At one point in the *Miscellanies* Edwards seems to accept this argument, but suggests that there may well be things in the world that, although they make sense, we will not be able to understand until their meaning is revealed to us in heaven. This, he suggests, is in fact quite likely, as it will give us a greater sense of God's perfections, and so lead to God being glorified all the more: *Miscellanies* 654 (unpublished).

God's perfections are most glorious in their exercise, and that justice is a perfection of God that is appropriately glorified, and that God's justice is best displayed in the awfulness of His judgement on sin, then some doctrine of hell does seem to follow. Equally, if the saints' sense of God's mercy and grace is stronger through seeing what they have been saved from, then again, hell would seem to be necessary. But the question presents itself: how many people must be in hell for God to be thus glorified? There is, of course, an obvious answer: one. And the Creed will tell us who that One is: 'He descended into hell . . . .'

Edwards was a Reformed theologian, so I will invoke a Reformed understanding of the *descensus*. Calvin, in the *Institutes*,[137] identifies Christ's descent into hell with His experiencing the pain of separation from the Father on account of sin on the cross. Whether we wish to adopt some further conception of the harrowing of hell or not, that Jesus Christ endured both the *poena sensus* and the *poena damni* on the cross seems beyond doubt. If it is really necessary for the saints in heaven to have a sight of what they have been saved from, if they really need some visual reminder of the strength of God's hatred of sin, then both are there for them: the Lamb bearing the marks of slaughter is seated on the throne; the 'wounds yet visible above' are indeed 'in beauty glorified'.[138] If God's justice must be displayed to be glorified, if His mercy may not be fully glorified without a sight of the terribleness of His anger, then the cross, not hell, must be where these things come to pass.[139]

This raises in an acute form the point I have mentioned in passing several times in the discussion in this chapter: in chapter 2 of this book I argued that Edwards' account of

---

[137] *Inst.* II.16.8–12.
[138] Edwards does in fact link the sufferings of the Christ with the sufferings of the damned in *Miscellanies* 516, but without drawing any theological conclusions.
[139] The cross as God's fundamental act of self-glorification is, of course, a prominent theme in John's Gospel. I shall have more to say about this in my critique of Edwards' overall understanding of glory in the final chapter.

God's self-glorification was Trinitarian, and indeed, that it would not work were it not so. In chapter 3, I sought to demonstrate that, for Edwards, creation glorifies God again in a Trinitarian manner, and by imaging forth the gospel story, and the same is true of redemption in chapter 4 and human life in the Church in chapter 5. Now, in his doctrine of hell, the same language is being employed – hell, too, is a locus for God's self-glorification – but the language must mean something different. The Trinitarian vision of God, and the overarching metanarrative of the gospel story, seemingly have no part to play here. This is the point where I believe that Edwards finally falls foul of Luther's outspoken challenge – here, in the depths of hell, God's glory is not seen through suffering and the cross.

I will return to this, my major theme, for the concluding comments of this chapter, but a further thought may usefully be made before that: a comparison of Edwards' doctrine with current writing on hell is instructive. A survey of recent works reveals that this debate has preoccupied philosophical theologians far more than exegetes or systematicians.[140] Some contributions are easily dismissed – for instance, Marilyn McCord Adams, whose rejection of the rationality of belief in hell depends on a series of analogies along the lines of 'if I were to do x, we would surely find it unacceptable if I were to be punished by y.'[141] All such a procedure proves, of course, is that the doctrine of hell is out of step with the general opinions of twentieth-century Western liberal intellectuals, which is hardly a startling result. More serious arguments are offered by writers such as Walls and Kvanvig,[142] who at least begin with data of revelation, in particular the claim that 'God is loving' or 'God is good'.[143]

---

[140] See, for instance, Jerry L. Walls, *Hell: The Logic of Damnation* (Library of Religious Philosophy vol. 9) (Notre Dame, IN: University of Notre Dame Press, 1992); Jonathan L. Kvanvig, *The Problem of Hell* (Oxford: Oxford University Press, 1993); Thomas Talbot, 'The Doctrine of Everlasting Punishment', *Faith and Philosophy* 7.1 (Jan. 1990) pp. 19–42.

[141] Marilyn McCord Adams, 'Hell and the God of Justice', *Religious Studies* 11 (1975) pp. 433–47.

[142] See n. 140.

[143] These two are often regarded as synonyms; see Walls, *Hell*, pp. 83–4 for an example.

On the basis of an analysis of what is entailed in making these claims, usually suggesting that 'God' at least implies omnipotence and 'loving' at least implies 'desires the happiness of every conscious creature', they arrive at a variety of modified doctrines of hell, ranging from John Hick's rejection of any concept of hell,[144] to attempts to defend a fairly traditional understanding by invoking libertarian ideas of free will.[145]

When these works are set alongside Edwards' defence of God's self-glorification by condemning certain creatures to hell, a number of points stand out. Firstly, my examination of Edwards' idea of God's self-glorification in general has demonstrated a concern for God's aseity, expressed in terms of all God's 'needs' finding perfect fulfilment in His life *ad intra* as Father, Son and Holy Spirit. Ideas of aseity and, much more significantly, of the Trinity, find little place in the recent philosophical-theological literature on hell. There is an assumption that if God is loving, that must mean He is loving towards us, an assumption that depends on interpreting 'God' monadically, and necessitates making the perfection of His existence dependent on His creatures. The latter point, and a departure from aseity, may be an acceptable modification to the Christian doctrine of God, but it appears that it is required only if the doctrine of the Trinity is denied, which is no modification but a simple departure from Christian theology.

Edwards' struggle with goodness as an attribute of God is significant here: his early *Miscellanies* entries suggested that goodness, of all God's attributes, needed to find

---

[144] Hick, *Evil*, pp. 341–5. Hick's point has been effectively rebutted by Plantinga, using a 'free-will' defence. See Alvin Plantinga, *God, Freedom and Evil* (London: George Allen & Unwin, 1975) pp. 29–64. Actually, Hick shrinks from full-blown universalism, because he believes that attributing freedom of indifference to human creatures, as he is committed to doing, holds out the possibility that some will continually reject God's proffered salvation (p. 343). An epigrammatic illustration of two fundamentally different approaches to theology offers itself here: Barth will not contemplate a universalist position, because he is afraid of compromising God's freedom; Hick, wanting to embrace universalism, ultimately has to refuse to do so in order to protect the freedom of human beings.
[145] Walls, *Hell*.

exercise to be perfect. As his thought moved on, it is clear that he realised that this was a threat to God's aseity, and found in the doctrine of the Trinity a way to speak of every attribute of God finding perfect exercise without any need for the creation. So, we read in the *Miscellanies*:

> The deists, unitarians and Socinians who deny the doctrine of the Trinity cannot explain how God is essentially good and just antecedently to and independent of the creation of finite [supply 'beings'] for God cannot be emanently [*sic*] good and just when there is no object of his beneficence and equity. If then to be essentially eternally & necessarily good and just he must be so in himself he must therefore find an infinite object within himself to whom he displays all his essential love beneficence and equity.[146]

Now, this defence is not by any means complete; an obvious argument may be made, for example, that, having chosen to create, God's goodness implies that He will be good to His creation. This is certainly the case, but an important move has been made, in that this is now a second order principle, not something bound up with God's ability to be Himself – there is, in a sense, more room. God's love is perfectly exercised *ad intra*; God will be loving *ad extra*, because that is His nature, but His *bene esse*, or even *esse*, is no longer bound up with His lovingkindness to His creation.

What comes out most clearly from this comparison, however, is how much depends on which words are privileged; Edwards (and more recent scholars who explicitly follow him) privilege words such as 'mercy' and 'grace', and insist that there can be no assumption or dependence upon such attributes – 'the quality of mercy is not strained',

---

[146] *Miscellanies* 1253, p. 5 of Schafer's transcript. Although the text is not entirely clear, this appears to be a quotation that Edwards recorded from Ramsay's *Philosophical Principles of Religion*. My discussion in chapter 2, however, will have indicated that the point is a regular one in Edwards' writings.

to quote Shakespeare.[147] Modern writers, with perhaps more immediate Biblical warrant, use words like 'love' and 'goodness', and insist that there can be no exceptions to the exercise of such attributes.[148] A way through this apparent *impasse* is offered by Aquinas' insistence on the simplicity of God.[149] Once this idea is taken seriously, the game of playing off one attribute of God against another is no longer a possibility. [150] Rather, we have to find a way of taking every perfection seriously in everything we say – a position that, of course, presents a challenge to both the modern discussions and to Edwards and his followers. The former stress God's love and fail to account for God's freedom; the latter (arguably) fail to take sufficient notice of the love and goodness of God in seeking to preserve an account of His freedom in their doctrines of grace. It is indeed 'the quality of mercy' not to be 'strained', but it is Allah who is called merciful; the God and Father of our Lord Jesus Christ is unambiguously identified with love.[151]

This points towards a deeper theological reason to be unhappy with Edwards' whole concept of God's self-glorification in the damnation of sinners, a reason that John

[147] *The Merchant of Venice* Act IV Scene 1; Portia makes this observation after stating 'Then must the Jew be merciful', eliciting the response 'On what compulsion must I? tell me that' from Shylock. For the point in Edwards, see for instance, 'Eternity of Hell Torments' *BT2*, p. 83; 'All God's Method's are Most Reasonable' *YE14*, p. 172. See also Davidson, *Reasonable Damnation*, in which I found the Shakespeare reference. Shakespeare's point is ironic of course; the remainder of the scene demonstrates the irrational nature of pure justice. Davidson seems to have missed this irony.

[148] Walker, *Hell*, Kvanvig, *Problem*.

[149] In fact, although this idea is associated with Aquinas, he found it in Augustine's *De Trinitate*. See *Summa* 1a q. 3 art. 7 and *De Trin.* VI.6–7, where simplicity is used to demonstrate that the difference between the Persons is not accidental but relational.

[150] Perhaps an example would be helpful at this point: there is a hymn that speaks of the cross as the 'trysting place where heaven's love and heaven's justice meet.' Whatever the merits of this as religious poetry, theologically it is ruled out by this point: 'heaven's love' and 'heaven's justice' can never be separated, and so cannot be thought of as meeting.

[151] The obvious references are 1 John 4 and 1 Corinthians 13, but I would also seek to argue that this point is required by the gospel narrative – if God is as He is in Jesus Christ, then 'love' must be an appropriate word to describe His perfection.

Colwell focuses on in his Drew Lecture.[152] On the basis of the gospel story we simply cannot accept that God glorifies Himself in two equal and opposite ways, in the display of His justice and the display of His grace. In speaking of the Father of Jesus Christ, we cannot speak of God's freedom without immediately also speaking of His love. Nor, contrary to the modern discussions of hell, can we speak of His love without immediately speaking of His freedom. This is language that calls to mind Karl Barth's basic statement about the reality of God in volume II of the *Church Dogmatics*: 'the One who loves in freedom'.[153]

To speak only of 'grace', 'mercy' and 'freedom', as Edwards does, leads inevitably to the double decree and the vision of God creating some people only to torture them for all eternity in unimaginable ways – although Edwards stood in a tradition that tried hard to help our imaginations at this point! To speak only of 'love' and 'goodness' leads to a variety of approaches ranging from Origenist universalism, through Hick's near-universalism, to broadly Wesleyan Arminianism. So it will not do to speak in either of these ways. We must acknowledge that God is God, against the latter, and that God is love, against the former, and so, as Barth does, deny universalism, but so affirm the grace and mercy of God that we are constantly drawn in that direction.[154] Only by doing this can we do justice to God's self-revelation in Jesus Christ.

A brief recapitulation will end the chapter. I began by seeking to place Edwards within his tradition, and so to highlight the 'vision across the chasm', the one feature of his doctrine of hell that was genuinely out of step with contemporary thought. On the basis of this, I sought to expose Edwards' underlying concerns in his discussions of

---

[152] Colwell, 'Glory', pp. 303–5: see n. 1 above.

[153] Title of §28 (CD II/1 p. 257) and expounded throughout the rest of II/1 and II/2.

[154] It is bizarre that there is still a debate about whether Barth was a universalist, given his repeated denials of the position. The question of how he thought he was able to avoid universalism is far more interesting. To my mind the best contribution is J. E. Colwell, *Actuality and Provisionality: Eternity and Election in the Theology of Karl Barth* (Edinburgh: Rutherford House, 1989).

hell, showing once again that the promotion of God's glory
was central. In discussing how Edwards saw God being
glorified here, I underlined the justice of hell as the
primary concern and argued that, from Edwards' own
position, this was finally indefensible. My discussion has
once again, from two different angles, sought to show that
this failure is a result of a prior failure to let the gospel
story inform his position sufficiently. This chapter has been
my most critical of Edwards. Here I have indicated the
point where I believe that his theology breaks down in a
major way – his own best instincts of God's Trinitarian,
gospel-shaped, self-glorification fail him. Finally, the
charge I have borrowed from Luther will stick.

7
God of Grace and God of Glory

Uncritical eulogies are out of fashion in theological histori-ography; perhaps unusually amongst intellectual fashions, this is probably to be welcomed. If, this side of the End, we can see only through a glass darkly; if the best of us are fallen, unrighteous and flawed, then there can be no place for simple assertions that such-and-such a writer was consistently insightful and simply correct in everything he or she produced. I have tried to expose a particular feature of Edwards' theology, and a linked flaw. It remains only to explain why I think that the positions I have been analysing in the previous chapters represent a theological triumph. I have quoted already Luther's uncompromising assertions: 'He deserves to be called a theologian who comprehends the visible and manifest things of God seen through suffering and the cross.'[1] In the previous chapter I suggested that this condition points directly to an obvious flaw in Edwards' theology; my major argument in this conclusion will be that this flaw is obvious only because Edwards was so much righter than the tradition he inhabited.

Summary and Prospect

A brief recapitulation of the main points of the argument is probably in order, however, before any attempt is made to interpret its significance. God created the world for the promotion of His own glory. That much is common to the tradition. What is somewhat less common, in the Reformed tradition at least, is any sustained discussion of what it might mean to say this. I have argued that Edwards described God's act of self-glorification using Trinitarian grammar, and so suggested that this was an act of divine

---

[1] From the Heidelberg Theses; see chapter 2 above, p. 76.

ekstasis, of the sending of the Son and Spirit by the Father. This *ekstasis* is directed towards a sharing or enlargement of the triune life, as the Church, finding its being in the Son and filled with the Spirit, shares God's own life and joys. A comparison with one of Edwards' sources, van Mastricht, sought to make the point that the surprisingly strong doctrines of immanence and *theosis* present in Edwards' account are a direct result of the Trinitarian nature of that account.

Having sketched the contours of this divine act of self-glorification, I have sought to show how it informs Edwards' theology in relation to various doctrines. With reference to the created order and its history, I suggest that Edwards' theology of creation is a largely successful attempt to hold to Trinitarian doctrine in the face of the philosophical ambiguities of modernity. Three points in particular are important here: firstly, Edwards needed to find an intellectually satisfying 'theistic Newtonianism' if he wished to give a teleological account of the created order, and that in what has been referred to as his idealism he succeeds in this; secondly, Edwards' metaphysics is much more robust than Bishop Berkeley's apparently very similar system – this again due to Edwards' thoroughgoing Trinitarianism; and thirdly, his typological scheme, freely extended to nature and history, is the content he gives to this teleological account; nature and history are simply the network of the self-revealing and self-giving of God, and can be interpreted as such through the gospel story. By asserting such positions, I suggest, Edwards was able to develop a remarkably robust and satisfying doctrine of the self-giving and so self-glorification of the triune God in creation.

Moving into the realm of soteriology, the gift of salvation is mediated by the Son and the Spirit, and so the gospel story is (for Edwards) a narrative of dynamic inter-Trinitarian relationships. It is remarkable here just how central Edwards makes the crucifixion of Christ, as he speaks of the cross as God's first and best thought. It is precisely at this point, however, that the first discordant note is heard, as the perdition of the damned seems to lack any Trinitarian logic. Given the logic of creation that I have uncovered here, this leaves the non-elect in the perilous position of lacking true humanity, or indeed true being – and one would have thought that their position was quite perilous enough in the old Calvinist logic without heaping this on them!

This concern is only amplified when we consider the two ways of being that are available to humanity. Although Edwards offers little in the way of systematic ecclesiology, those positions that he does adopt concerning life in the Church make entire sense when expounded in terms of this Trinitarian logic of God's self-giving, whereas they appear at least incongruous if not explained this way. Edwards' account of life beyond the boundaries of the Church, however, whilst still using the language of God's self-glorification, appears to rely on a different logic. In particular, I have argued that the specific ways in which Edwards claims hell promoted God's glory finally rely on unsustainable positions concerning the nature and visibility of divine justice, and that the failure here was precisely that Edwards' doctrine of perdition was neither Trinitarian in form nor crucicentric, this latter point being supported by using comparisons with Barth and the more recent philosophical tradition.

Having argued these points, I now attempt in this final chapter to make use of them, and that in two different ways: first by exploring the relevance of such an account for the interpretation of Jonathan Edwards' thought, and so attempting to make some contribution to our under-standing of the work of this significant and creative theologian; second, I will consider what light my conclu-sions may shed on the systematic task of understanding the relationships and coherence of Christian doctrinal claims.

Edwards' Vision of Glory

There is a question to be asked concerning the interpret-ation of Edwards' theology here. 'In a theologian of

Edwards' stature', asserts Conrad Cherry, 'there are a number of fundamental and distinctive motifs operative, and his outlook cannot be reduced to any one of them. Nevertheless, any one of a number of motifs may serve as a window though which we may observe other aspects of his thought'. Whilst accepting Cherry's point that there can never be one major theme in, one right way to approach, any theologian, we may observe that particular approaches give a better view of the whole, are larger and better-placed windows, so to speak.[2]

Given that, it would be audacious in the extreme to claim that the concept of divine self-glorification was *the* central theme of Edwards' theology, and such a claim would require an analysis of a number of other themes that scholars have identified as important to Edwards to demonstrate their peripheral nature. I will, however, address the question of the central categories of Edwards' thought in a more modest way. Generally, no doubt because of the popularity of the revival writings, Edwards has been analysed in terms of human response to God. So, for example, Conrad Cherry centred his discussion on faith, several commentators have found the question of the nature of 'the sense of the heart' to be determinative, and Anri Morimoto looked at salvation.[3] The chief contribution, in my estimation, of a more recent work, McClymond's *Encounters with God*,[4] lies in the assertion that Edwards' thought was God-centred. This was not missed by earlier commentators (Holbrook's description of 'theological objectivism' springs to mind[5]) but it has perhaps never been given the prominence it deserves. In stressing a reflexive act of God as a significant theme in Edwards' thought, I have tried to lend weight to the idea that one gets closer to the centre of that system by focusing on God in Himself, rather than on human relationships to God.

---

[2] Cherry, *Theology*, p. 7.
[3] Cherry, *Theology*; Morimoto, *Catholic Vision*.
[4] M. J. McClymond, *Encounters*. See particularly pp. 4, 28–30.
[5] Holbrook, *Ethics*, pp. 2–7.

I also hope, however, to have moved that claim forwards slightly: it is not the bare fact of God, but the dynamic life of God, that is so central to Edwards. Hence my repeated stress on the Trinity: the being and history of the world is a generous overflowing of the being and life of the Triune God, and finds its meaning in the eschatological enlargement of that life. Such a vision would be either meaningless or pantheistic without a robust and active doctrine of the Trinity.

As I have indicated, this is a point of emphasis rather than a new approach to Edwards. Of more interest, perhaps, is the place of the 'flaw' I have found in my interpretation of Edwards: to return to the 'windows' metaphor, is this a minor issue, which merely looks large from this particular viewpoint, or is it a major structural problem?

Interestingly, most students of Edwards' theology seem to believe that there is some sort of a contradiction at the heart of it. To use only the most famous illustration, most theologians who have studied Edwards would broadly agree – as would I – with the following opinions of Douglas Elwood:

> ... as the foundation of goodness in God, Edwards ... stressed absolute beauty ... God is sovereign because he is good, not good because he is sovereign ... God is not so much power-itself as he is love-itself. In creating a world he is moved not by a lust for power but by the power of love.[6]

But Edwards could, and did, preach passages such as the following:

> The bow of God's wrath is bent, and the arrow made ready on the string, and justice bends the arrow at your heart, and strains the bow, and it is nothing but the mere pleasure of God, and that of an angry God, without any promise or obligation at all, that keeps the

---

[6] Douglas J. Elwood, *The Philosophical Theology of Jonathan Edwards* (New York: Columbia University Press, 1960) p. 30.

arrow one moment from being made drunk with your blood . . .[7].

Perry Miller tried to rehabilitate Edwards by bracketing his theology *in toto*; the more recent fashion has been to bracket the imprecatory sermons,[8] to claim that these are not a major part of the corpus (true), not representative of much of it (also true) and so can be safely ignored (which of course does not follow).[9] Any complete account of Edwards' theology should illuminate and identify the disjunction that is clearly present here.[10]

To take one example, from the best study, Jenson identifies what he sees as the flaw in Edwards' theology: the lack of ontological weight given to the word in all its forms. This, however, sheds no light on the recurrent problem of the imprecatory sermons, and so is ultimately unsatisfactory as a complete criticism, however useful it is in a

[7]   'Sinners in the Hands of an Angry God', 'Application' (*BT2*, p. 9).
[8]   Norman Fiering remarks on 'the efforts of some modern interpreters to make the doctrine of hell merely a footnote to Edwards's other speculations': (*Moral Thought*, p. 200).
[9]   I am not sure I have ever seen this argument made explicitly, but the first two points are regularly made and then, with no further reason offered, these sermons are ignored. It is difficult to see what other reasoning may be operative. This tendency has become so marked that the author of one recent study on Edwards' doctrine of salvation argued that his logic allowed for a 'wider hope' without feeling any need to refer to the imprecatory texts (Morimoto, *Catholic Vision*, pp. 62–8). As it happens, I agree with the point; but it surely cannot be made without a detailed discussion of texts that point so strongly in the opposite direction.
[10]   Robert Lowell's poem, 'Jonathan Edwards in Western Massachusetts', illustrates that this is not just a problem perceived by the theological community. To extract some stanzas:
   Poor country Berkeley at Yale,
   you saw the world was soul,
   the soul of God! The soul
   of Sarah Pierrepont! . . .
   Then God's love shone in sun, moon and stars,
   on earth, in the waters,
   in the air, in the loose winds,
   which used to greatly fix your mind. . . .
   You gave
   her Pompey, a Negro slave,
   and eleven children.
   Yet people were spiders . . .
(From *For the Union Dead*, London: Faber & Faber, 1966, pp. 40–4.)

variety of other areas. I have repeatedly referred to the 'flaw' in Edwards' theology; in crystallographic terms, a 'flaw' is a fault where well-arranged structures on either side fail to meet. On the one hand, Edwards holds to a Reformed and Puritan doctrine of perdition that makes sense on its own terms; on the other he reformulates doctrines of God and creation in the face of the growing Enlightenment challenge. But the two will not hold together – and my analysis in the previous chapter of his attempts 'to justify God's ways to man' in this area suggest strongly that he was aware that this join would not hold. My discussion, I suggest, illuminates the nature of this flaw; it does not explain its origin. To explore this further, it is necessary to move from historical questions to systematic ones.

The Cross as the Locus of God's Self-Glorification

The first systematic question to be asked is the most basic: Edwards gives a theological account of God's glorification; in exploring that account, I have thus far asked about its internal and theological coherence without relating it particularly to the Scriptures. This section is an attempt to do that, to ask if Edwards' account is not just coherent but right, when measured by the canon of Scripture. I suggest that it is: in the gospel stories, it is not the works of power which primarily declare God's glory, although this is a feature. It is not even the resurrection and ascension that do this. Rather, it is the condescension, suffering and death of Jesus. This is the force behind Luther's bold assertions.

This is true in all four gospels, although in different ways. Amongst the synoptics, Luke's account of the birth of Jesus has the angels declaring the *gloria in excelsis* – but declaring it to shepherds, not kings, and declaring it to announce an act of divine self-limitation. The words and works of Jesus lead those around to marvel and so to glorify God throughout the first three gospels,[11] but the

---

[11] For example, the healing of the paralytic in Mt. 9:1–8 (parallels Mk 2:1–12 and Lk 5:17–26), results in all three gospels in the crowds giving glory to God.

crowds are precisely those who desire to 'look upon the visible things of God as though they were clearly perceptible in those things which have actually happened', and so to 'call good evil and evil good', to quote Luther once more.[12] The crowds, that is, are those who seek a Messiah after the patterns that Jesus rejected when tempted by Satan. The theme is particularly interesting in Luke's Gospel, with its pictures of the way the Gentiles are more open to God's plan than God's people of old. It is the centurion who glorifies God when he sees Jesus die, not the people who 'were entrusted with the oracles of God' (Romans 3:2).

It is the fourth gospel, however, with its rich usage of the language of glory in connection with the cross, that makes the point most emphatically. Apart from the comment that Jesus 'had not yet been glorified' in chapter 7, and the reference to Jesus beginning His ministry in 2:11, the linked concepts of Jesus' glorification and the glorification of the Father in Jesus that form such a strong motif throughout the latter part of the gospel begin in chapter 11 – Lazarus' illness is to be the occasion for God's glory to be revealed and for Jesus to be glorified. As a work of power, this may seem to disprove my point, but this miracle leads directly to the plot to kill Jesus, and so is precisely the occasion for God's glory to be revealed in the way I have suggested. As the narrative moves on, repeated references to Jesus' death as God's act of triune self-glorification are part of the literary dynamic that pushes towards the cry of *Tetelestai* ('It is done!') that is the moment of climax in the gospel. In 12:23–4 'the hour has come for the Son of Man to be glorified', an assertion immediately followed by the image of a grain of wheat dying in order to be fruitful; 'Father, glorify your name!' is the prayer of obedience that Jesus offers when He will not pray 'Father, save me from this hour' in the Johannine parallel to the events of Gethsemane. Judas' decision to betray his master is followed by another description of the reflex glorification of Father and Son in the event of the cross in 13:31–2 – and

---

[12] Heidelberg Theses 19–21.

so on through the farewell discourses, until the great priestly prayer of Jesus in chapter 17 begins with assertions and petitions about the glory that the Son gives to the Father and the glory that the Father will give to the Son at Calvary. Strikingly, in the chapters that describe the resurrection appearances of Jesus, there is only one further reference to God's glory, in 21:19, and concerning the way that the apostle Peter would glorify God in his own death. The link between the display of God's glory and the cross is evident.

Space precludes the extension of this argument into areas of Scripture other than the gospels, but the point could, I think, be carried there also: In the Old Testament, *kavod* and its derivatives refer (when applied to God) always to an act of self-manifestation, of revelation of God's character. In particular, the presence of God in the tabernacle and then the temple is the presence of God's glory,[13] and the later chapters of Isaiah link the glory of God with His salvific action.[14] These two themes, and the general theme of God's presence or self-revelation, could form the basis of an argument that the crucifixion is the culmination of the language of glory in the Old Testament.[15] Equally, in the New Testament, whilst the language of glory is more eschatological, describing the honour that will be given to God when what He has done is finally understood, what God has done is centred on the death and resurrection of Jesus.

If all this is correct, what does it mean for a theological account of God's self-glorification? Here I return to Edwards' analysis, as I described it in chapter 2 above. God's glory is the display and communication of His perfections, which are known and loved by His creatures.

---

[13] Ex. 40:34ff.; 1 Kgs. 8:11.

[14] For example, Is. 40:3ff.; 43:7.

[15] One might also refer to the reference to Jesus' glory in the Johannine Prologue, where the language gathers up many of these Old Testament motifs – the tabernacle, the Exodus, later, the temple – and points forwards towards the new locus of glorification that the cross will be. See also on this my comments on von Balthasar's reconstruction of the Biblical language of glory in chapter 2.

It is clear that Edwards believed that God is known primarily through the gospel story, and thus particularly through the humiliation and death of Jesus Christ, so the Cross is indeed the primary locus for the display of God's perfections, and hence our knowledge of them. Christian worship is the central expression of creation's love for the Creator – worship that finds its beginnings in baptism in the Spirit and into Christ's death, and which finds its consummation in the invitation 'Take, eat – this is my body, broken for you', as Christ's offering is shared by His Church in the power of the Spirit. So, again, our love for God's perfections is Cross-centred. Finally, the communication of God's perfections: Edwards interpreted this by using categories of participation, of indwelling the Son and being indwelt by the Spirit. Without extensive discussion of Biblical texts, it is clear that these are at least major Pauline pictures of salvation, and the argument might be made that they are *the* central categories. Soteriology, of course, is centred on the gospel. It seems appropriate, then, to claim that, if Edwards' definitions of God's self-glorification are adequate to the task he puts them to, of describing God's purposes for the world, then he was right to insist that these purposes are gospel-centred, and wrong at the point where he fell away from his own best insight, and spoke of God being glorified in abstraction from the gospel story.

All of which, however, is still not enough, and a final question needs to be asked: is Edwards correct to identify God's purposes in the world with self-glorification, as he describes it? The question here is one of substance, not terminology: I have indicated that the language of 'glory' was common in this connection, but also that the content that Edwards gives to this language was original, and so it would be possible to conclude that the language was appropriately used, but that Edwards filled it out in an inadequate way. Equally, it would be possible to conclude that Edwards' account of God's purposes in creating the world is of great value, but that the traditional language of glory is inadequate to it.

I have already, in my initial exposition of Edwards'

discussion, addressed some of the more obvious questions that could be raised:[16] the suspicion of Neoplatonist emanationism can easily be laid to rest; equally, Edwards has a ready defence to the charge that his account is unworthy of God in that it makes Him appear selfish; the account is coherent on its own terms, and appears to be solidly based in Scripture. The point has now come when this issue needs to be explored more systematically; in what follows, my agreement with, and borrowings from, Edwards' own discussions will be clear.

The first point is one of possibility: can we know God's basic purposes? It might seem that a pious and humble confession of ignorance is appropriate here but, as the Reformed tradition never tired of reminding us in discussing predestination, whatever God has revealed of Himself to us is for our own good, and we do ourselves disservice and God dishonour if we fail to confess what He has revealed, just as much as if we pretend to know that which He has not. More than this, however, there are three pressing systematic reasons for insisting that we can know. Firstly, simple ignorance concerning God's first purposes is likely to lead to the worst forms of nominalism – whilst we know, believe in and love the God who saves us, there will be a God behind this God about whom we know nothing, a prior purpose in God that lies hidden and makes everything we do know second-order, and so untrustworthy. Secondly, this postulate is likely to lead to a sectarian theology, in that theology is able to deal adequately with the Church, but not with the world – professing ignorance of its being and purpose.[17] Thirdly, and most tellingly, whether we construct it more philosophically in terms of God's simplicity, or in a more narrative-based manner in terms of faithfulness and singlemindedness, if we claim to know any of God's ultimate purposes, we must assume to have some knowledge of them all. God does not intend

---

[16] See chapter 2, above, particularly p. 59.
[17] I suspect that this error could be charged to at least some of the various Anabaptists and Spiritualists who formed what has become known as the 'Radical Reformation'.

one thing when He creates and quite a different thing when He redeems; His purposes are at least coherent and arguably identical. Edwards' arguments, therefore, about God having one chief end in creating the world, are sound.

So, God's purpose in creating should be knowable and should be unified – and unified with His purposes in redeeming as well. What is this purpose? Here, Edwards' arguments may be accepted almost without qualification; his examination of Biblical texts is thorough and convincing and, whilst he does not always keep the wider sweep of the Scriptural narrative in the foreground, the conclusion he comes to, that God's purpose is that He should be known, loved and experienced through the giving of His Son and Spirit, coheres very well with the central thrust of the gospel.

What are we to make of this? Firstly, Edwards was right in linking the revelation and overflow of God's glory so thoroughly to the gospel story. It is not just that God is active in the world in making His character known, a character that is so overwhelmingly beautiful that all who see and under-stand will necessarily be drawn to praise and glorify Him; it is that God makes His character known only and precisely through His self-giving in the gospel – fundamentally, through the death and resurrection of Jesus. Secondly, Edwards' failure to carry this through with relation to the doctrine of perdition was not just a failure of logic or coherence in his particular system, but a failure of theology – it lacks coherence, not just with the rest of Edwards' thought, but also with the Biblical texts. Any theology that claims to be Biblical must, amongst many other conditions, refuse to speak of God's self-glorification apart from the cross and resurrection of the Lord Jesus Christ.

This failure is, however, theologically interesting. Edwards borrowed his basic assertion that God created the world for the promotion of His own glory from the tradition, although he developed it in distinctive ways. Further, his account of perdition is no more than in line with broad strands of the tradition. This sug-gests that, by offering a modified account of God's self-glorification, he exposes problems within a tradition of doing theology that may be illuminating in understanding that tradition.

The History of Reformed Theology

By 'Reformed theology' I am referring to the broadly coherent tradition of Christian thought and practice that, in its continental European manifestations, defined itself against the Lutheran and Roman Catholic traditions and in its Anglophone versions defined itself against Roman Catholicism and Anglicanism. Space precludes the inclusion of an argument against the idea of the doctrine of predestination as the defining point of 'Reformed theology', but it is an idea that I am unhappy with. A less sweeping and, I think, more defensible suggestion is that one of the distinctive features of Reformed theologies is a particular, and broadly similar, view of predestination. Whilst I cannot argue this point fully in the present context, some pointers as to the direction the argument might move in can be given.

When Loraine Boettner wrote on the doctrine of the divine decrees in the early part of this century, he felt able to entitle his treatment *The Reformed Doctrine of Predestination*.[18] Barth responded sharply to this study,[19] but he responded because he felt that the Reformed doctrine was inadequate,[20] not because of any quarrel with the idea of presenting several centuries of Reformed thinking on this subject in such a monolithic way. More recent historical study has, of course, muddied the waters somewhat. Two ongoing discussions in particular stand out: the recognition that federal Calvinism was something

---

[18]   n.p: Presbyterian and Reformed, 1968.
[19]   *CD* II/2, pp. 36–8; 46–7.
[20]   '... it cannot be our present task simply to take one of the classical forms of the traditional doctrine and to present it as integrally as possible – as, in the case of the Calvinistic form, Loraine Boettner has recently attempted to do ...' (*CD* II/2, p. 13).

different from the thought of Calvin himself;[21] and a series of arguments concerning the nature of faith and the relationship between Christ and the decree that have usually been treated by the same authors, sometimes in a fairly heated manner, and can be summed up by the sobriquet: the 'Calvin against the Calvinists' debate.[22] However, these do not prevent a distinctive, and still remarkably coherent, Reformed tradition stretching from Calvin through Dort to Warfield and Barth. I suggest that two features define this tradition: the attempt to use the doctrine of predestination to give assurance, and the shape given to expositions of the doctrine.

The latter point is an observation relating to the Remonstrance and the Synod of Dort. In virtually all Reformed theology, the doctrine of predestination is expounded in terms of the five points – whether the writer is defending them, attacking them or seeking to make modifications, still the questions asked by the Remonstrants define the shape in which the doctrine is

---

[21]   The arguments as to whether federalism is merely a systematisation of ideas already present or latent in Calvin, or whether it is something new (perhaps learnt from Bullinger) that changes the system decisively, need not be addressed here. For various contributions see, J. Wayne Baker, *Heinrich Bullinger and the Covenant: The Other Reformed Tradition* (Athens, OH: Ohio University Press, 1980); Jens G. Møller, 'The Beginnings of Puritan Covenant Theology', *Journal of Ecclesiastical History* 14 (1963) pp. 46–67; Holmes Rolston III, 'Responsible Man in Reformed Theology: Calvin versus the *Westminster Confession*', *Scottish Journal of Theology* 23 (1970) pp. 129–56; Charles S. McCoy, 'Johannes Cocceius: Federal Theologian', *Scottish Journal of Theology* 16 (1963) pp. 352–70; Stoever, *'A Faire and Easie Way to Heaven'*; Stephen Strehle, *Calvinism, Federalism and Scholasticism: A Study of the Reformed Doctrine of Covenant* (Bern: Peter Lang, 1988); von Rohr, *Covenant*; David A. Weir, *The Origins of the Federal Theology in Sixteenth Century Reformation Thought* (Oxford: Clarendon Press, 1990).

[22]   Notable contributions are: Basil Hall, 'Calvin against the Calvinists', in G. Duffield (ed.) *John Calvin: A Collection of Distinguished Essays* (Grand Rapids, MI: Eerdmans, 1966) pp. 19–37; Paul Helm, *Calvin and the Calvinists* (Edinburgh: Banner of Truth, 1982); R. T. Kendall, *Calvin and English Calvinism to 1649* (Oxford: Oxford University Press, 1979); Muller, *Decree*; James B. Torrance, 'Covenant or Contract? A Study of the Theological Background of Worship in Seventeenth Century Scotland' *Scottish Journal of Theology* 23 (1970) pp. 51–76.

expounded.[23] Supralapsarianism and infralapsarianism
are alike positions which accept the five points; even
Amyraldianism was discussed in these terms.[24] Just as it
was impossible after Nicea for the Greek-speaking church
to discuss the Trinity without using the word *homoousios*,
however unhelpful some might have felt it, so Dort gave a
particular   agenda   to   discussions   of   predestination
amongst those who regarded that Synod as having some
level of authority, which is to say, within the Reformed
tradition.

The former point relates to the most innovative of
Calvin's contributions in this area: there is nothing
particularly original about his doctrine of predestination,
but the use he gives it, of replacing sacramental theology
as the grounds for Christian hope, is certainly original. In
the medieval church the combination of efficacious sacraments and a doctrine of purgatory meant that theological
reassurance was available for anyone disposed to
question their salvation, or troubled by fears of hell. The
Reformation removed the 'safety net' of purgatory – but
in its Lutheran form at least retained the efficacy of
the sacraments and (particularly) the proclamation of the
Word. The Zwinglian version of Reformed theology,
however, did away with this also, leaving no answer to
the terrible question, 'But how can I know I am saved?' for
religiously serious people. The Anabaptist response –
assurance comes from my consciousness of having done
the right things – was, of course, no assurance at all, and
in any case rank Pelagianism; Calvin's alternative was to

---

[23] Evidence for this contention can be found in the works cited above.
[24] '... unquestionably the predominant design of [the Saumur
theologians] was to restore what [they] firmly believed to be the teaching
of Scripture, Calvin and the Dort Canons concerning the matter of predestination' (Brian G. Armstrong, *Calvinism and the Amyraut Heresy: Protestant
Scholasticism and Humanism in Seventeenth-Century France* [London:
University of Wisconsin Press, 1969], p. 142). Again, 'Amyraut himself
often asserted that his position was the same as that of Dort.' (G. Michael
Thomas, *The Extent of the Atonement: A Dilemma for Reformed Theology from
Calvin to the Consensus (1536–1675)* [Carlisle: Paternoster, 1997]).

locate assurance in the promise of God, specifically election.[25]

It is clear from Calvin's treatment that this is his purpose. Within the first paragraph on election in the 1559 *Institutes*, Calvin insists that '[w]e shall never be clearly persuaded, as we ought to be, that our salvation flows from the wellspring of God's free mercy until we come to know his eternal election . . .'.[26] As the account moves on we read that 'Satan has no more grievous or dangerous temptation to dishearten believers than when he unsettles them with doubt about their election.' And again:' . . . the mind could not be infected with a more pestilential error than that which overwhelms and unsettles the conscience from its peace and tranquillity towards God'.[27]

However, when Calvin introduces the idea of temporary faith in his discussion of reprobation, this purpose fails.[28] Those with 'temporary faith', according to Calvin, may have 'signs of a call that are similar to those of the elect' but lack 'the sure establishment of election'.[29] In this case, however, the question is surely still open: how can worried believers know whether what they experience is a 'sure establishment' or merely 'signs . . . that are similar'? I will return to this question.

The tradition that followed Calvin was thus faced with an important pastoral question. Whatever may be thought of the central thesis of R. T. Kendall's *Calvin and English Calvinism*, his evidence surely demonstrates his contention that 'the fundamental concern in the theology of Perkins and his followers centres on the question, How can one

---

[25] Given Calvin's doctrine of the sacraments – the faithful fulfilment of God's promise by His Spirit – a new, and I think more satisfying, version of sacramental assurance was theologically available to him. Whilst his introductory statements concerning the Lord's Supper suggest that this was at least in his mind (*Inst.* IV.17.1), he offers alternative loci for assurance (particularly election), and does not particularly stress this one. In response to Lutheran polemic, later Reformed theologians tended to adopt a Zwinglian view of sacrament where this possibility was not open, and so assurance remained linked to election.

[26] *Inst.* III.21.1.

[27] Both from *Inst.* III.24.4.

[28] *Inst.* III.24.7–9.

[29] Both *Inst.* III.24.7.

know he is elect and not reprobate?'[30] Wallace identifies a 'Reformed tradition' of predestinarian teaching from the earliest days of the Reformation, and highlights the desire to give 'comfort and assurance' as one of the distinctives of this tradition. As he traces through the anglophone developing tradition, he indicates that this distinctive grows in importance.[31] The Puritan tradition was perhaps more devoted to explicitly practical theology than continental Reformed theology,[32] but the point may also be found there:[33] 'The uses of this doctrine are many and outstanding in the Church of Christ. But these uses reach their full effectiveness, only when the elect are made surer of their election' claims the Leiden Synopsis.[34] Turretin also insists on absolute assurance of predestination.[35]

Finally, one may comment that the great concern in Barth's presentation of the doctrine of election is that it should be gospel. Not only is this clear from Barth's first comments on election, as he discusses the orientation of the doctrine, it is also abundantly clear from the discussion of rejection, which Barth defines as an attempt by a human person to live as if he or she were not the elect of God, in the face of God's decision that he or she is elected. The sense that assurance lies here is very clear in Barth's exposition.[36]

---

[30] Kendall, *Calvin*, p. 1.

[31] On this see Dewey D. Wallace, *Puritans and Predestination: Grace in English Protestant Theology 1525–1695* (University of North Carolina Studies in Religion) (Chapel Hill, NC: University of North Carolina Press, 1982), particularly, for example, his suggestion that Elizabethan alterations in the Articles of Religion were prompted by 'the growing Reformed use of predestination for providing assurance'. (pp. 31–2).

[32] See also my comments on this in chapter 5, pp. 171–3.

[33] Joel R. Beeke, *Assurance of Faith: Calvin, English Puritanism, and the Dutch Second Reformation*, American University Studies Series VII: Theology and Religion vol. 89 (New York: Peter Lang, 1991) begins with the assertion that 'one of the great struggles of the theologian and pastor of the post-Reformation churches lay within the area of personal assurance of faith . . . .'

[34] Leiden Synopsis XXIV, 41–2, quoted by Heppe, *Reformed Dogmatics*, p. 178.

[35] *Inst. Elenc. Theol.* IV.13 – see the statement of the question, and particularly §§13, 22 and 27 – this latter asserting that 'this certainty is necessary . . .'.

[36] And made all the more so if alternative loci are considered. Baptism, for example, is an ethical response to the prior assurance of God's election, not a ground for assurance in itself.

Thus there are continuities of purpose and of contour throughout the history of Reformed Orthodoxy, if not a precise continuity of theological content. To some extent, these continuities precede the period usually considered as 'Orthodoxy' – in Calvin, for instance – and also extend beyond it – in Warfield's defence of the five points,[37] or Barth's use of election to give assurance to the believer. If, however, there is a broadly coherent tradition of Reformed theology in the area of predestination, it seems that there is also now a broad agreement that this tradition does not work. Criticisms are rife within the tradition, whether the complaints come from the Remonstrants, Amyraut, eighteenth-century evangelicals or nineteenth-century liberals. But the welcome given to Barth's recasting of the doctrine suggests that these isolated attacks have been replaced by a near-universal rejection of this way of formulating the doctrine, amongst mainstream theologians at any rate. Whilst some still defend five-point Calvinism, there is wide agreement that what Boettner called 'The' Reformed doctrine of predestination is unsatisfactory. Where there is less agreement is in the nature of the problem.

Barth, and a series of scholars broadly following his critique, have focused on Christological issues, claiming that the Decree ousts Christ from His rightful place as the index of all God's acts. Barth made this criticism of Calvin, as well as the tradition that followed him; later scholarship has tended to revise this judgement by suggesting that Calvin was appropriately Christological, but the tradition went wrong soon after – Beza often being blamed.[38]

---

[37] Warfield, *Works*. One might almost say *passim* on this point, but see particularly 'Predestination' in vol. 2, *Biblical Doctrines* I, pp. 3–67; 'Calvinism' in vol. 5, *Calvin and Calvinism*, pp. 353–69; and vol. 6, *The Westminster Assembly and its Work*, particularly pp. 3–151. This latter makes the point that it is Westminster Calvinism more than that of Dort which Warfield defends – but the Westminster Divines held as firmly to the five points as any Anti-Remonstrant.

[38] As I have indicated already, the less careful form of the criticism made by some scholars following Barth, that in the tradition the doctrine of predestination was not Christological at all, is not supported by the evidence. A comment of Heppe's that I have already quoted makes this point sufficiently well to warrant repetition: '*Of course* the person of Christ is the foundation of election. To a certain extent he is the sole object of it . . . .' (p. 168; my italics).

Edwards is interesting in this regard: there is little doubt that his doctrine of election is appropriately Christological, and yet he can – fairly, in the sense that it is true to sermons that he preached and never disowned – be held up as an example of this tradition at its worst. It may be that a consideration of Edwards will shed theological light on a – perhaps the – central question that has been asked of the Reformed tradition of theology.

Although it has been done before, it will be instructive to review a response to this charge as levelled against Calvin:[39]

Whilst the final edition of the *Institutes* must be considered the basic source for Calvin's theology, the development of his treatment of election is instructive; through the various editions of the *Institutes* it grows in importance and, crucially, occupies different positions in the theological scheme.[40] The vital change in 1559 is to separate predestination from providence and to place it squarely under the work of the Spirit in applying Christ's benefits. So, as I have noted already, the end of Book III, 'The way we receive the grace of Christ' is the locus for predestination, in contrast to the medieval tradition, which made predestination a special case of providence, or to Augustine and Bucer, who had placed the doctrine under ecclesiology.

It is important at this point that the movement of later Reformed orthodoxy is not read back into Calvin. This doctrine is not, for Calvin, the first word concerning

---

[39] Many studies of Calvin's understanding of predestination have appeared – indeed, a disproportionate number, related to the importance of the doctrine in his own theology, if not in relation to that of those who followed him. Those I have found most instructive include Muller, *Decree*; Wilhelm Niesel, *The Theology of Calvin* (tr. Harold Knight) (Lutterworth Library vol. XLVIII; London: Lutterworth Press, 1956); J. K. S. Reid, 'The Office of Christ in Predestination', *Scottish Journal of Theology* 1 (1948) pp. 5–19 and 166–83; F. Wendel, *Calvin: The Origin and Development of His Religious Thought* (tr. Philip Mairet) (London: Collins, 1963). In addition, Barth's interactions with any scholar in history are instructive, and he carries out a long and rich (if slightly misconstrued, in my opinion) dialogue with Calvin throughout *CD* II/2.

[40] See Wendel, *Calvin*, pp. 263ff. for an instructive survey covering not just the *Institutes*, but other writings such as the *French Catechism* of 1537.

humanity in light of which all other words must be understood. Perhaps it should be – Barth certainly felt so[41] – but to give the doctrine a place different from the one Calvin assigns and then to criticise him because it fails to fulfil that role is hardly a fair, let alone an appropriately generous, way to do theology. Barth suggests a *via media*: that, for Calvin, 'election was a final (and therefore a first) word on the whole reality of the Christian life, the word which tells us that the existence and the continuance and the future of that life are wholly and utterly of the free grace of God'.[42]

The first part of this formulation is acceptable, but dangerous. In reading Calvin, as compared to later Reformed dogmatics, I would want to insist on the radical difference between 'a final (and therefore a first) word' and a first (and therefore a final) word. For Calvin, election is the first word spoken concerning the Christian life, but it is this *a posteriori* – the position of election at the *end* of Book III cannot be stressed too strongly. If election is made the *a priori* basis for a doctrine of salvation, the oft-lamented hardening of the doctrine of predestination that we see historically is almost inevitable. By this placement, Calvin avoids teaching a limited atonement,[43] is able to insist that assurance is found in Christ, not in the Decree, and

---

[41] *CD* II/2, p. 86.

[42] *CD* II/2, p. 86.

[43] This 'grim doctrine' does indeed 'logically follow' from the 'conception of predestination' that Barth claims Calvin taught – see *CD* IV/1, p. 57 – but, as will become clear, I believe Barth misread Calvin at this point in several important particulars. Sometimes it is argued that Calvin does in fact teach limited atonement (e.g. Helm, *Calvin*, pp. 13–23); these arguments, if examined carefully, tend to turn on a logical deduction: Calvin taught irresistible, personal election, and did not teach universal salvation, so he must have taught a limited atonement. This argument is not watertight logically (it requires an unstated premise that the atonement is the only efficient cause of salvation), but even if it were, showing that a position may be deduced from someone's theology is some distance from showing that that theologian realised this and accepted the position. There is no textual evidence that Calvin taught a limited atonement and so it is difficult to assert that he did. The most other arguments may show is that he was illogical in not doing this. Kendall's criticisms on this point are useful, although his alternative position (that the atonement was unlimited, but the heavenly intercession of Christ is limited to the elect) is less convincing (p. 17).

generally maintains the fluidity of his treatment, preserving both a strongly evangelical and universalising appeal to all to repent and believe, and a doctrine of God that insists on His sovereignty and priority. This balance is necessary in any account of the doctrine which will offer assurance to the believer: the 'all' of the promises is vital (as Calvin recognises[44]) to assure me that I am among the elect, and the sovereignty of God is vital to assure me that my faith rests on His constancy, not my weakness.

The standard criticism of Calvin concerns the 'hidden decree'; if this stands, then there is no assurance in Calvin's account – election and rejection are alike secret decisions of God, and I cannot know which applies to me. Reid makes this charge forcefully, with the help of a 'chance phrase' in III.22.1: '... election precedes grace. If this is true, then one's worst forebodings are fulfilled. The God and Father of Jesus Christ is a God of grace. Who, then, is this God who determines men's election before grace becomes operative?'[45] Certainly, as Reid contends, the idea that election belongs to the eternal, secret, absolute will of God is a *leitmotiv* in Calvin's account; the question remains, however, whether this eternal, secret and absolute will can be revealed. The placement of the doctrine under the work of Christ, and the Christological focus of Calvin's under-standing of revelation, suggest that this may be the case. Further, if, as I have argued, Calvin's aim in treating election is to give assurance to believers, then, making the assumption that he was not blind to the most glaring contradictions in his own theology, it seems likely that this will is indeed revealed.

All revelation, for Calvin, is revelation of the Word, Jesus Christ, who is with God and is God (I.13.7, echoing John 1). Thus revelation is God revealing Himself by means of Himself. 'For this purpose the Father laid up with

---

[44] 'But why does he say "all"? It is that the consciences of the godly may rest more secure ...' (III.24.17).

[45] Reid, p. 12. Reid misreads Calvin at this point; the phrase 'election precedes grace' occurs as part of a rhetorical question, and Calvin's whole intention is to deny the possibility that this might be true, as the context makes clear. See *Inst*. III.21.1. (I am grateful to Colin Gunton for pointing this out to me.)

his only-begotten Son *all that he had* to reveal himself in Christ so that Christ ... might express the true image of his glory.' (III.2.1; my emphasis). There is nothing of God that is not in Jesus Christ.[46] This gives content and force to Calvin's repeated insistence that we look to Christ for assurance of our election (III.24.5): 'If we have been chosen in him, we shall not find assurance of our election in ourselves; and not even in God the Father, if we conceive of him as severed from his Son. Christ, then, is the mirror where we must, and without self-deception may, contemplate our own election'.

Election, for Calvin, is in Christ, and known only in Christ. This enables Jacobs to assert that, for Calvin, 'Christ and election belong to one another inextricably – as inseparable as water and a fountain; Christ, correctly understood, is the "index": Christ is election itself.'[47] But Calvin goes further than this – in III.22.7, Christ is called the *auctor electionis*. *Auctor* (the Latin word will carry such senses as 'creator', 'maker' and 'founder', as well as the etymologically similar 'author') implies that Christ for Calvin is something more than the decree, not less, as Reid and Barth imply. In this same section Christ is represented as claiming, with the Father, 'the right to choose'. Christ is the source of the decree, not just its channel. He is the One who elects, who elects Himself to be the means by which others are elected. Calvin does not spell this out, and so perhaps leaves himself open to misunderstanding, but the conception is nevertheless there.

Given this, I would contend that the standard criticism of Calvin's account, of the concept of hiddenness, is unfair. Calvin is straining hard to offer as clear a view as he is able of the certainty of perseverance and final salvation for all who have come to Christ in faith. Having said this, there are two further areas where I believe there are weaknesses, and damaging ones, in the account of predestination

---

[46] Calvin's statement (at least) of the *extra calvinisticum* is clear in asserting that there is nothing of the Son that is not incarnate, although the Son cannot be limited to the humanity of the incarnation. See *Inst.* II.13.4.
[47] Quoted in Muller, *Decree*, p. 35.

Calvin offers. The two locations are the doctrine of eternity, and the decree of reprobation.

Firstly, the related issues of the work of the Spirit and the nature of eternity: Calvin, almost in passing, offers an adequate definition of eternity as all things being present to God (III.21.5), but then appears to treat election as something that happened before all time and is fixed, rather than offering a dynamic, pneumatological account of something that happens in time because it is happening in eternity. Any conception like this is in grave danger of lapsing into simple fatalism, as humanity is reduced to a puppet theatre, playing out scenes written long before. Certainly, Calvin does not make so gross an error, but perhaps he does not guard sufficiently against it either in these passages – his account of fallen human freedom in II.2–5 is far more careful.

Secondly, the decree that is genuinely Christless and hidden in Calvin's account is the decree of reprobation. The point at which he appears to engage in special pleading in his attempt to give assurance to believers is when he speaks of 'temporary faith' (III.24.7–9). Those with this 'temporary faith', according to Calvin, 'never cleaved to Christ with the heartfelt trust in which the certainty of election has, I say, been established for us'. They may indeed 'have signs of a call that are similar to those of the elect', but lack 'the sure establishment of election' (III.24.7). But of course such phrases achieve the very opposite of their intention, raising the spectre that there is something that masquerades as true faith but is not. How can any believer know whether he or she feels a 'sure establishment' or whether it is merely 'signs of a call similar to those of the elect'? The invitation for years of morbid introspection by later believers is surely here: with these phrases in my ears, I cannot be sure of my own salvation. There is no assurance, and so the doctrine fails in its purpose. The weakness in Calvin's account of predestination is that the doctrine of reprobation is detached, Christless, hidden in the unsearchable purposes of God. As such it bears no comparison with the doctrine of election, but remains something less than a Christian doctrine.

There is, in Calvin's account, a fundamental difference between election and reprobation. *Contra* Barth, Calvin's failure is not that he teaches a symmetrical double decree (Barth speaks of 'the classical doctrine with its opposing categories of "elect" and "reprobate" '.[48]), but that he has almost no room for the doctrine of reprobation in his account.

This difference, this asymmetry, is 'a very amiable fault'; it gives insight into Calvin the pastor, whose heart and mind were full of the glories of God's gift of salvation in Christ – so different from the caricature so often painted. Calvin's doctrine fails not because the 'No' is equal to the 'Yes', as Barth would have it, but because the 'No' does not really enter his thinking. It is a logical result of the 'Yes', and necessary for the 'Yes' truly to be 'Yes', but whereas election is bound up in his theology, it is the very fact that he is seemingly not interested in reprobation, that he has not brought it within the Trinitarian scope of his system, that makes it such a weak point. Amiable or not, it was a disastrous fault, however, because the failure to give the assurance Calvin longed to give is here, and so here is the root of all the long history of the *syllogismus practicus*. Calvin's account, then, is directed towards displaying the glories of God's grace clearly and only in the face of Jesus Christ, but remains possessed of an 'Achilles heel' which, on the witness of history, was indeed the point at which the fatal blow was struck.

So, I suggest that the problem in Calvin is to do with his doctrine of reprobation, rather than his doctrine of election, or predestination in general. If this is correct, then an interesting comparison is available: I have argued throughout this book that the same is true of Edwards. This suggests an interesting line of enquiry:

Barth's doctrine of election in *Church Dogmatics* II/2 has perhaps excited more interest than any other area of the *Dogmatics*, and has been widely praised. However, the very inventiveness of Barth's contribution makes it more difficult to decide what it is that is decisive in making this account theologically satisfying in a way that the earlier

48   *CD* II/2, p. 326.

Reformed tradition was not – particularly as it has not, perhaps, been sufficiently recognised that, for all its novelty, this remains a contribution from within Reformed theology.[49] My discussion of Calvin and Edwards suggests that the earlier lack was in the area of reprobation, rather than election, and a glance at Barth suggests that this may well be key: one of his most original moves was to offer a Christologically determined doctrine of reprobation.

For the Reformed tradition, to be reprobate was, by definition, to be separated from Christ. This point was made towards the end of chapter 4, but bears reiteration. The elect were in Christ, and so whatever might happen in the way of temporary backsliding, they remained secure. The reprobate were separated from Christ by 'a great gulf fixed', and so any goodness, religious practice, or apparent faith on their part was worthless. This is true of Calvin, and true of Edwards. It is not true of Barth.

In discussing Barth's understanding of election, the appropriate point at which to begin is again in considering the placement of the doctrine; Barth, with his encyclopaedic knowledge of theological history, believes himself to be the first person to place election as part of the doctrine of God.[50] The implications of this are immense: '[i]t is indissolubly part of the very being and essence of God that he elects. This cannot be put too strongly. The Christian God is one who elects. To be the Christian God *is* to be the one who elects, chooses, predestines.'[51] These last

---

[49] A glance at the second index, of names, demonstrates this most effectively, enabling not only a tracing of the detailed running debate with Calvin, but also the regular discussions of the various Reformed Symbols, seven references to Cocceius, eight to Polanus, five to van Mastricht, six to Wollebius' brief treatment, and so on. Bruce McCormack's recent magisterial study of the development of Barth's theology makes this point powerfully. He argues that Barth's first attempt to write a theology text, *The Göttingen Dogmatics*, was conceived after the medieval model of the 'Sentence Commentary', with Heppe's synopsis of the Reformed tradition taking the place of Peter Lombard. See Bruce McCormack, *Karl Barth's Critically Realistic Dialectical Theology: Its Genesis and Development 1909– 1936* (Oxford: Clarendon Press, 1997) pp. 329–50.

[50] *CD* II/2, p. 76.

[51] C. E. Gunton, 'Karl Barth's Doctrine of Election as Part of his Doctrine of God', *Journal of Theological Studies* NS 25 (1974) pp. 381–92, p. 381.

words illuminate a second theme: that predestination is election. Barth is emphatic in his rejection of double predestination.[52] There is no balance, no equivalence, the 'No' must be heard for the 'Yes' to be heard, but this 'No' has its existence only as part of the 'Yes' of God. God is free, but He is free to love.

Following his introduction to the doctrine, Barth rejects the standard temptation of asking about the election of an individual first. He treats first the election of Christ, then the elect community, and only once these are in place will he address the question of the individual. Christ is both the electing God and the elected man. Jacobs' words are, in the light of this section, far more true of Barth than of Calvin – Christ is the Decree. Given this, the decree for humanity is only to life, and knowledge of the decree is unambiguous gospel. Christ is the decree, however, and that includes the decree of rejection – Christ is the rejected one – God chooses for Himself the suffering, death and rejection that are the inevitable concomitant of the decree of life – the 'Yes' has a 'No' swallowed up in it, but nevertheless there – the light of God's grace casts a shadow; but this 'No', this shadow, is Christ's alone.[53]

The elect community mirrors this dual role; the one community, consisting of both Israel and the Church, is both the passing form of the community that resists God's election and the coming form of the community that witnesses to its election. The one reveals God's judgement, the other God's mercy, but both are part of the one elect community. Barth's point here is made forcefully by his consideration of Pontius Pilate:[54] in Pilate, the Gentiles join with the Jews in bringing the fulfilment of Israel's hope – 'Thus the death of Jesus unites what was divided, the elected and rejected.'[55] We see the story of Jesus Christ in the story of the elect community.

---

[52] At least as the phrase was traditionally understood. Barth, as I shall argue, teaches a double decree far more effectively than the tradition in his insistence that Jesus Christ is both the Elect and the Rejected One.
[53] *CD* II/2, pp. 162–8.
[54] *CD* II/2, p. 229.
[55] *CD* II/2, p. 229.

After this, Barth is prepared to turn to the election of the individual.[56] Each human person wills his or her own rejection by God; but God wills his or her election. Jesus Christ bears all rejection, so there is no possibility of living in the rejection that we will for ourselves. The only possibility is to live as the elect of God, to live as people loved by God.

Nevertheless, there are those who try to live in the impossible way, and they are the 'rejected'; Barth's crowning example is the long and rich section on Judas.[57] Fundamentally, as the actions of giving bread and wine and washing feet show, Jesus was for Judas, although Judas was against Jesus. The outcome of this is not revealed: we cannot conceive that Judas' choice will eventually be determinative, but neither can we presume on the grace of God. We can only hope.

Here, then, is a gloriously evangelical asymmetry – 'death is swallowed up in victory'. But for this to be truly gospel, the reality of death must be preserved. Not because death has any rights, but because God owes nothing to any person, and so we must not reach a place where we think we can presume on His grace. If we do so, it ceases to be grace and we cease to preach the gospel of grace. The question, then, turns on how Barth maintains the 'impossible possibility', how he avoids the necessity, if not the possibility, of universal salvation.

The first point to make is that those critics who try to make Barth fit the standard Reformed structure of alternatives, where the only possible positions are Calvinism, Arminianism or universalism, are simply missing the point.[58] Barth regularly and explicitly denies each of these. All people are elected; God's choice is sovereign; hell remains a possibility. The best current solution[59] seems to centre on the concept of eternity in Barth's theology. If

---

[56] CD II/2, pp. 306–506.
[57] CD II/2, pp. 458–506.
[58] J. D. Bettis, 'Is Karl Barth a Universalist?', Scottish Journal of Theology 20 (1967) pp. 423–36, suggests both Brunner and Berkouwer use this structure.
[59] So Bettis; Colwell, Actuality.

election is something happening to time, not something that has happened before time, then the problem is lessened considerably. However this serves only to replace a temporal priority with a logical one, which is undoubtedly an improvement, but perhaps not a full solution. My own suspicion, although in the absence of any serious work it remains little more than that, is that further illumination must be sought in Barth's theodicy – it is, after all, ultimately the inevitability of the 'shadow' that first causes him to speak of the decree of rejection.[60]

The very fact that Barth's doctrine has been seen as dangerously close to universalism is, of course, a point in its favour – the question for Christian theology in the light of what God has done in Christ must surely be how this can fail to affect any given human being, how anyone can fail to be saved. Thus the radical asymmetry Barth gives to the doctrine of individual election by means of his symmetrical doctrine of the predestination of Christ is entirely appropriate, and indeed necessary for *evangelical* theology. What I hope is clear, however, is the way Barth succeeds in offering a theology that is genuinely gospel – good news – by giving Christological content to perdition. To sum up in an epigram: Barth succeeds where Calvin fails because Barth had a doctrine of reprobation, where Calvin did not.

What has all this to do with my study on Edwards? I have suggested in the course of this study that Edwards' non-Christological doctrine of reprobation was incoherent, because of his doctrine of creation. Edwards has a much more Trinitarian account of the being of the world than the tradition in general,[61] and so even those who are reprobate, in that they are created beings, must have some connection to Christ and the Spirit. The earlier Reformed doctrine was coherent in its own terms – although it failed in its purpose of providing assurance; but, we may ask, were those terms

[60] *CD* II/2, pp. 169–75.
[61] This criticism will even stand for Calvin, whose doctrine of creation in Book 1 of the *Institutes* lacks the careful Christological and pneumatological shaping that characterises so much else in the work. See Gunton, *Triune Creator*, pp. 152–3.

satisfactory? It was not just a removal of Christ from the being of the reprobate, but a prior removal of Christ from the being of the created world that was the problem. The Spirit, too, becomes an ecclesial reality, no longer in any theologically relevant sense the 'Lord and Giver of Life'.[62]

Returning briefly to the tradition, this failure may have something to do with the prevalence of the infralapsarian position. Under this understanding, creation and fall are potentially part of a different order from redemption, and at best a prior, and opaque, part of the same order. Human beings were already created and fallen – and this by the decree of God – before redemption became an issue. Our knowledge of God's character and purposes, however, begin only at this point. In the supralapsarian scheme, creation was the first event in the gospel narrative; for the infralapsarian, it is a different story. Given this, God's showing of Himself to be Father, Son and Spirit in the gospel story could possibly fail to be determinative for the act of creation, according to an infralapsarian theology.

Whether for this reason or others, it is clear that the tradition was not thoroughly Trinitarian in its construction of the doctrine of creation, and so created, fallen humanity could be what it is without reference to the Son and Spirit – and so reprobation and perdition could be constructed as Christless, Spiritless doctrines. This is, as I have said, coherent in its own terms – but in Christian terms it is inadequate. As Edwards saw and argued, the God who creates is Father, Son and Spirit, and so no creaturely reality can be Christless and Spiritless. Edwards' embracing of a Trinitarian ontology was a necessary correction to the tradition. However, Edwards failed to make the second correction that this move made necessary, that of recognising that in speaking of human perdition, as

---

[62] So, for instance, Wollebius' doctrine of creation is an exposition of the six days, with the only reference to the Holy Spirit coming in an aside concerning the Incarnation. See Beardslee's translation in *Reformed Dogmatics*, pp. 54–8. It may not be too fanciful to trace from this the narrowing of the doctrine of the Spirit that has been one of the chief ironies of the rise of Pentecostal and Charismatic movements.

much as in speaking of human salvation, we can only speak in Christological and pneumatological terms.

I have argued that the failure of the Reformed doctrine of predestination was its failure to be a Christian doctrine – that is, a doctrine built and based on the gospel story – and so a refusal to speak of God's agency without speaking of God's Son and God's Spirit. I have further suggested that this relates to a deeper failure within the Reformed tradition, a failure to construct the doctrine of creation Christologically and pneumatologically. Edwards, precisely because he goes halfway towards rectifying these failures, demonstrates these theological connections with great clarity.

The first heresiarch in the Christian tradition was Marcion, whose particular ministry to the Church (in common with all the heresiarchs) was to expose the dangers that constantly face Christian theologians in a particular area. The tradition, in speaking of the Creator God and the God who redeems by different names and with different grammar, was dangerously close to the intellectual territory that bears Marcion's name. Certainly, when we read in Perkins the suggestion that Adam fulfils the same role for the reprobate as Christ does for the elect,[63] we must disagree most strongly: this may be a sophisticated form of Marcionism, but sophistication is not enough to rescue a doctrine from the anathemas.

A Modest Systematic Proposal

It is often asserted that Karl Barth has taught theologians to understand all things through the interpretative matrix of Christology; my own admiration for, and debt to, Barth's magisterial achievements in the *Church Dogmatics* will be abundantly clear by now, but I think that this statement

---

[63] Perkins speaks of God loving the elect 'in Christ with an actual love' and hating the reprobate 'in Adam with an actual hatred'. This is in connection with the creation of humanity, so we must conclude that some ontology is intended. Perkins, 'An Exposition of the Symbol' in *Works* vol. I, p. 238.

needs more care. It has been a commonplace, certainly of the Reformed tradition of theology, and one could say of the Christian tradition in general, to assert that Christ is God's full and final revelation to the world; Barth's theological advance was to see very clearly, in one or two areas more clearly than any of his predecessors perhaps, what we are committed to through saying this.

In some ways, the achievements of Jonathan Edwards two centuries earlier were very similar; my constant theme has been how a particular vision of the gospel story informs every area of his thought, from technical adjustments of the federal theology to metaphysical interpretations of Newton's physics. It is of the very essence of theology that it must claim to be able to interpret all realities; Christian theology – as Barth, and Edwards before him, and a great cloud of witnesses along with them both, saw – must interpret all things through Jesus Christ.[64]

However, Edwards failed to follow his own best insights when he spoke of those who are in rebellion against God. This the gospel narrative will not allow, and that for two reasons. First, at least one of the canonical forms of the gospel story begins with the assertion that in Jesus Christ *Immanuel* – God is with us; again, inasmuch as Jesus Christ is the 'image of the invisible God', all who are created in that image, which is to say all humanity, cannot be separated from Him; this Edwards saw, although he constructed it differently. Second, and more pointedly for the particular issue of the reprobate, the crux of the narrative is a cross; Jesus Christ becomes sin, becomes a curse, hung on a tree, amongst criminals, by gentiles – and it is this Jesus who is vindicated in resurrection, and who will reign as Lord of all. However we seek to talk

---

[64] Thus my point made in passing about Edwards' apocalyptic speculations, which was not intended to be merely humorous: the modern tendency to find such attempts to interpret history theologically no more than amusing looks more like paganism masquerading as sophistication than any intellectual advance. Edwards' interpretations were, I think, almost totally wrong, predicated as they were on the assumption that John's Revelation describes the career of Antichrist, identified with the Roman See. That he happened to be wrong should not blind us to the appropriateness of what he was trying to do.

theologically about those who are finally found in rebellion we must take with due seriousness this point that these people, also, cannot be thought of as anything other than in 'the closest conceivable proximity to Jesus Christ'.[65]

We may, as Edwards did, talk about the lost as the bearers of God's wrath. This echoes Scriptural language, and is probably the majority line in the tradition. It can, however, be sustained only if we immediately acknowledge that Jesus Christ also bore God's wrath on the tree. This is not a plea for universalism: I am not suggesting we refuse to speak about hell; instead, I am insisting that if we do speak about it we do so Christianly – a procedure which, I suspect, may finally be the only way to avoid the current stampede towards universalism in the Church. The intellectual achievement of Jonathan Edwards was breathtaking; his vision of the overarching narrative of the gospel story of God glorifying Himself through the gift of His Son and His Spirit to His unworthy creatures sought to bring all things in heaven and on earth within its compass. I am merely arguing for a correction by which whatever things may be under the earth are brought within the same narrative, so that in all, and through all the only God, the Father, Son and Holy Spirit may be glorified for ever.

---

[65] A phrase borrowed from Barth again (CD II/2, p. 458) in his long and rich discussion of Judas Iscariot, chosen for special honour by Christ, as the paradigmatic Scriptural example of the individual living as if he were rejected by God. Barth's account of reprobation in CD II/2 is the closest approach I know to what I am envisaging here.

Bibliography

(All Biblical quotations are from the Revised English Bible)

Jonathan Edwards

Collected Works

Yale Edition (referred to as *YE1, YE2*, etc.):

The Works of Jonathan Edwards, Yale University Press, New Haven, 1957–

1. *Freedom of the Will* ed. P. Ramsey, 1957
2. *Religious Affections* ed. J. E. Smith, 1959
3. *Original Sin* ed. C. A. Holbrook, 1970
4. *The Great Awakening* ed. C. C. Goen, 1972
5. *Apocalyptic Writings* ed. S. J. Stein, 1977
6. *Scientific and Philosophical Writings* ed. W. E. Anderson, 1980
7. *Life of David Brainerd* ed. N. Pettit, 1985
8. *Ethical Writings* ed. P. Ramsey, 1989
9. *A History of the Work of Redemption* ed. John F. Wilson, 1989
10. *Sermons and Discourses 1720–1723* ed. W. H. Kimnach, 1992
11. *Typological Writings* ed. W. E. Anderson, M. I. Lowance and D. Watters, 1993
12. *Ecclesiastical Writings* ed. David D. Hall, 1994
13. *The "Miscellanies", a–500* ed. Thomas A. Schafer, 1994
14. *Sermons and Discourses 1723–1729* ed. Kenneth P. Minkema, 1997
15. *Notes on Scripture* ed. Stephen J. Stein, 1998
16. *Letters and Personal Writings* ed. George S. Claghorn, 1998

Banner of Truth Edition (reprint of the Dwight/Hickman edition 1834; referred to as *BT1, BT2*)

The Works of Jonathan Edwards 2 vols, Edinburgh, Banner of
  Truth, 1974

Separate Works

Images or Shadows of Divine Things ed. Perry Miller, Yale
  University Press, New Haven, CN, 1948
'The Mind' of Jonathan Edwards: A Reconstructed Text ed.
  Leon Howard, University of California Press, Berkeley,
  CA, 1963
The Philosophy of Jonathan Edwards from his Private Notebooks
  ed. Harvey G. Townsend, University of Oregon
  Monographs Studies in Philosophy no. 2, University of
  Oregon, Eugene, OR, 1955
Remarks on Important Theological Controversies J. Galbraith,
  Edinburgh, 1796
Treatise on Grace and other Posthumously Published Writings
  ed. P. Helm, James Clarke, Cambridge, 1971
*Selections from the Unpublished Writings of Jonathan Edwards
  of America* ed. Alexander B. Grosart (printed for private
  circulation, 1865)

Unpublished Works

Box and folder numbers are given in the text to works from
the Jonathan Edwards Collection, General Collection,
Beinecke Rare Book and Manuscript Library, Yale
University. Particular works referred to in the text from
this collection are:

Blank Bible	Box 17, Folder 1216
Book of Controversies	Box 15, Folder 1203
Catalogue	Box 15, Folder 1202

As explained in the Author's Note, references to unpublished entries from the *Miscellanies* are taken either from
Thomas Schafer's transcripts, or from the versions being
prepared for publication by the *YE*.

Other Primary Sources

The Westminster Confession of Faith Free Presbyterian Publications, Glasgow, 1994 (also contains the *Catechisms, Covenants, Directories for Worship*, etc.)

Anselm, *Cur Deus Homo* in *Basic Writings* ed. Charles Hartshorne, tr. S. W. (i.e. N.) Deane, Open Court Publications, La Salle, 1962[2]

Aquinas, Thomas, *Summa Theologica* Latin text with English translation in 61 vols, general editor: Thomas Gilby, Blackfriars, London, 1964–6

Augustine works collected in *The Nicene and Post-Nicene Fathers, First Series* vols 1–8, general editor: Philip Schaff, Hendrickson, Peabody, MA, 1994 (reprint of London editions of previous century)

Barth, K. *Church Dogmatics* tr. and ed. G. W. Bromiley and T. F. Torrance, T&T Clark, Edinburgh, 1956–77

Baxter, Richard *Works* vol. 22 James Duncan, London, 1830

Beardslee, John W. *Reformed Dogmatics* Baker Book House, Grand Rapids, MI, 1977 (contains a complete translation of Wollebius' *Compendium Theologiae Christianae* and selections from Voetius and Turretin)

Berkeley, George *Works* in 9 vols ed. A. A. Luce and T. E. Jessop, Thomas Nelson and Sons, London, 1948–57

Beza, Theodore 'Summa Totius Christianismi...' in *Tractationum Theologicarum* (Secunda Æditio) Eustathii Vignon, Anchora, 1576, pp. 170–205

Bunyan, John *Christian Behaviour; The Holy City; The Resurrection of the Dead: Miscellaneous Works* vol. 3 (ed. J. Sears McGee, Clarendon Press, Oxford, 1987)

Calvin, J. *Institutes of the Christian Religion* 2 vols tr. F. L. Battles; ed. J. T. McNeill, Westminster, Philadelphia, 1960

Descartes, René *Meditations on First Philosophy* tr. and ed. John Cottingham, Cambridge University Press, Cambridge, 1996[2]

Heimart, Alan, and Miller, Perry (eds), *The Great Awakening: Documents Illustrating the Crisis and its Consequences* Bobbs–Merrill, Indianapolis, 1967

Heppe, Heinrich *Reformed Dogmatics* rev. and ed. Ernst Bizer, tr. G. T. Thomson, George Allen & Unwin, London, 1950

Hobbes, Thomas *Leviathan* ed. Richard Tuck, Cambridge University Press, Cambridge, 1991

Irving, Edward *Works* vol. V (of five) ed. G. Carlyle, Stahan, London, 1865

Locke, J. *Essay Concerning Human Understanding* 2 vols ed. A. C. Fraser, Clarendon Press, Oxford, 1894

Lowell, Robert *For the Union Dead* Faber & Faber, London, 1966

Luther, Martin *Works* (ed. Helmuth Lehmann) vol. 31: *The Career of the Reformer 1* Muhlenberg Press, Philadelphia, 1957

Owen, John *A Discourse Concerning the Holy Spirit* in *Works* vol. III (of sixteen) ed. William Goold, Banner of Truth, Edinburgh, 1965

Pannenberg, W. *Systematic Theology* vol. 2 tr. G. W. Bromiley, Eerdmans, Grand Rapids, MI, 1994

Perkins, William *Works* vol. I Cambridge, 1612

Taylor, John *The Scripture Doctrine of Original Sin Proposed to Free and Candid Examination* J. Wilson, London, 1740

Turretin, François *Institutio Theologiæ Elencticæ* (3 vols) John D. Lowe, Edinburgh, 1847

— *Institutes of Elenctic Theology* (tr. G. M. Giger; ed. J. T. Dennison) 3 vols, Presbyterian and Reformed Publishing, Phillipsberg, 1992–7 (translation of the above)

Van Mastricht, Petrus *Theoretico-Practica Theologia qua per Singula Capita Theologia, pars Exegetica, Dogmatica, Elenchtica et Practica, Perpetua Successione Conjugantur* ed. nova, Thomæ Appels, Rhenum, 1699

Urs Von Balthasar, Hans, *The Glory of the Lord: A Theological Aesthetics* (7 vols) tr. Erasmo-Leiva-Merikakis; ed. Joseph Fessio and John Riches, T&T Clark, Edinburgh, Warfield, 1982–89

Warfield, Benjamin B. *Works* (10 vols), Baker Book House, Grand Rapids, MI, 1981

Secondary Works

Adams, Marilyn McCord 'Hell and the God of Justice' *Religious Studies* 11 (1975) pp. 433–47

Almond, Philip C. *Heaven and Hell in Enlightenment England* Cambridge University Press, Cambridge, 1994

Armstrong, Brian G. *Calvinism and the Amyraut Heresy: Protestant Scholasticism and Humanism in Seventeenth-Century France* University of Wisconsin Press, London, 1969

Baker, J. Wayne *Heinrich Bullinger and the Covenant: The Other Reformed Tradition* Ohio University Press, Athens, OH, 1980

Bauckham, Richard 'The End of Secular Eschatology' (unpublished 1998 Drew Lecture; script held by the library of Spurgeon's College)

Beeke, Joel R. *Assurance of Faith: Calvin, English Puritanism, and the Dutch Second Reformation* American University Studies Series VII: Theology and Religion vol. 89, Peter Lang, New York, 1991

Bettis, J. D. 'Is Karl Barth a Universalist?' *Scottish Journal of Theology* 20 (1967) pp. 423–36

Boettner, Loraine *The Reformed Doctrine of Predestination* Presbyterian & Reformed, n.p., 1968

Braaten, Carl E. and Jenson, Robert W. (eds), *The Two Cities of God: The Church's Responsibility for the Earthly City* Eerdmans, Grand Rapids, MI, 1997

Brand, David C. *Profile of the Last Puritan* Scholars' Press, Atlanta, GA, 1991

Bromiley, G. W. *Introduction to the Theology of Karl Barth* T&T Clark, Edinburgh, 1979

Camporesi, Piero *The Fear of Hell: Images of Damnation and Salvation in Early Modern Europe* tr. Lucinda Byatt, Polity Press, Cambridge, 1990

Chai, Leon *Jonathan Edwards and the Limits of Enlightenment Philosophy* Oxford University Press, Oxford, 1998

Cherry, Conrad *The Theology of Jonathan Edwards: A Reappraisal* Doubleday, Garden City, NY, 1966; repr. Indiana University Press, Bloomington, IN, 1990

Colwell, J. E. *Actuality and Provisionality: Eternity and*

Election in the Thought of Karl Barth Rutherford House, Edinburgh, 1989

— 'The Glory of God's Justice and the Glory of God's Grace: Contemporary Reflections on the Doctrine of Hell in the Teaching of Jonathan Edwards' *Evangelical Quarterly* 67/4 (1995) pp. 291–308

Copleston, Frederick C. J. P. *A History of Philosophy* vol. V *Hobbes to Hume*, Burns, Oates & Washbourne, London, 1959

Danaher, William J. 'By Sensible Signs Represented: Jonathan Edwards' Sermons on the Lord's Supper' *Pro Ecclesia* VII (1998) pp. 261–87

Daniel, Stephen H. *The Philosophy of Jonathan Edwards: A Study in Divine Semiotics* The Indiana Series in the Philosophy of Religion Indiana University Press, Bloomington, IN, 1994

Daniélou, Jean *From Shadows to Reality: Studies in the Biblical Typology of the Fathers* tr. Wulstan Hibberd, Burns & Oates, London, 1960

Davidson, Bruce W. 'Reasonable Damnation: How Jonathan Edwards Argued for the Rationality of Hell' *Journal of the Evangelical Theology Society* 38/1 (1995) pp. 47–56

Delattre, Roland A. *Beauty and Sensibility in the Thought of Jonathan Edwards* Yale University Press, London, 1968

Derrida, Jacques 'Structure, Sign and Play in the Discourse of the Human Sciences' in David Lodge (ed.) *Modern Criticism and Theory: A Reader* Longman, London, 1988 pp. 108–23

Dodds, Elisabeth D. *Marriage to a Difficult Man: The 'Uncommon Union' of Jonathan and Sarah Edwards* Westminster Press, Philadelphia, 1971

Downey, James *The Eighteenth Century Pulpit: A Study of the Sermons of Butler, Berkeley, Secker, Sterne, Whitefield and Wesley* Oxford University Press, Oxford, 1969

Duffield, G. (ed.) *John Calvin: A Collection of Distinguished Essays* Eerdmans, Grand Rapids, MI, 1966

Elwood, Douglas *The Philosophical Theology of Jonathan Edwards* Columbia University Press, New York, 1960

Erdt, Terrence *Jonathan Edwards: Art and the Sense of the*

Heart, University of Massachusetts Press, Amherst, MA, 1980

Fiering, Norman *Jonathan Edwards's Moral Thought and its British Context* University of North Carolina Press, Chapel Hill, NC, 1981

Frei, Hans W. *The Eclipse of Biblical Narrative: A Study in Eighteenth and Nineteenth Century Hermeneutics* Yale University Press, London, 1974

Gay, Peter *The Enlightenment: An Interpretation*, Vol. 2: *The Science of Freedom* W. W. Norton, London, 1977

Gerstner, John H. *The Rational Biblical Theology of Jonathan Edwards* 3 vols Berea Publications, Powhatan, VA, 1991–3

Gilkey, Langdon *Maker of Heaven and Earth: The Christian Doctrine of Creation in the Light of Modern Knowledge* University Press of America, London, 1959

Goppelt, Leonhard *Typos: The Typological Interpretation of the Old Testament in the New* tr. Donald H. Madvig, Eerdmans, Grand Rapids, MI, 1982

Gorringe, Timothy G. *God's Just Vengeance: Crime, Violence and the Rhetoric of Salvation* Cambridge University Press, Cambridge, 1996

Gunton, Colin E. 'Karl Barth's Doctrine of Election as Part of his Doctrine of God' *Journal of Theological Studies* (NS) 25 (1974) pp. 381–92

— *The Actuality of Atonement: A Study in Metaphor, Rationality and the Christian Tradition* T&T Clark, Edinburgh, 1988

— (ed.) *God and Freedom: Essays in Historical and Systematic Theology* T&T Clark, Edinburgh, 1995

— (ed.) *The Doctrine of Creation: Essays in Dogmatics, History and Philosophy* T&T Clark, Edinburgh, 1997

— *The Triune Creator: A Historical and Systematic Study* Edinburgh University Press, Edinburgh, 1998

Haroutunian, Joseph *Piety vs Moralism: The Passing of the New England Theology* Harper & Row, New York, 1970

Hatch, N.O., and Stout, H. S. (eds), *Jonathan Edwards and the American Experience* Oxford University Press, Oxford, 1988

Helm, P. *Calvin and the Calvinists* Banner of Truth, Edinburgh, 1982

Hick, John *Evil and the God of Love* (revised edition) Macmillan, London, 1985

Holbrook, Clyde A. *The Ethics of Jonathan Edwards: Morality and Aesthetics* University of Michigan Press, Ann Arbor, MI, 1973

Holmes, Stephen R. 'Edwards on the Will' *International Journal of Systematic Theology* 1/3 (1999) pp. 266–85

— 'The Upholding of Beauty: A Reading of Anselm's *Cur Deus Homo*' *Scottish Journal of Theology* (forthcoming)

Jenson, R. W. *America's Theologian: A Recommendation of Jonathan Edwards* Oxford University Press, Oxford, 1988

Jones, Howard Mumford *O Strange New World: American Culture: The Formative Years* Chatto & Windus, London, 1965

Kendall, R. T. *Calvin and English Calvinism to 1649* Oxford Theological Monographs Series, Oxford University Press, Oxford, 1979

Kendrick, T. D. *The Lisbon Earthquake* Methuen, London, 1956

Kvanvig, Jonathan L. *The Problem of Hell* Oxford University Press, Oxford, 1993

Lampe, G. W. H., and Woollcombe, K. J. (eds) *Essays on Typology* SCM Press, London, 1957

Lee, Sang Hyun *The Philosophical Theology of Jonathan Edwards* Princeton University Press, Princeton, NJ, 1988

Levin, David (ed.) *Jonathan Edwards: A Profile* American Profiles Series, general editor Donald Aïda DiPace Hill & Wang, New York, 1969

Lowance, Mason I. *The Language of Canaan: Metaphor and Symbol in New England from the Puritans to the Transcendentalists* Harvard University Press, London, 1980

McClendon, James W. *Systematic Theology:* vol. 1: *Ethics* Abingdon Press, Nashville, TN, 1986

McClymond, M. J. 'God the Measure: Towards an Understanding of Jonathan Edwards' Theocentric Metaphysics' *Scottish Journal of Theology* 47 (1994) pp. 43–59

— *Encounters with God: An Approach to the Theology of Jonathan Edwards* Oxford University Press, Oxford, 1998

McCormack, Bruce *Karl Barth's Critically Realistic Dialectical*

Theology: Its Genesis and Development 1909–1936 Clarendon Press, Oxford, 1997

McCoy, Charles S. 'Johannes Cocceius: Federal Theologian' *Scottish Journal of Theology* 16 (1963) pp. 352–70

May, Gerhard *Creatio ex Nihilo: The Doctrine of Creation out of Nothing in Early Christian Thought* tr. A. S. Worrall, T&T Clark, Edinburgh, 1994

Miller, Perry *Jonathan Edwards* American Men of Letters Series, William Sloane Associates, n.p., 1949

— *The New England Mind: From Colony to Province* Harvard University Press, Cambridge, MA, 1953

— *The New England Mind: The Seventeenth Century* Harvard University Press, Cambridge, MA, 1954

— *Errand into the Wilderness* Harvard University Press, Cambridge, MA, 1956

— *Orthodoxy in Massachusetts 1630–1650* Beacon Press, Boston, 1959[2]

— and Johnson, Thomas H. *The Puritans* (revised edition) Harper and Row, New York, 1963

Moberly, Walter *The Ethics of Punishment* Faber & Faber, London, 1968

Møller, Jens G. 'The Beginnings of Puritan Covenant Theology' *Journal of Ecclesiastical History* 14 (1963) pp. 46–67

Morimoto, A. *Jonathan Edwards and the Catholic Vision of Salvation* Pennsylvania State University Press, University Park, PA, 1995

Morris, William S. *The Young Jonathan Edwards: A Reconstruction* Carlson, Brooklyn, 1991

Muller, R. A. *Christ and the Decree*: *Christology and Predestination in Reformed Theology from Calvin to Perkins* Baker Book House, Grand Rapids, MI, 1988[2]

Murray, Iain H. *Jonathan Edwards: A New Biography* Banner of Truth, Edinburgh, 1988

Niesel, Wilhelm *The Theology of Calvin* tr. Harold Knight, Lutterworth Library, volume XLVIII, Lutterworth Press, London, 1956

Oberg, Barbara B., and Stout, Harry S. (eds), *Benjamin Franklin, Jonathan Edwards, and the Representation of American Culture* Oxford University Press, Oxford, 1993

Parrington, Vernon L. *Main Currents in American Thought:*

An Interpretation of American Literature from the Beginnings to 1920 vol. 1: *1620–1800: The Colonial Mind* Harcourt, Brace and Co., New York, 1930

Plantinga, Alvin *God, Freedom and Evil* George Allen and Unwin, London, 1975

Prestige, G. L. *God in Patristic Thought* SPCK, London, 1952

Preus, James S. *From Shadow to Promise: Old Testament Interpretation from Augustine to the Young Luther* Harvard University Press, Cambridge, MA, 1969

Reid, J. K. S. 'The Office of Christ in Predestination' *Scottish Journal of Theology* 1 (1948) pp. 5–19 and 166–83

Rolston, Holmes 'Responsible Man in Reformed Theology: Calvin *versus* the *Westminster Confession*' *Scottish Journal of Theology* 23 (1970) pp. 129–56

Ruland, Richard, and Bradbury, Malcolm *From Puritanism to Postmodernity: A History of American Literature* Penguin, London, 1992

Russell, Bertrand *A History of Western Philosophy: And its Connection with Political and Social Circumstances from the Earliest Times to the Present Day* George Allen & Unwin, London, 1961[2]

Sairsingh, Krister 'Jonathan Edwards and the Idea of Divine Glory: His Foundational Trinitarianism and its Ecclesial Import' unpublished Ph.D. Dissertation, Harvard University, 1986

Schwöbel, C., and Gunton, C. E. (eds), *Persons Divine and Human* T&T Clark, Edinburgh, 1991

Shedd, W. G. T. *The Doctrine of Endless Punishment* Banner of Truth, Edinburgh, 1986

Simonson, H. P. *Jonathan Edwards: Theologian of the Heart* Eerdmans, Grand Rapids, MI, 1974

Stewart, Ian 'Zero, Zilch and Zip' *New Scientist* 2131 (25 April 1998) pp. 41–4

Stoever, W. K. B. *'A Faire and Easie Way to Heaven': Covenant Theology and Antinomianism in Early Massachusetts* Wesleyan University Press, Middletown, CT, 1978

Storms, C. Samuel *Tragedy in Eden: Original Sin in the Theology of Jonathan Edwards* University Press of America, London, 1985

Strehle, Stephen *Calvinism, Federalism and Scholasticism: A*

Study of the Reformed Doctrine of the Covenant Basler und Berner Studien zur Historischen und Systematischen Theologie Band 58, Peter Lang, Bern, 1988

Talbot, Thomas 'The Doctrine of Everlasting Punishment' *Faith and Philosophy* 7/1 (1990) pp. 19–42

Tennant, F. R. *The Origin and Propagation of Sin* Cambridge University Press, Cambridge, 1902

Thomas, G. Michael *The Extent of the Atonement: A Dilemma for Reformed Theology from Calvin to the Consensus (1536–1675)* Paternoster, Carlisle, 1997

Torrance, James B. 'Covenant or Contract? A Study of the Theological Background of Worship in Seventeenth-Century Scotland' *Scottish Journal of Theology* 23 (1970) pp. 51–76

Torrance, Thomas F. *Space, Time and Incarnation* T&T Clark, Edinburgh, 1997[2]

Tracey, Joseph *The Great Awakening* Banner of Truth, Edinburgh, 1976

Trueman, Carl R. 'Heaven and Hell: 12 in Puritan Theology' *Epworth Review* 22/3 (1995) pp. 75–85

— and Clark, R. S. (eds) *Protestant Scholasticism: Essays in Reassessment* Paternoster, Carlisle, 1999

von Rohr, John *The Covenant of Grace in Puritan Thought* AAR Studies in Religion no. 45, Scholars Press, Atlanta, GA, 1986

Wainwright, W. J. *Reason and the Heart: A Prolegomenon to a Critique of Passional Reason* Cornell University Press, London, 1995

Walker, D. P. *The Decline of Hell: Seventeenth-Century Discussions of Eternal Torment* Routledge & Kegan Paul, London, 1964

Wallace, Dewey D. *Puritans and Predestination: Grace in English Protestant Theology 1525–1695* University of North Carolina Studies in Religion, University of North Carolina Press, Chapel Hill, NC, 1982

Walls, Jerry L. *Hell: The Logic of Damnation* Library of Religious Philosophy vol. 9, University of Notre Dame Press, Notre Dame, IN, 1992

Weir, David A. *The Origins of the Federal Theology in Sixteenth-Century Reformation Thought* Clarendon Press, Oxford, 1990

Wendel, François *Calvin: The Origins and Development of his Religious Thought* tr. P. Mairet, Collins, London, 1963

Williams, Norman Powell *The Ideas of the Fall and Original Sin: A Historical and Critical Study* Longmans, Green & Co., London, 1929

Winslow, Ola E. *Jonathan Edwards 1703–1758: A Biography* Octagon Books, New York, 1973

Young F. '"Creatio ex Nihilo": A Context for the Emergence of the Christian Doctrine of Creation' *Scottish Journal of Theology* 44 (1991) pp. 139–51

Index